At Work in Homes:
Household Workers in World Perspective

Roger Sanjek and Shellee Colen, Editors

American Ethnological Society Monograph Series, Number 3
James L. Watson, Series Editor

Copyright © 1990 by the American Anthropological Association
All rights reserved
Printed in the United States of America
Production Editor: Medea M. Ranck
ISBN 0-913167-39-8

Library of Congress Cataloging-in-Publication Data
At work in homes : household workers in world perspective / Roger Sanjek
 and Shellee Colen, editors.
     p.   cm. — (American Ethnological Society monograph series ; no. 3)
   Includes bibliographical references.
   ISBN 0-913167-39-8
   1. Domestics.   I. Sanjek, Roger, 1944-   II. Colen, Shellee.
III. Series.
HD8039.D5A86   1990
331.7′6164046—dc20   90-33353
                                                                          CIP

Copies may be ordered from:

American Anthropological Association
1703 New Hampshire Avenue, N.W.
Washington, D.C. 20009

Contents

Conclusion

Introduction

1
At Work in Homes I: Orientations

Shellee Colen
Roger Sanjek

At Work in Homes presents a global perspective on household work and those workers who are recruited to perform a variety of reproductive tasks in households other than their own. The case studies in this volume, from Africa, Asia, the Caribbean, and North America, include several little-studied locales of household work. In this introduction we will argue that the structuring of work in homes not only provides reproductive labor to employing households, but simultaneously reinforces relations of power and inequality within each local society where it is found. Together these essays force us to reexamine household work, to expose its distinctive transcultural features, and to question received generalizations.[1]

We intend that this volume will affirm the value of historically situated study of household workers, and help to develop theoretical models that locate household work in a world economic system perspective. We hope *At Work in Homes* will contribute to the growing scholarly attention to household work, to debate about social policy, and to activism around improved working conditions and social justice for household workers in many national and local settings worldwide.

Household Workers: Concept and Definition

We choose the term "household worker" because it better describes the situation of workers in homes than such stigmatized terms as "servant," "domestic," or "domestic worker." We use household worker as an inclusive term to cover the many types of work in homes portrayed in this volume, as well as others such as home care of the infirm and the frail elderly.

1

Household workers are persons who are recruited from outside the employing household to perform some portion of its reproductive work.[2] This may include housecleaning, laundering, repair of clothing or other household items, cooking, child care, marketing, firewood provision, bill paying, and telephone answering. The tasks may involve indoor or outdoor work, and have material and mechanical aspects, as well as emotional and psychological dimensions. Although household work may be performed by core household members, as defined by kinship, or by lodging and boarding arrangements (Lamphere 1987), and by slaves or indentured servants, our primary concern is with hired household workers (whether kin or not), who are paid by wage or in kind for their labor.

Differential access to power between employers and workers is central to household work. Workers are recruited from households that are less powerful, poorer, and socially disenfranchised to some degree in relation to the households of employers. Imposing differences of class, race, or ethnicity, or more subtle differences of social or geographical positioning, usually mark off employers' households from those of workers. Not infrequently, several axes of social differentiation are compounded.

Household workers may be adults or children; they may be extrahousehold kin, or nonkin from local or distant communities. When individuals—whether kin or not—are recruited from outside primarily to do household work, we consider them to be household workers. While most of the cases in this volume concern adult workers, Sanjek's essay focuses on child household workers in Ghana who are often recruited through kinship ties. The child does not choose to become a household worker, but is transferred to the employer's household by the adults involved. The child worker's status is distinct from core household members—in terminology, in the extent of household work they perform, and most notably in the lack of extrahousehold opportunities for training or employment relative to other children in the household (compare Watson in press, on Hong Kong child workers).

In other cases discussed in this volume, the decision to enter household work is made by the adult worker. Yet, at times, the line between voluntary and involuntary conditions of household work may blur. When employment opportunities are circumscribed for certain populations by colonialism, unequal accumulation, or economic and social domination, choice becomes a slippery concept. This is clearly so when we look at employment "choices" for Black South African women under apartheid (Cock 1980; Preston-Whyte 1978), or for African Americans who during long periods of United States history were considered a service caste by white society (Davis 1981). The conditions of household work, particularly live-in situations, may resemble those of coerced labor, and may similarly constrain workers' lives (see Colen, this volume; Silvera 1983). Yet, while many household work situations stretch the meaning of "voluntary," strictly speaking a measure of personal choice by the worker is involved.

Slaves and indentured servants have been responsible for performing domestic work in several historical periods,[3] but domestic workers are distinct from slaves, no matter how controlled their waking lives may be by their employers. Household work contrasts with several of the distinctive features of slavery cataloged by Lovejoy (1983:1–8). Unlike slaves, household workers retain kinship ties and status outside their household of work; household workers are not recruited through the direct violence of warfare, raids, or kidnapping; household work entails an element of "voluntary" choice for the worker (and on the part of their parents in the case of child household workers) that enslavement does not; unlike those of slaves, household workers' sexual and biological reproductive capacities are not controlled by their employer (even if their employers abuse their rights); household workers select their own marriage partners; household worker status is not inherited as is slave status.[4]

Household workers are workers, sometimes waged, sometimes paid in kind. At root in all cases is an employer-worker relationship. Household worker labor is put to the tasks of reproduction rather than production.[5] While housework does not produce capital directly, workers perform socially necessary household maintenance, food preparation, child care and socialization, and other reproduction tasks for a wage.[6] The value of household workers' labor is transferred to members of the employing household, permitting them to allocate their time and energies in other ways—to more remunerative or prestigious productive work, leisure, or investment in social relations. The essential point is that the workers' *labor* is utilized to maintain and advance the position of members of the employer household (see Colen, Hansen, and Sanjek, this volume).[7] The labor for which employers pay frees them for other, generally preferred, activities.

To fail to see household work as an employer-worker relationship is to succumb to the mystification of kinship, custom, and language that so frequently accompanies it. This mystification is particularly strong in the case of Ghanaian and Hong Kong (Watson in press) kin-recruited child workers, and Kano "royal slaves." "Royal slave" in contemporary northern Nigeria is a status claim to palace residence and employment; it is not slavery with the entailments listed by Lovejoy. And while the Hong Kong *mui jai* is referred to by a kin term, it is

a term tellingly applied to no one else. Similarly, the language of incorporation into the 18th-century French patriarchal household ob-
scured the reality that household workers were there primarily as
workers; over time custom melted, and contract prevailed (Maza 1983;
Fairchilds 1984). Today, when employers use the ideology of family
membership ("she's one of the family") to soften the edges of exploitative capitalist wage relations, workers reject it.[8] Household workers
are in employing households to work; they are neither "daughters" as
in Ghana, nor "maids," or equivalent terms. Those for whom they
work we prefer to call employers, and not "masters," "patrons,"
"mothers," or other local terms of address or reference.

Contemporary Western society is plagued with its own mystification—the ideological separation made between the household and
the workplace. With capitalist organization of industrial production in
the 19th century, much productive work moved outside the home to
new workplaces. Most reproductive activity remained in the household, performed primarily by women. "Work" became something one
did for a wage in a "workplace"; the home was no longer seen as the
site of "work," and paid "housework" was regarded by employers as
low status, even stigmatized work, or not *real* work at all. In addition
to its ideological implications for gender, this separation interferes
with our capacity to see the home as a workplace, and to conceptualize
the interpenetration of production and reproduction.[9]

The tasks of household work may be performed either by household members—most frequently defined by kinship—who are motivated by obligation, necessity, or "love," or by paid household workers. The association of some household tasks with these kinship-as-
sociated motivations contributes to the mystification of household
work by employers, if not by workers. Especially in the situations of
live-in household workers and daytime or 24-hour child-care workers,
job performance requires intimate involvement in the employing
household members' lives. As in other forms of service work, part of
the job is pleasing the employer beyond the performance of physical
and material tasks (cf. Hochschild 1983). The emotional and psychological element in household work may involve maintaining a pleasant
demeanor and assessing the employer's mood in order to avoid un-
pleasantness, reprimand, or dismissal. The "emotion work" of child
care goes far beyond the physical tasks of feeding, diapering, and
bathing. It is not surprising, in these cases, that employers may attempt to reconcile these contradictions by creating a kind of fictive kinship to address and refer to household workers. The complicated role-
set of employer-worker-child can product its own mystifications
(Colen, this volume).

Household work has been treated most frequently by anthropologists within studies of kinship, gender, or migration. While more research, and more careful consideration of existing research, will enhance comparison and theory on these topics, studies of household work also have much to contribute to the anthropology of work and labor systems. It is here, theoretically and substantively, that we believe the impact of these essays, and the work of other scholars of household work, will be greatest.

Intensification of Inequality

In a broad sense, household work does more than provide reproductive labor for employer households and wages for workers. As Rollins suggests (1985, this volume), it also reproduces the relations of inequality in its local society, the very relations that structure recruitment of workers.[10] These relations of inequality include gender, age, ethnicity, race, class, and migration status, and most often compound two or more of these axes of differentiation.

How, precisely, does this reproduction and reinforcement of inequality happen? First, the household worker-employer relationship itself is unequal. Workers are less powerful than their employers, and must comply daily with orders to preserve their positions. Second, the value of household workers' labor is at the disposal of the classes which employ them. This affords a measure of power that reinforces or expands class dominance. Freed from burdens of many of their own reproduction tasks, employers may put this value to productive use, invest it in intensification of existing social relations, or use it in display or leisure. Third, the inherent inequality of the relationship is an overlay on the existing social differences of gender, age, ethnicity, race, class, and migration status between worker and employer populations. These forms of social difference matter in many social contexts beyond that of the household worker-employer nexus.

Household work marks such differences for both populations because of its inherent inequality. This is possible because household work in all class societies results in a measure of stigma. Household labor, including housecleaning, kitchen work, and clothes washing, generally is seen as lowly, devalued work, associated with dirt and disorder.[11] Household workers are paid to do this reproductive work for others, work that others can do themselves without being paid. When people can afford to pay for this transfer of household work tasks, they no longer do it themselves, but assign it to those who accept payment and subordination, often having little choice.

The stigma arising from the household situation affects both workers and the populations or social categories from which they are recruited.[12] Watson (in press) notes that when rural Hong Kong women sought to disparage the dowry amounts of other women, they said they were married like a *mui jai* (child household worker), thus branding the marriage and bride with low status. When a Nepalese Nyishang villager visits an urban relative and is received cooly, he or she speaks of being treated like a "household worker" (Cooke, this volume). Employers often view household workers only through their work roles, and not as fully human persons. In addition, the time demands of household work frequently constrain workers from maintaining their own households and participating fully in their own intimate family relationships.[13] These circumstances reinforce employer rationalizations of exploitive behavior, and augment the social stigma of household work. When household work comes to characterize a social group, it stigmatizes in a way that other working-class occupations that involve productive work and permit fuller family and personal life—such as mining, agricultural labor, factory work, or clerical employment—do not.

More than the household worker-employer role partners are involved. When certain kinds of people do household work, and others do not, a social message is carried far beyond workers and employers themselves. The more widespread the practice, the more powerful the message. In this manner, household work can reproduce ideologically many forms of inequality, as well as reinforce such concepts culturally and psychologically for those individuals who themselves do household work, or employ household workers. We now examine these relations of inequality, as structured by gender, age, ethnicity, race, class, and migration status, while recognizing that these relations rarely occur separately in concrete historical situations.

Gender.   Concepts of gender inequality are reinforced in societies where reproductive work is assigned to women, and women are also the majority of household workers. In these situations, the underlying sexual division of labor is maintained within employing households, and it is seen as "natural" in the culture at large that women perform household work, the tasks of reproduction. Such rigid cultural definition is not reproduced exclusively by household work, but is certainly deepened and entrenched by its presence. In such societies, as in Hong Kong (Watson in press) and northern Nigeria (Mack, this volume), notions of male noninvolvement in household social reproduction are extremely tenacious (compare Horowitz 1974).

In contemporary Zambia (Hansen 1989, this volume) and Tanzania (Bujra n.d.), where men are the more favored and more frequent household workers, at least for higher income employers, men's assumption of paid household work is itself seen as "natural." This situation arises from the particular histories of the region in which the assumption of wage labor by men, including household work, mining, and other tasks, is longstanding. Men are expected to engage in wage labor; women, to perform child rearing and domestic duties in their own homes. This raises the question of whether there is any less rigidity in gender allocation of reproductive work in natal, solitary, male roommate, and conjugal Zambian and Tanzanian households versus those in Hong Kong or northern Nigeria. Does the male assumption of paid household work have any effect on men's performance of such tasks in their own households?

Age. Age as an axis of inequality may be intensified in situations where household workers are most frequently children, as in early 20th-century Hong Kong and in Ghana. While social class differences are involved, we want to focus upon the issue of age difference. Our argument is that the widespread deployment of child household workers reinforces notions of difference between children and adults, making societies where we encounter child household workers in large numbers more accommodating to the general use of child labor than other societies. In Adabraka, Sanjek encountered universal expectations that children do household tasks, both for other adults in their residential buildings as well as for adults of their own households. In Zambia (Hansen, personal communication) and Tanzania (Bujra n.d.), informal child household labor is encountered in lower income urban areas; as one ascends the class ladder, however, households are more likely to employ adult males, unlike Ghana where girl "maid servants" are encountered at all class levels.

Ethnicity. Ethnicity is often a central factor in differentiating household workers and employers. Cooke's Nepal case even suggests that the forging of Nyishangte employer ethnic identity occurs in the context of the increasing employment of Gurung household workers. Clearly Nyishangte experiences outside Nepal have contributed to ethnogenesis as well, but the sense of ethnic boundedness in one small valley—versus surrounding populations whom others would see as similar—seems to emerge in large part from the recruitment patterns and social relations of household work.

When patterns of labor migration and uneven development result in Sri Lankans doing household work in Kuala Lumpur, Filipinas in Hong Kong, and Haitian, Dominican, and St. Lucian household workers in Martinique, class differences meld with ethnic differences. If such recruitment patterns persist will not notions of ethnic hierarchy be reinforced by the widespread employment of such household workers?

The earlier employment in U.S. history of Irish household workers, and their gradual movement out of the occupation in the context of wider social change, bolsters our contention. Anti-Irish prejudice was reinforced by widespread employment of Irish household workers. We suggest such sentiments diminished in scope and force as the Irish left the occupation for other jobs. With the growing employment of ethnically and culturally distinguishable immigrant household work forces in Third World cities, the accompanying emergence or hardening of ethnic identity and prejudice deserves directed research.

Race. Race is more than ethnic difference. Unlike ethnicity, racial differences are built into the legal structures of states, and are maintained by many institutions over long historical periods (Banton 1983; Ringer 1983; Sanjek 1984). When recruitment of household workers is structured by racial difference, as occurs in many settings, our question is how this institution plays a role in reinforcing racial inequalities.

In the United States, African-American women have constituted much of the household work labor force during the 20th century. As the work of Rollins and others indicates, this situation has reinforced notions of racial inequality, mainly among white North Americans. Popular media—in Hollywood films the ubiquitous African-American "maid," or the now less-frequent Chinese or Japanese "houseboy"— build racist stereotypes on the bare bones of social-racial-demographic work realities.

How have the representations of racially different groups and concepts of racial inequality held by North Americans shifted as different groups moved in and out of household work? Household work does not exist apart from other institutions or events. New images of China and Japan in the 20th century, as well as new immigration and the opening of other occupations to Asian Americans, no doubt affected perceptions of Chinese- and Japanese-American men and women in conjunction with their large-scale move out of stigmatized household work.

For African-American women the issue may be one of contested representations. How has their move away from household work, and their public visibility in other occupations, affected the image of African-American women in the dominant, white American culture? How does the current strong presence of West Indian household workers, many also of African descent, figure in this situation? Is there today a contest among mass media images of African-American women where the household worker is now less prominent, African-American working-class and professional women just barely visible, and the "Black welfare mother," played upon by the media and white American politicians, blown out of proportion? Such questions need finer definition and directed research.

Class. Class differences commonly structure all household work relations, though frequently other axes of inequality are present as well. Yet, as this volume's essays on Malaysia, Zambia, and Ghana show, there are certainly societies in which workers and employers do not differ in terms of ethnicity and race.[14] In these societies, persons of each ethnic group may be found as both household workers and employers. (We discount, for the sake of analysis here, the expatriate white employers.)

In these postcolonial societies racial inequalities formerly coincided with the hierarchy of political power. With independence, political elites of local ethnic origin assumed power. As many have argued, the class structures of the colonial era did not depart with the Europeans. If household work reinforces class difference how should this be studied in the contemporary setting? The answer is complicated because in these societies employment of household labor is found at middle, and even lowly, social levels; it is not restricted to the elite.

It is easy to argue that pervasive social inequality is reinforced, but a more subtle approach is needed. Research needs to be directed, in the same nation or city, to household work at all social levels: in Third World settings, to both the elite groups studied by Armstrong in Malaysia, and the middle- and lower middle-level groups studied by Sanjek in Ghana. Hansen's book (1989) provides extensive treatment of household work in contemporary Zambia, and moves such study forward.

In Western settings, such as the United States, the circumstances of middle- and lower middle-class employers of household workers seem especially important to study. Where class differences are large and obvious, less may be learned than where class differences between employer and worker are narrow. Here the ideological as well as psychological aspects of how household work reinforces class inequalities may be particularly significant (see Rollins 1985, this volume).

Migration status. In the contemporary world, migration is frequently implicated in the recruitment of household workers. State policy concerning the international movement of labor and capital has created highly exploitable groups of household workers in several national settings. For the United States Colen documents how noncitizen and nonpermanent-resident migration status for undocumented workers creates vulnerabilities upon which recruitment of household labor thrives (this volume; see also Ruiz 1987; Silvera 1983). As populations grow whose legal employment rights are severely restricted by immigration status, or by the absence of statuses permitting formal sector waged work, the relative cost of household labor falls. Interests of choice and of necessity are served by the perpetuation of such a situation; interests of the state, business, employers, and workers all coincide. Household work is certainly not the only occupation in which this self-reinforcing situation is found, nor is the United States the only nation in which immigration flourishes in a situation of non- or semiprotection. South African pass laws bear comparison with United States immigration law. We need more comparative work probing how household work may operate to extend the new inequalities of documented and undocumented labor.

Our argument, to summarize, is that household work always operates in situations of inequality, and that through household work the multiple axes of inequality dividing household workers and employers intensify and harden. Social relations, social sentiment, and legal structures may all serve to separate and distance household worker and employer populations where household work is widespread.

Organization of the Volume

There is no broad, comprehensive, world systemic theory that accounts for the emergence of household work everywhere. While we stress a global perspective, we do not aim at developing universal theories of household work. The juxtaposition of different studies of household workers—female and male, adult and child, urban and rural, from Africa, Asia, the Caribbean, and United States—opens up points for more probing analysis of each case. To understand how gender, class, age, ethnicity, and race cohere in many different settings of household worker-employer relations refreshes the terms we bring to each case, and jogs us to ask questions that we might not otherwise entertain.

While the following essays could be arranged in other ways, we have grouped them in three categories—indigenous African and Asian, Euroamerican, and neocolonial forms of household work. These categories invite comparison, and reflect our interests in historically informed study of household work within a global framework. The three categories are not sequential in evolutionary or developmental terms. We stress that all the cases in this volume are contemporary. The categories derive from the particular development of the forms and social relations of household work, and do not aim to identify the larger political or social contexts within which they are found.

The indigenous cases from Kano, Ghana, and Nepal are non-Western in form. They present sets of household work relations different from the European and North American cases that have become paradigmatic for studies of household work. These situations are less contractual than Western cases; kin terms, or variations on kin terms, for household workers are frequently used by both worker and employer; and the workers are more closely incorporated into the employer households than in Western forms. They are indigenous in that they are not forms of labor imposed from without, but they nonetheless reflect world systemic forces that intensify and direct labor utilization in response to capitalist development. The Nepal household labor situation, relatively new and clearly shaped by the articulation of local region and larger economic realm, is more contractual than the other cases, but still indigenous in form. All three cases suggest that where indigenous forms of household work obtain, they may undergo growth, as well as decline.

The Euroamerican cases are forms that originated in Western Europe and were transported to (and transformed in) North America. Our cases in this volume from the United States (Rollins, Colen) both find adult women of color—specifically women of African-American or Caribbean cultural background—working in relations of a more contractual nature than those of the indigenous cases. Yet, contractual elements historically have been hard won (see Palmer 1987), and pale beside contractual work standards for other forms of work, including service sector jobs. In these Euroamerican cases of household work, what Rollins (1985, this volume) calls "maternalism" and other manifestations of differential power hinging on race and class mystify the contractual worker-employer relationship. Continuing terminological treatment by employers of household workers by first name, like children, reflects this.

The neocolonial forms in Zambia and Kuala Lumpur represent Western European household labor forms transplanted, and now developing on their own, in former European colonies. Employers today are native to the local societies, though expatriates continue to employ local household workers as well. In these two cases, ongoing relations with the workers' own families appear to be easier and more open than in either the indigenous cases, where such relations are severed during the period of employment (except for the "royal slaves" in Kano), or the Euroamerican cases, where the relations are problematic, especially in live-in contexts. Although Martinique is a Depart-

ment of France and household work there is subject to regulation by
the national government, the social relations of household work as described by Laguerre are neocolonial in form.

The ethnographic fieldwork of the contributors to this volume de-
marcates three stages in the recent tide of research on household
work. Sanjek in Ghana in the 1970s, and Armstrong in Malaysia and
Cooke in Nepal in the 1980s, studied household work as one facet of
broader research which had other major goals. Hansen followed up
earlier urban research during the 1970s with a major study of household workers in the 1980s; Laguerre's short, directed 1985 study of
household work in Martinique also followed other Caribbean research. During the 1980s, Rollins, Colen, and Mack each studied work
in homes, in the United States and in northern Nigeria, as their dissertation topic. Their work suggests the direction ethnographic studies of household work are likely to take in the 1990s.

We hope that the 1990s also will see further developments in the
comparative and theoretical anthropology of household work. More
such work is needed to examine both the ideologies and the social relations of this form of labor. It is to the tasks of setting local pictures in
a global frame, connecting reproductive and productive labor, and af-
firming household work as work, that we present the essays that follow. We hope this volume will spur debate, and promote critical thinking about household work and workers.

Notes

1. The essays in this volume were presented at an American Ethnological
Society Invited Session at the American Anthropological Association 1985 annual meeting in Washington, DC. Papers also presented by Elsa Chaney, To-
moko Hamada, and Rubie Watson are being published elsewhere. Enid
Schildkrout and Karen Sacks served as discussants for the panel. For comments on our "At Work in Homes" and "Household Workers in World Perspective" essays, we would like to thank Janet Bujra, Eugene Cooper, Deborah D'Amico-Samuels, Karen Tranberg Hansen, Louise Lamphere, Michael
Landy, Beverly Mack, Lani Sanjek, James L. Watson, Rubie Watson, and an
anonymous AES reader.

2. See Edholm et al. (1977) for a useful discussion of the distinctions between social reproduction, reproduction of the labor force, and biological reproduction. References to all works cited in this introduction are found following the concluding essay, "Household Workers in World Perspective."

3. See Graham (1988) on Brazil, Joshel (1986) on ancient Rome, and Origo
(1955) on medieval Italy.

4. No definition is foolproof. The *mui jai* household workers Watson writes of did not choose their own husbands. The household workers of "royal slave" status in the Kano Emir's palace household described by Mack are recruited from within—and there lie their kinship ties. Yet, they are not slaves in Lovejoy's sense, even if their apical enslaved ancestors were.

5. On this point see Cock (1980, 1981), Colen (1986), Edholm et al. (1977), Gaitskell et al. (1984), Jelin (1977), and van Onselen (1982).

6. See Benston (1971), Berk (1980), Dalla Costa and James (1972), Oakley (1974, 1976), and Secombe (1974) on unpaid housework.

7. This point is also made in Brandewie (1973), Bunster and Chaney (1985), Cock (1980, 1981), Jelin (1977), and Rubbo and Taussig (1977).

8. Hence the irony of Childress's title, *Like One of the Family* (1956); see also Cock (1980), Colen (1989), and Silvera (1983).

9. These points are elaborated by Kelly (1979), Lamphere (1987), and Rapp (1978).

10. Compare Cock (1980, 1981), Colen (1986), Katzman (1978), and Rubbo and Taussig (1977).

11. This may be less true for child-care work, which seems to carry less stigma in contemporary North America than other tasks, but this varies historically and culturally; see Joshel (1986) on wet nurses in ancient Rome.

12. This stigma is different from the concept as developed by Goffman, which he assigns to physical deformity, blemishes of individual character, or inherited subordinate status (Goffman 1963:4). We see the stigma of household work as social rather than personal, and historically constituted (and therefore transcendable) rather than inherent to a person or social group.

13. This point is illustrated in Colen (1986, 1989, this volume), Preston-Whyte (1978), and Watson (in press).

14. See also Brandewie (1973) on the Philippines, and Tellis-Nayak (1983) on India.

Indigenous African and Asian Forms of Household Work

2
Service and Status: Slaves and Concubines in Kano, Nigeria

Beverly B. Mack
George Mason University

Today in Kano, Nigeria,[1] there is a royal wife whose ancestry is testimony to the social functions of slavery and concubinage in Kano:[2] she is the great-granddaughter of a slave woman *(kuyanga)*[3] who was captured at age seven. The young slave and her slave husband had a daughter who became a royal concubine *(k'wark'wara)*, which status guaranteed that *her* children and subsequent generations would be free. That concubine was the grandmother of today's royal wife.

Now living in the same area of the Kano palace is a concubine of about the same age as the royal wife. She was accepted as a concubine after presenting evidence of her slave lineage back through several generations. All her children are free. Her son is as likely to become an emir as the sons of a royal wife, and her daughters will probably marry other emirs or noblemen of the region. They may become royal wives through the same system of social change that for generations has both restricted and freed Hausa/Fulani women of slave status in northern Nigeria.

Slavery and Concubinage in Northern Nigeria

Kano is a Muslim city in northern Nigeria, inhabited by Hausa and Fulani whose shared cultures have resulted in a mixed Hausa/Fulani society. Here, as in other societies, the practice of slavery has allowed for the establishment of concubinage among the wealthy.

From the Middle Ages until its prohibition in 1901, slave-raiding was an integral part of the economic and political competition among groups in the area. Along with slave-raiding there developed the *harim* (Arabic) system, and the practice of wife seclusion. While the extent to which slavery—and therefore concubinage—were practiced in the Sudan prior to the introduction of Islam is not clear, both institutions were well established by the 14th century.

Many historical accounts underline the importance of slavery in the area; considerably less is recorded concerning concubinage. It is known, however, that the Prophet Mohammed himself owned slaves and kept concubines, continuing a modified version of pre-Islamic Arab practices (Willis 1985a:22, 1985b:viii). The question of which peoples could be taken as slaves and concubines soon became a prime doctrinal issue among Sudanic *'ulama* (Willis 1985a:16–23) and by 1614 the Muslim scholar Ahmad Baba was protesting the practice of slave-raiding among Muslim Hausa states (Lovejoy 1983:62). Sarkin Kano Muhammad Rumfa (1463–99) took slaves in battle, as did the 17th-century warlord of the Jukun when he sacked Kano. The Kano *sarki* Kutumbi (c. 1623–48) put women in harems (Lovejoy 1983:71, 113). The *jihad* and Islamic reform led by Usman Dan Fodio from Sokoto in 1804 did not diminish the practice of slave-raiding, but did engender philosophical tracts on the subject, most of which encouraged a Muslim slaveowner to free his slaves upon their conversion to Islam—a demand not likely to inspire wealthy men to such displays of devotion. Thus, slavery continued long after the Shehu's *jihad*, and concubinage along with it. The Shehu Usman Dan Fodio himself kept a concubine (Boyd and Last 1985:294), and by 1826 the British explorer Clapperton estimated a slave-freeborn ratio of 30:1 in Kano (Clapperton 1966 [1829]:171).

Enslavement was central to the aims of the Sokoto Caliphate, for which the practice was a "crucial institution . . . [with] political order based on systematic enslavement" (Lovejoy 1981b:201). Ideologically the conversion of non-Muslims—an implicit aim of the *jihad* itself—was best accomplished through the acculturation of young captives, especially concubines and children born into slavery. Taxes demanded by the Caliphate were often paid in slaves; Richard Lander reported meeting slaves destined for the Sokoto Caliphate: "On our journey [east of Kano] we met, on their way to Soccatoo, as a tax paid to Sultan Bello from a neighboring country, thirty slaves, men, women, and children, who were ill with the smallpox" (Lander 1830, II:112). Nearly 30 years after the *jihad* slaves were still being taken and women were still being traded or exchanged as concubines among powerful men.

Toward the end of the 19th century, the Kano emir Tukur was known for public executions of his enemies, and was accused of having sold free people into slavery (M. G. Smith n.d.: Ch. 6, p. 20). Even as he was driven from Kano, Tukur continued to depend on slave-raiding to increase his ranks; in 1894 Robinson observed that

> Tukur, on leaving Katsena, retreated [further] to Kamri, one of the towns subject to Kano, the inhabitants of which were powerless to prevent his entry into their town. The result is that the King of Kano burnt this town and carried off its inhabitants as slaves. [M. G. Smith n.d.: Ch. 6, p. 64]

Aliyu Babba, who overthrew Tukur, ostensibly to protest such slave-tyranny, was not much different from Tukur in practice:

> When Aliyu first entered the palace, his followers began to break into people's compounds, confiscating their property . . . some [people were] to be killed, some to be sold, some women to be secluded in harems; some were enslaved directly and remain so to this day [1933]. [M. G. Smith n.d.: Ch. 6, p. 32]

At the turn of the 19th century a spy for the British colonial administrator Lugard observed slaves—"women, men, and children"—for sale in a market near Zaria, just south of Kano (M. G. Smith n.d.; Ch. 6, p. 65).

Thus slavery and concubinage existed for centuries as an integral part of both traditional indigenous and orthodox Islamic practices, until both the institutions were finally affected by the intervention of the British at the beginning of the 20th century, when

> The British . . . became experts in Islamic law and . . . interpreted the provisions on slavery in a manner that would justify its continuation, with modifications. Slave officials were eased out of office, but concubinage was left intact. [Lovejoy 1983:264]

Technically the abolition of slavery necessitated the abolition of concubinage, since free women cannot be concubines. In fact, colonial policy toward slavery was based on the realization that enforced and wholesale abolition would prove economically and socially disastrous. Consequentially, a gradualist approach was adopted and concubinage, together with other aspects of domestic slavery, was not interfered with. The British abolished slave-raiding and sale, as well as the legality of slave status for those born after April 1, 1901. But the social status of slave has endured into the 20th century; people still identify themselves as slaves when such status can be beneficial, in particular by connecting them with the royal community.

Royal Slaves and Concubines

Much has been written on the hierarchy of slaves in Hausa society at large (see especially M. G. Smith 1960), but the situation of female slaves and concubines within the palace community remains largely unexplored. The existence of slaves to support royalty is a given: "Every royal family is also a slave family. The two go together. You don't get kings without slaves. You don't get slaves without kings" (Armah 1979:300). Slave labor supports and sustains the royal community; in return, some slaves acquire titles and attendant privileges.

As has been discussed elsewhere, slave status did not prevent upward mobility within Hausa society (Lovejoy 1983; M. G. Smith 1960). Although slaves were retained primarily as laborers, they were also employed "as messengers, retainers, and domestic servants . . . while females filled the harems of the wealthiest officials . . . [and] because palace establishments were often very large, many women were also needed to prepare and cook food" (Lovejoy 1983:196).

Certain benefits of becoming a trusted retainer are obvious, especially given the uncertainty of life in rural regions during the long period of civil war that preceded the invasion of the British. In return for security and privilege, royal slaves provided loyal service, guaranteed by their assimilation into the system. Cut off from their own homes and family ties, they necessarily became members of a new family; in the case of the palace community, it was one into which they were easily co-opted. Once given titles and authority as representatives of the Emir, throne slaves found themselves in opposition to people of social status other than royal. Royal slaves acquired a certain respectability by association with the palace and thus were distinguished as slaves of privilege and special status. A male slave could achieve power and high status by association with the throne. His children, however, would maintain their slave status unless their slave father had married a freeborn woman, an unlikely arrangement among the Hausa (M. G. Smith 1960).

Since women were precluded from public participation in the ruling process, their opportunities to aspire to comparable titled positions were more limited than those of men.[4] However, there did exist a mechanism through which their children could divest themselves of slave status to become royalty. A female slave or her daughter—if they were captured together—could become a concubine. A concubine's children shared the same rights and privileges as a legal wife's children. For the children of the emir, this meant that all sons of concubines were eligible for the kingship. The daughters of both royal wives and concubines were, as a rule, married to wealthy and influential men.

Thus it appears that women had little choice but to be used to increase the number of royal family members, thereby increasing the royal family's power. Viewed in the context of a slave-raiding society, when very few people—male or female—had much control over their lives, the institution of concubinage offered women a means of some control over their children's, if not their own lives. It guaranteed that one's children were of royal status upon their birth, and it bought free status for all future progeny.

In accordance with Islamic law, even an emir may have only four wives. This practice, often viewed in the West as excessive, was originally a restriction imposed by Mohammed, who changed laws of polygyny that prevailed in his time. Some argue that this restriction actually raised women's position in society (Hogben and Kirk-Greene 1966:26). Hill points out, however, that despite the limitation of four wives, men were permitted to have unlimited numbers of concubines, thereby increasing legally the number of women in a household. Since the colonial period this practice has become "the prerogative of exalted chiefs, perhaps only of Emirs" (1977:293).

Thus, except for an emir's four wives (and possibly some of his own sisters residing there briefly), the rest of the women of the palace are slaves or concubines, social statuses that have persisted despite their legal abolition. Both of these constitute service roles, although they vary in terms of attendant privileges. Being a royal slave or concubine in a northern Nigerian palace has been described as a relatively enviable position, but the circumstances of concubinage have varied enormously. Margery Perham in 1932 reported less than positive impressions of concubinage after a visit to the women's quarters of Sarkin Kaita, the district headman of the northwestern town of Kaita:

> I go in and stand back in amazement. Standing, silent, posed, dressed in all their motley finery, are row upon row of women. . . . These women hardly, if ever, go outside this little inner yard; they live in this warren of caverns surrounding it. . . . The man's multitudinous progeny hang from their backs, cling to their legs or crawl in the dust. The women seem to me inert; their eyes are lifeless. As their owner calls them up for inspection, they shuffle forward with arms drooping. [Perham 1983:97]

This is the description of the concubines kept by a man who obviously had more interest in his own prestige than money to support women as his religion dictated.

By contrast, when Perham visited the women's quarters of more affluent, "exalted" chiefs in the same year, she found

> a miracle of progress [in the girl's school, with] waves of little girls. The
> Emir has provided them with a uniform, which they put on in my honor,
> homespun cream tunics with pink collars and gay little turbans of white
> silk striped with pink and yellow. They looked free and happy, crawling
> about or squatting as they sewed little mats with coloured threads or
> played with instructive kindergarten toys. Some of the Emir's wives were
> helping with them. . . . [One is] an extremely fine-looking woman, with
> grave, courteous, yet independent manners. [Perham 1983:107]

Current social and religious standards ensure that prestige, affluence,
and physical security are guaranteed to royal slaves and concubines.
Together they form an elite group of servants whose circumstances are
distinct from those of most others of slave status in the region.

Inherited Status

Hausa/Fulani society is organized around a wide range of distinct
statuses that are inherited from one generation to the next. Along with
blacksmiths and other stigmatized individuals, slaves normally are
found at the lowest stratum of the social hierarchy. But royal slaves
are unofficially ennobled by association with royalty. Thus their social
status, as well as their social esteem, changes by virtue of attachment
to the royal community; "as property the status of a slave depends on
that of his/her owner, other things being equal. . . . [T]he Emir's
slaves are superior to free men."[5] Membership in the palace community is a privileged position, for it guarantees social and economic security besides conferring prestige by affiliation with one's royal patron.

In 1901 colonial legal decree stated that children born to slave parents would no longer be considered slaves, but slave social status continues to be passed through successive generations, following a uter-
ine line of descent. Individuals descended from throne slaves continue
to recognize and identify themselves as slaves. Their children are considered to be subjects to their patron, the emir.

Free status was distinct from royal slave status. Historically, male
slaves had no certain means of acquiring their freedom. They might
purchase it, and sometimes freedom was granted by their masters, but
there was no guaranteed mechanism for male slaves to acquire freedom.[6] The next best move was to guarantee freedom for one's children; this could be accomplished by marrying a free-born woman.
Adult male slaves, traditionally captured elsewhere and brought to
Kano, were outsiders; by marrying a free-born woman, a male slave's
children were assimilated into the local community through blood ties

with a local woman. In addition, his daughter would be eligible to be-come a *jakadiya,* or royal messenger.[7] An enslaved man's marriage to a free-born woman, however, was a rare occurrence owing to the cost of acquiring such a woman as a wife (Lovejoy 1983:14; M. G. Smith 1960). Smith notes that such high cost was indicative of the Hausa/ Fulani opposition to such unions (Personal communication, December 1986).

Female slaves, however, were able to change their inherited sta-tus. During the era of slave-raiding, if a mother and daughter were captured together, the mother could be made a concubine to her cap-tor, and her daughter could be given to the captor's son; they would not be made concubines of the same man.[8] Later, after the period of slave-raiding had ended, the daughter of two slave parents (socially, although not legally, considered to be a slave) could become a concu-bine to an emir or someone else of high status. In this way she could guarantee not only her own freedom, but also free status for her chil-dren.[9]

Only free men, not slaves, have concubines. The children of these men are free, inheriting their fathers' free status just as the children of an emir inherit their father's royal status. The children of concubines traditionally have the right to the same benefits as the children of wives. As the current Emir of Kano, Alhaji Ado Bayero, recalls:

> When I was growing up I remember my father [the emir] would give equally to each of us, his children, regardless of whether our mothers were concubines or wives—in fact if a concubine's son was even one day older than I, he'd receive first, and if that was the last thing, too bad. [Personal communication, March 1983]

The children of royal concubines, as the biological heirs to an emir, share his royal status and enjoy attendant privileges that are irrever-sible. These children are the product of liaisons between descendents of slaves and their patrons, but neither they nor their descendants can become slaves or concubines in Hausa society, now that they have at-tained free status.[10]

Moreover, as noted, sons of royal concubines are eligible to suc-ceed to the throne. The current Emir of Kano is himself the son of a concubine, and Barth provides another example from the mid-19th century, observing that "Sadiku [Sidiku], son of Mallam Omaro or Ghomaro who had been eight years governor [emir] of Kat-sena, . . . is not a pure Pullo, being the offspring of a Bornu female slave" (Barth 1857:81).

Slave Women's Titles

When a man ascends the throne, his mother—very often a former concubine—inherits the honorary title *Mai Babban 'Daki* ("one who owns the big hut")[11] and can move into the royal residence near the palace designated for the title holder. If the mother dies while her son is still in office, a daughter—sister to the emir—may inherit the title and residence for the duration of his reign.[12] *Babban 'Daki*, the building itself, is said to have been built in the 15th century by Mohammed Rumfa, who is also said to have established the honorary title for his mother. Other women of slave status are appointed to titled positions in the Kano palace. Although such titles carry no property rights, they do confer prestige in relation to royalty and authority as designated agents of the emir himself

Two women attend to the daily affairs of the whole of the palace, with a special focus on the women's quarters *(cikin gida)* at its center. The *'uwar soro* (literally, mother of the household, or overseer) is responsible for the concubines, concerned with everything that goes on in the palace, and is especially responsible for the welfare of the emir's daughters. Such responsibility extends to the daughters' homes after marriage, and the *'uwar soro* is likely to visit them there to carry gifts or news from the palace. The *mai soron baki* (overseer of palace guests) focuses her concern on the living quarters of the palace, particularly the women's quarters. Anyone who wishes to visit women in the *cikin gida* area must be cleared through the *mai soron baki*. Even messages from the high slave officials like the *sallama* and the *shamaki*, who work directly with the emir elsewhere, must go to the emir through the *mai soron baki* when the emir is in the *cikin gida*.

Two other titled positions concern attention to specific areas. These are the *'uwar gida* (overseer of the household) and the *'uwar waje* (overseer of the area outside the main living quarters). There are two types of *'uwar gida* (overseer of the household): one is concerned with the areas where royal wives reside, *'uwar gidan matan aure*, the only titled position discussed here that is not held by a slave. The other, the *'uwar gidan k'warak'warai*, attends to the concubines' areas. As of 1983 in the Kano palace there was one *'uwar gidan matan aure*, but the position for *'uwar gidan k'warak'warai* was vacant. The position of *'uwar waje* theoretically is held by some 10 to 15 women, each of whom supervises the needs and complaints of women in the living units within her area. In 1983 there was, however, only one slave woman with this title.

Historically the most important single structure in the palace, *soron mallam*, is the place where a newly appointed emir must stay for

several days after being turbaned. It is said that the Emir Ibrahim Dabo
(1819–46) lived here. Formerly 10 to 20 concubines lived in this area,
but now there are none living there, and part of it has been attached
to the quarters of one of the emir's wives. Although there is no title
holder now, the *mai soron mallam* was the slave woman responsible for
the care and upkeep of the area.

Two other titled positions now vacant were of central importance
in the daily affairs of the palace. The *'uwar kuyangi*, or senior slave
woman, who traditionally resided in the Yelwa section of the palace,
was responsible for the living conditions of all slave women in the palace. The *'uwar tuwo*, or head cook, supervised all cooking done in the
centralized kitchen of the palace Yelwa quarters. The several daily
meals prepared in this kitchen would feed palace residents as well as
those *talakawa* (commoners) who were attached to the nearby Central
Mosque.

Finally, the *jakadiya*, or messenger, was a slave woman who acted
as an official trusted messenger, carrying news between the emir and
his retainers and the women (especially the wives) secluded in the enclosed interior area *(cikin gida)*. Such women reside in the palace, so
they are no longer attached to a connubial home. Often the *jakadiya* is
a widow who has been married to a slave who also served the palace,
or she is related to other important titled slave retainers, such as the
royal builder, *sarkin gini*. Each *jakadiya* is responsible for carrying messages in a certain area of the palace—they are dispersed throughout
the palace's network of passageways, situated so that there is always
someone nearby to carry news to the restricted areas of the women's
quarters in the heart of the palace. In 1983 there were approximately
ten such women in the Kano palace. Baba of Karo described a *jakadiya*
of her childhood:

> A *jakadiya* is different from a concubine, you don't put her in a hut and
> keep her inside the compound as you do a concubine, and a *jakadiya*
> doesn't take her turn with the cooking, either. The *jakadiya* comes to fetch
> her master if he is in the women's quarters and someone comes to see
> him; his men cannot come inside the compound where the women live,
> so she brings him the message. [M. Smith 1981:235]

Thus, as with slave men, titled positions established important
roles for slave women as influential members of the royal community
of women. The roles described above, like those of titled slave men,
involved monetary and material rewards, as well as residence in the
palace. This meant that slave women with royal appointments and titles enjoyed security and privilege as royal servants.[13]

Legal and Social Rights under Concubinage

Regardless of whether her son succeeds to the throne, a concubine's own status is changed simply by bearing children for the emir. Under Islamic law, concubines who have borne a child for free masters can no longer be sold as slaves.[14] Furthermore, upon the death of a concubine's master, she is guaranteed freedom, and her children are guaranteed inheritance rights according to Islamic law.[15]

"But if a concubine had children she would hardly ever leave," observed Baba of Karo (M. Smith 1981:41). How much truer is this for royal concubines, very few of whom leave the palace, which has become their home. Lovejoy comments that "even concubines had to be watched closely for fear they might get away" (Lovejoy 1981b:228). While this might be true of the concubines of nonroyal men, for royal concubines the palace community provided stability, security, and an easier life than that which they might find outside the palace. Protection from attack was virtually insured, food and clothing were guaranteed, and there were many other women around with whom to associate and share household tasks. Furthermore, a royal concubine enjoyed status higher than that of all other palace women except the emir's wives, mother, and perhaps sisters. She was irrevocably tied to the royal family through kinship, and was not likely to leave her children, who, according to Muslim law, would remain under their father's guardianship.

Examples of attempts to free concubines are often cited to indicate women's own attitudes toward concubinage. In 1926 the Emir Alhaji Abdullahi Bayero fulfilled a promise to the British by declaring manumission for all the slaves in the palace, without ordering them to quit its precincts (Fika 1978:226). They remained, continuing the symbiotic relationship that exists among those who both serve and comprise the royal community. Smith describes this as conversion from bondage to voluntary association. (M. G. Smith n.d.: Ch. 8, pp. 12–15). It also explains the pride with which older slaves and former concubines who remain in the palace speak of their slave backgrounds. Ironically one old woman in the Kano palace refuses to be called a Fulani—an association of which most would be proud—but insists on saying she is a slave because "it proves you have a background."[16] The former Emir of Katsina, Alhaji Muhamman Dikko offered a purse and freedom to his concubines as he was dying in 1944. It is said they all refused both money and the offer of freedom.[17]

The current Emir of Katsina is said to have no concubines, and the Emir of Kano has only those few given to him in friendship by other titled men, and those who have requested admission as concubines.[18] To qualify as a concubine, a woman must present irrefutable evidence of her slave lineage on both sides of her family. However, such "papers" can prove only one's social status as a slave. Since colonial decree forbade legal slave status for anyone born after 1901, tracing one's lineage would seem to be a pointless exercise, since all concubines younger than four score and nine years are technically illegal (Smith, personal communication, December 1986). However even now some women prefer affiliation with royalty through concubine status to life as the secluded Muslim wife of a less affluent man; therefore they still attempt to qualify as royal concubines.

Rights of residence are inherent in concubine status. Describing a concubine of former Emir of Kano Aliyu (1895–1903)—a woman who was in 1982 still living in the Kano palace—it was said that she had "bought her freedom with a child, and the [current] Emir can't send her away, or refuse her anything, or sell her."[19] Former concubines or widows of former emirs have the right to be housed in the palace that has been their home, even if they are absent for many years, and these rights are often exercised. These women, along with numerous others with less legitimate claim to palace residence, can create a tremendous economic burden for an emir. In recounting the members of the royal community, a former colonial officer observed:

> Then there were the male members of his staff, his own household police, the scribes, the craftsmen and so on, and their immediate relatives and dependents. Worst of all there were more than a hundred old women—all they could do was eat, the Emir said—willed to him by various deceased men who had had little or no personal connections with the ruler. Under Islamic law it was possible for anyone, so far as we could see, to bequeath his widow to the state, i.e., to the Emir. There was no earthly means of getting rid of them: only Heaven could intervene and carry them off, and that took time. For an Emir to refuse his pious duty would be to lose a great deal of face. . . . So the Emir went on supporting them and being made the target of innumerable complaints from their voracity. [Niven 1982:128]

It is an emir's religious obligation to provide a home to any woman who requests his protection, with no questions to embarrass her and no demands. The wives of former emirs will often return to the palace to live in their later years after having resided with their families, or having lived for a while on their own.

Through the system of inherited status in the Kano royal community the emir increased the numbers of people over whom he had control and for whom he bore responsibility, whether through concubinage or slavery. The institution of concubinage has traditionally served to expand the royal family beyond the number of children an emir's wives could bear.[20] Since the state electoral council usually chooses the emir's successor from the pool of those who are eligible, greater numbers of children increased the chances that his line would be continued in the next reign. But concubinage was not without its reciprocal rights and opportunities, which included both material and social comforts. A young Western educated Hausa/Fulani woman remarked in 1969, "I would prefer to be a concubine in this interesting educative home, with many fascinating women to talk to and no worries or responsibilities than to be the wife and equal partner of a peasant farmer" (Trevor 1975:264–265). Since its inception in Hausa/Fulani society, concubinage has been both imposed on the reluctant, and chosen by others, who were willing to trade their freedom for the social status, material comfort, and guarantee of freedom that it provided for themselves and their children.

Seclusion

During the slave-raiding of the 18th and 19th centuries the practice of wife seclusion became a useful means of assimilating captured women into the upper ranks of Hausa/Fulani society. This practice forbade wives and concubines from having social relations outside their husbands' or masters' compounds, in accordance with traditional interpretations of the religious mandate that men should protect their women. While wife seclusion among the affluent existed prior to 1804, it was reinforced by *jihad* leader Usman Dan Fodio, who promoted the seclusion of women among his cohorts, the Fulani who replaced traditional Hausa leaders.[21] After the *jihad* increasing numbers of affluent urban women were secluded, unless they had been widowed. Interviews with women of the Kano palace confirm that seclusion continues today, as both wives and concubines reside in the heart of the palace, where no men except members of their immediate family are allowed.

Royal wives, because of their high status, are the most strictly secluded, never leaving the compound of several rooms that comprise their own living quarters. Even though their quarters are surrounded by the compounds of other wives and concubines, they cannot visit back and forth across the common courtyard they share. On the rare occasions they are allowed to leave the palace, permission is granted only for exceptional events, like visiting the clinic for childbirth, making the *hajj* to Mecca, or accompanying the emir on a trip abroad. In each case, the woman must be accompanied by a chaperone—a woman slave—and the wife is expected to behave with discretion.

Although restricted to the *harim* area, concubines are not so strictly secluded. They are free to move about the network of compounds and courtyards that comprise the women's quarters of the palace. It is the concubine who is attracted to a royal wife as her servant, and who communicates messages for a wife to other members of the women's quarters. Traditionally, each royal wife had a concubine-handmaiden called *'uwar wajenta* (literally, mother of her place) but now the *'uwar soro* is the only one with such a designated assistant.[22]

Indicative of her somewhat lower status, the concubine has smaller, less lavish, and less strictly fixed living quarters than a royal wife. She is more frequently moved from one area of the women's quarters to another as space is reallocated according to changing needs. For the concubines there are no permanent private quarters, but there are areas designated as "birthing rooms" for their residence.[23] And although a concubine has access to all areas of the palace women's quarters—unlike a royal wife, who is confined to her own compound—concubines may not go beyond the women's quarters without the express permission of the emir. Their lower social status allows concubines more freedom within the women's quarters, but ultimately they are as shielded from the outside world as wives.

Slave women are servants to concubines and wives. Their lower status is reflected both in their smaller living space and their greater freedom of movement. Slave women, often messengers between the public domain of men and the privacy of the women's quarters, may live in the palace corridors they oversee as a part of their duties. They are neither secluded nor prevented from moving about outside the palace compound. Those who reside in the women's quarters are usually attached to the titled women described above.

Not all slave women are messengers or titled retainers, however. Some may reside in the slave quarters at the back of the palace. Usually their husbands are slaves to the emir. Although slavery has long been outlawed, successive generations of royal dependents who trace their ancestry to slaves have continued to call the palace their home, paid allegiance to the emir, and reaped the rewards he bestows as a part of their quasifamilial relationship. The women who live in the palace and who identify themselves as slaves may work for the women of the palace, running errands for them in the city, making textile craft items, or acting in other capacities on behalf of royal women. Like those who act as official messengers, these women shuttle freely between the women's quarters and the public areas of Kano city.

Household Work

As indicated above, in the palace of traditional Kano, inherited status determines one's function, and thus the tasks one is expected to perform. Technically, both slaves and concubines are of slave status, and continue to identify themselves as such. But concubines are slaves in the process of transition to free status. As such, they enjoy some of the economic benefits and social esteem afforded to royal wives, and are almost as restricted in their freedom of movement. It is a matter of pride among Muslim Hausa to be affluent enough to be secluded; a man must be able to provide servants for his secluded women. The seclusion of women requires the labor of servants to conduct their public market errands, and to provide the necessary household tasks, such as carrying firewood and water. Further, such servants must fulfill several criteria: first, they should be women in order to have access to secluded women; and second, they themselves must have liberty to move about in public without shaming themselves or those they serve. Therefore, preadolescent girls or slave women are the only individuals suited to serving secluded women, whether wives or concubines.

In the palace it is slave women resident in the women's quarters who perform the bulk of household work.[24] There was until recently a central palace kitchen where they cooked each day for everyone in the palace community; now the cooking is done for smaller groups throughout the palace, but it is still primarily a slave's task. Slaves also are responsible for labor-intensive food preparation prior to cooking, such as winnowing and pounding grains, harvesting and preparing vegetables, and procuring meat from the palace supply.

Another important task provided by slave women is child care. Royal wives and concubines still depend on slaves to care for their infants past weaning age. These children are free to run about the women's quarters, visiting and playing wherever they like but each is monitored closely by a slave nanny, with whom a close bond is established. With economic assistance from the child's biological mother, the slave-status foster mother is responsible for the child's health, feeding, clothing, cleanliness, and behavior. The child is usually sent back to the mother's compound to sleep at night, but may stay with the nanny if he or she chooses. When the children reach school age, the nanny has less control—especially of the boys, who spend very little time in the women's quarters after adolescence—but there remains a kinship-like bond between a slave nanny and her charge.

In addition to meal preparation and child care, the slave woman runs errands, carries messages, and acts as chaperone to the wife or concubine on the rare occasion that either of them leaves the palace. Any spare time slave women have is spent on their own income-generating projects, such as cooking snacks, embroidering Muslim caps, knitting, or making spaghetti noodles. These items are sold outside the palace as well as within the women's quarters; they are hawked by the women's daughters, who are free to wander anywhere before they reach marriageable age (Schildkrout 1983; M. Smith 1981).

It is in these income-generating activities that wives, concubines, and slaves are most likely to share their time. Such work is also undertaken by wives and concubines, who, freed from daily chores, are able to spend their time as they choose—chatting with those who visit them, teaching other women how to read and write, and sewing, knitting, crocheting, or making snacks for sale. Slaves and concubines sit in the courtyard of the women's quarters, embroidering caps and chatting together in the afternoon. Slaves and concubines freely visit the royal wives, either on errands or simply paying their respects. Very often royal wives—usually better educated than other palace women—will teach the Quran, literacy, mathematics, or history to women who come in from the town for tutoring. They are also consulted regularly to arbitrate conflicts between other women or among children, or for advice on matters of social propriety.

Thus the women of the harem community—four royal wives, some concubines, and a majority of slave women—interact with one another on a daily and intimate basis. While tasks are allocated according to one's status, there is a great deal of overlap: royal wives often cook meals for their children, or do their own laundry, although they are not obligated to do so; child care responsibilities are often traded off to meet the needs of the women involved; craft-making capabilities are traded among women of all statuses, depending on who has learned the necessary skill that is marketable.

Conclusion

In 1826 Hugh Clapperton described one member of his traveling party in Hausaland:

> The most useful, and as brave as any one of us, was an old female slave of the sultan's, a native of Zamfara, five of whose former governors [kings] she said she had nursed. She was of dark copper color. In dress and countenance very like one of Captain Lyon's female Esquimaux. She was mounted on a long-backed bright bay horse, with a scraggy tail, crop-eared, and the mane as if the rats had eaten part of it; and he was not in high condition. She rode a-straddle; had on a conical straw dish-

cover for a hat, or to shade her face from the sun, a short dirty white
bedgown, a pair of Houssa boots, which are wide, and came up over the
knee, fastened with a string around the waist. She also had a whip and
spurs. At her saddle-bow hung about half a dozen gourds, filled with
water, and a brass basin to drink out of; and with this she supplied the
wounded and the thirsty. [Clapperton 1966(1826):188]

Arguably the most "useful" members of a Hausa/Fulani Muslim
household are the women, whose religious mandate involves responsibility for the maintenance of the home. This is equally true for the
royal community, a Hausa/Fulani Muslim household on a grand scale,
with several thousand residents whose daily needs must be met. Although the day-to-day maintenance of the palace has been largely the
responsibility of women, whether royal, slave, or concubine, their
roles remain virtually unrecognized in historical accounts. Such neglect is by no means unique to Kano society. In a description of his
organization of a Kano base of British intelligence operations in 1939,
Sharwood-Smith commented that the Government House plan was
that he "would be given two other French-speaking Northern D.O.'s
to assist me, and my wife could run the office and do maps and cy-
phering" (Sharwood-Smith 1967:132). In the Kano palace, as in many
other places, women's roles have been taken for granted, and have
gone unrecorded.[25]

Concubinage and slavery are terms that often engender images of
deprivation and oppression. Certainly the role of women and children
as *diyya*, or "plunder for lives pledged in *jihad*," is an unhappy one
(Willis 1985a:22). Islam stipulates that women's roles are separate from
and subordinate to those of men.[26] The woman is the designated
guardian of the household scene, and her role is necessarily one of
economic and social dependence. Dependence was an integral part of
the situation of women during post-*jihad* Islam, so concubinage and
the situation of women slaves in the Kano palace must be considered
within this religious context.

However, within the institutions of dependency that marriage
and concubinage surely were (Lovejoy 1981a:13), concubinage provided one of the few mechanisms for a woman's control of her life
within the framework of 19th-century slave-raiding Hausaland. It constituted the chief means of transition from slave status to freedom for
the concubine, her children, and subsequent generations. Working
within the social system, those women who became concubines
played the game as far as possible to their best advantage. During a
period when individuals were being captured as slaves, any situation
that provided security—to say nothing of guaranteeing free status—

was an enviable position; there were many, and much worse, roles than that of concubine or royal slave.

In the women's quarters of the Kano palace, inherited status simultaneously limits a woman's social identity, and provides the opportunity to supersede those limits. Among slaves and concubines one's status defines the services one must perform; slaves and concubines have specific obligations to royal wives by virtue of their subordinate status. Theoretically, this is a rigid hierarchical social system, but it is this sharp definition of roles that allows for flexibility. Examination of the ways in which these roles are practiced reveals that the duties incumbent upon slave women are not enforced absolutely. There is room for congeniality and some degree of reciprocity in the sharing of tasks among women of the palace. However, it remains clear to all these women that a royal wife retains the prerogatives of her position, and ultimately slaves are subject to the demands of royal wives. Thus the attraction inherent in concubinage lies in its being a mechanism for advancement within the system, a means of moving from slave to free, if not royal, status.

The benefits of concubinage are evident only in relative terms. In larger emirates concubines may enjoy more privileged situations than their counterparts in less affluent circumstances, where women may be kept against their will as concubines.[27] However, the fact that concubinage has endured underlines its social importance. Concubinage endows a theoretically rigid social system with fluidity, providing greater numbers of candidates for leadership, ensuring the incorporation of conquered peoples into the royal family, and guaranteeing the expansion of control that inheres in such measures. It is not surprising, therefore, that concubinage has survived, despite major social changes, to this day.

Notes

1. I refer the reader to the following works for commentary on Hausa/Fulani slave women and concubines: Dunbar (1977), Lovejoy (1981a, 1981b, 1983), Smith (1981), M. G. Smith (1978), Robertson and Klein (1983).

I am grateful to the following for commenting on this study: His royal Highness Alhaji Ado Bayero, Emir of Kano, Allan Christelow, Catherine Coles, Robert Harms, David Henige, Robert Henry, Mervyn Hiskett, Paul Lovejoy, A. Neil Skinner, Mary F. Smith, and M. G. Smith.

2. The following examples and information contained in this study are from my own research among the women of the Kano palace during the periods 1979–80 and 1982–83.

3. For further explanation of this and all subsequent Hausa terms the reader is referred to Abraham (1968).

4. In a personal communication with His Royal Highness, the Emir of Kano, 9 March 1983, the Emir remarked that "Islamic law under the *jihad* abolished women's roles in public office."

5. M. G. Smith, personal communication, December 1986.

6. See Lovejoy (1981, 1983), and M. G. Smith (1960), for discussions of *murgu* (buying one's freedom) and other means of achieving freedom.

7. Personal communication, Hajiya Abba Bayero 26 April 1982.

8. Personal communication with Hajiya Abba Bayero 26 April 1982.

9. Personal communication, His Royal Highness the Emir of Kano, Alhaji Ado Bayero 9 March 1983.

10. Personal communication, Hajiya Abba Bayero 26 April 1982.

11. Smith notes that the various wives head various *"daki,* i.e., subdivisions of the husband's family and offspring. Thus *Mai Babban 'Daki* is 'the woman whose *daki* dominates the rest'." Personal communication, December 1986.

12. This and all the following information on titles was conveyed in a personal communication with His Royal Highness, Alhaji Ado Bayero on 9 March 1982.

13. M. G. Smith notes that "In Zaria the District Head I knew did otherwise. His *jakadiyu* [pl.] were his concubines and very jealous of one another. The wives didn't matter a hoot to them. He also had one nonconcubine *jakadiya,* married to a client, a bright Fulani woman who did his serious work." Personal communication, December 1986.

14. See Lovejoy (1983:6–14), Hill (1977:204), and Smith (1960:83) for further discussion of this as well as its application to concubines of nonroyal men.

15. In a personal communication with His Royal Highness the Emir of Kano, Alhaji Ado Bayero, the Emir commented that upon an emir's death or deposition his wives, concubines, and titled women may go with him to his place of exile, or, in the event of his death, may exercise any of the following options: (1) go to live with their grown children; (2) be married off (if still young); (3) be divided among the emir's brothers as their wives or concubines; (4) take their freedom; or (5) remain in the palace if they feel it has become their home.
Smith comments that a man's slaves and infertile concubines were inherited by his children (M. G. Smith 1978:49). See also Hinchcliffe (1975).

16. Personal communication, Hajiya Abba Bayero 26 April 1982.

17. Personal communication, Hajiya Abba Bayero 26 April 1982.

18. Personal communication, Hajiya Abba Bayero and His Royal Highness, Alhaji Ado Bayero, 26 April 1982 and 14 May 1982. Mediating personal preferences and traditional expectations can be difficult; if an emir prefers to have women continue their education and be free, it is difficult to convince

young women who wish to become concubines that an education might be better for them.

19. Personal communication with Hajiya Abba Bayero 21 May 1982. The woman described died during the summer of 1986, *Allah ji'kan ta, Amin.*

20. See also Willis (1985a:16–26).

21. According to the Kano Chronicle, Rumfa is said to have established the custom of wife seclusion in Kano in the 15th century, but it appears to have remained restricted to the upper classes until quite recently. Robinson (1896:205–6) noted that royal women were just about the only ones secluded in Hausaland at the end of the 19th century, and Polly Hill emphasizes that the practice of wife seclusion is "innovatory, not traditional" (1972:24).

22. Personal communication, Hajiya Abba Bayero 26 April 1982.

23. Personal communication, Hajiya Abba Bayero 9 May 1982.

24. See Willis (1985b:viii) for collaboration of this view.

25. See Tucker (1985) for a discussion of this situation.

26. Note, for example, that under Islamic law one man's testimony is equivalent to that of two women.

27. Mary Smith (1981) notes that Sarkin Kama Namoda, then in his seventies, had four wives and nine concubines in 1972, and many of the latter had been installed against their will. M. G. Smith comments that these concubines were "almost all surely freeborn" (Personal communication, December 1986).

References Cited

Abraham, R. C.
   1968   Dictionary of the Hausa Language. London: University of London Press.
Armah, Ayi Kwei
   1979   The Healers. London: Heinemann African Writers Series.
Barth, Heinrich
   1857   Travels and Discoveries in North and Central Africa 1849–1855. 3 Vols. New York: Harper and Brothers.
Boyd, Jean, and Murray Last
   1985   The Role of Women as "Agents Religieux" in Sokoto. Canadian Journal of African Studies 19(2):283–300.
Clapperton, Hugh
   1966[1829]   Expedition into the Interior of Africa From the Bight of Benin. London: Frank Cass.
Dunbar, Roberta Ann
   1977   Slavery and the Evolution of Nineteenth Century Damagaram. *In* Slavery in Africa. Suzanne Miers and Igor Kopytoff, eds. Pp. 155–181. Madison: University of Wisconsin Press.
Fika, Adamu
   1978   The Kano Civil War and British Overrule, 1882–1940. Ibadan: Oxford University Press.

Hill, Polly
 1972 Rural Hausa: A Village and a Setting. Cambridge: Cambridge University Press.
 1977 Population, Prosperity, and Poverty: Rural Kano 1900 and 1970. Cambridge: Cambridge University Press.
Hinchcliffe, Doreen
 1975 The Status of Women in Islamic Law. *In* Conflict and Harmony in Education in Tropical Africa. Godfrey Brown and Mervyn Hiskett, eds. Pp. 455–466. London: Allen and Unwin.
Hiskett, Mervyn
 1984 The Development of Islam in West Africa. London: Longman.
 1985 The Image of Slaves in Hausa Literature. *In* Slaves and Slavery in Muslim Africa, I, Islam and the Ideology of Slavery. John Ralph Willis, ed. Pp. 106–124. Lanham, MD: Littlefield, Adams & Company.
Hogben, S. J., and A. H. M. Kirk-Greene
 1966 The Emirates of Northern Nigeria: A Preliminary Survey of Their Historical Traditions. London: Oxford University Press.
Lander, Richard
 1830 Records of Captain Clapperton's Last Expedition to Africa. I and II. London: Colburn and Bentley.
Lovejoy, Paul
 1981a Slavery in the Context of Ideology. *In* The Ideology of Slavery. Paul Lovejoy, ed. Pp. 11–38. Beverly Hills: Sage Publications.
 1981b Slavery in the Sokoto Caliphate. *In* The Ideology of Slavery. Paul Lovejoy, ed. Pp. 201–244. Beverly Hills: Sage Publications.
 1983 Transformations in Slavery. Cambridge: Cambridge University Press.
Niven, Sir Rex
 1967 Nigeria. London: Ernest Benn, Ltd.
 1982 Nigerian Kaleidoscope: Memoirs of a Colonial Servant. Hamden, CT: Archon Books.
Perham, Margery
 1983 West African Passage. London: Peter Owen.
Pittin, Renee
 1983 Houses of Women: A Focus on Alternative Life-Styles in Katsina City. *In* Female and Male in West Africa. Christine Oppong, ed. Pp. 291–302. London: Allen and Unwin.
Robertson, Claire, and Martin Klein
 1983 Women and Slavery in Africa. Madison: University of Wisconsin Press.
Robinson, C. H.
 1896 Hausaland, or Fifteen Hundred Miles through the Central Soudan. London: Sampson Low, Marston & Company.
Schildkrout, Enid
 1983 Dependence and Autonomy: The Economic Activities of Secluded Hausa Women in Kano. *In* Female and Male in West Africa. Christine Oppong, ed. Pp. 107–126. London: Allen and Unwin.
Sharwood-Smith, Sir Bryan
 1967 Recollections of British Administration in the Cameroons and Northern Nigeria 1921–1957: "But Always as Friends." Durham, NC: Duke University Press.

Smith, Mary
    1981   Baba of Karo: A Woman of the Muslim Hausa. New Haven: Yale University Press.
Smith, M. G.
    1955   The Economy of Hausa Communities of Zaria. Colonial Research Studies No. 16. London: HMSO.
    1960   Government in Zazzau. London: Oxford University Press.
    1978   The Affairs of Daura. Berkeley: University of California Press.
    n.d.   The History of Kano. Unpublished manuscript, files of the author.
Trevor, Jean
    1975   Western Education and Muslim Fulani/Hausa Women in Sokoto, Northern Nigeria. *In* Conflict and Harmony in Education in Tropical Africa. Godfrey Brown and Mervyn Hiskett, eds. Pp. 247–272. London: Allen and Unwin.
Tucker, Judith
    1985   Women in Nineteenth Century Egypt. London: Cambridge University Press.
Willis, John Ralph
    1985a   Jihad and the Ideology of Enslavement. *In* Slaves and Slavery in Muslim Africa, I, Islam and the Ideology of Slavery. John Ralph Willis, ed. Pp. 16–26. Lanham, MD: Littlefield, Adams & Company.
    1985b   Preface. *In* Slaves and Slavery in Muslim Africa, I, Islam and the Ideology of Slavery. John Ralph Willis, ed. Pp. vii–xi. Lanham, MD: Littlefield, Adams & Company.
Wright, Marcia
    1975   Women in Peril: A Commentary on the Life Stories of Captives in Nineteenth Century East-Central Africa. *In* African Social Research, 20:800–819.

3

Maid Servants and Market Women's Apprentices in Adabraka

Roger Sanjek

Asian/American Center, Queens College, CUNY

Ghana has been the scene of much research on the issue of child fostering since Esther Goody's paper of 1966, the source point for most of this work. There she defined fostered children as those who "during an important part of their childhood and adolescence . . . live and learn, not in their parents' homes, but under the care and authority of parent surrogates" (1966:2). In that paper she opened up two areas for further research: (1) the roles that fostered children may play; and (2) the relationships between the children and their "parent surrogates." Goody identified four roles—student, "housemaid," apprentice, older person's caretaker—that I shall distinguish even more sharply than she did. In terms of relationships, she discussed the question of whether child and surrogate parent are kin or nonkin. It is this formal aspect of fosterage that has received much of the attention by subsequent researchers in Ghana (Azu 1974; Brydon 1979; Oppong 1969; Schildkrout 1972), more so than that given to the substantive issue of the roles fostered children play, or to the wider significance of child fosterage in Ghanaian society.[1]

Among the other issues she raised, several of which have been pursued in her further writings (Goody 1970, 1973, 1982), Goody also asked about the magnitude of fostering—"How common is it?" To this she was only able in 1966 to report on her own work in eastern and central Gonja, where between 18 and 26 percent of children resident in villages studied were fostered-in, and on some retrospective data for adults living in two southern Ghanaian villages. In these, 29 percent of the adults in an Ewe village had been fostered as children, as had 32 percent of the adults in a Fanti village. Subsequent fieldwork has turned up similar results—with either localities or samples of adults, as units of assessment (Goody 1982:39, 113, 152, 157; Pellow 1977:177)—but such numbers or rates are difficult to compare with each other. To my knowledge, no more comprehensive answer to the question "How common is it" has been offered.

Here I attempt a broader answer to this question. Although national census data for Ghana provide no direct information on fostering, some ethnographically informed inferences from census figures can be made. These data, so examined, show hitherto unrecognized regional differences in sex ratios for the age cohorts of 5 to 9 years, and 10 to 14, the prime years in which fostering occurs. Some regions are losers of girls in relation to boys, while other regions, and the three largest Ghanaian cities, are gainers of girls.[2] Furthermore, national totals show as many or more boys in these age groups as girls, a situation opposite to what we should expect, given that demographers have found child mortality rates in Ghana to be higher for boys than for girls. I suggest that some of the girls missing in the census count are child household workers who went unenumerated.

I also raise some new questions about fostering in southern Ghana, particularly in the cities: From where do the "maid servants" and market women's apprentices come? At what ages do they join their mistresses? What are the social characteristics of the rural families they leave? What are the social characteristics of the women who foster them? What is the significance of this pattern of childhood urbanization for understanding class formation and differentiation among urban Ghanaian women?

Historical Background

Much of the research on Ghanaian child fostering, as noted, has focused on the relationships between children and parent surrogates, and not on the roles children undertake. Consequently, the literature has treated the phenomenon as a problem in kinship and social organization, rather than one of work and labor systems. Goody's long-term research and thinking on fostering, brought together in *Parenthood and Social Reproduction: Fostering and Occupational Roles in West Africa* (1982), embodies the strengths and weaknesses of the focus on relationships.

With full command of the ethnographic literature on West Africa, Goody places the contemporary evidence of child apprenticeship and household work within "a basic West African conception of parenthood which is consistent with the delegation of certain aspects of parental roles under certain conditions" (1982:252). Using this literature structurally rather than historically, she develops a sequence of formal transformations through which this "basic" West African cultural pattern becomes what is observed in cities such as Accra today (1982:250–281). From this perspective, she states,

> There appears to be a general tendency to shift from fostering by kin to analogous arrangements with strangers who can provide either a training in modern skills or a chance to gain familiarity with urban ways. . . . For girls, in addition to [training in] skills in sewing, baking and trading, there has evolved the institution of "housemaid." I say evolved, because there does not appear to have been anything similar in the traditional societies of West Africa, with the possible exception of children who were lent to a creditor as surety for a debt. [1982:183]

The ahistorical, structural approach reveals its limitations here. Goody's evidence for fostering in "the traditional societies of West Africa" consists of ethnographic research dating from the 1920s through the 1970s. During these decades, and for centuries earlier, labor patterns in West Africa were distorted from any "basic West African" essence by the transatlantic slave trade, by the intensification of internal slavery, and by colonial demand for labor. Age, gender, and kin roles in the social provisioning and reproduction of labor were shuffled as urban and rural labor power was redirected by an increasingly internationalized demand system. The labor of "housemaids" must be located within this broader set of stresses on local labor allocations. I shall return to this point in my conclusion. Here we need briefly to place female household workers into this historical context.

From the past decade's reappraisals of slavery in Africa (Cooper 1979; Klein 1978; Lovejoy 1983; Lovejoy, ed. 1981; Miers and Kopytoff, eds. 1977; Robertson and Klein, eds. 1983; Watson, ed. 1980), we now know that slavery *within* the continent expanded throughout the centuries of the external trade, and that the majority of the enslaved within Africa were women. In trading communities like Accra, female slaves were used by free women to increase their productive activities (Robertson and Klein 1983:15–16). For Ghana, at least, it appears that Goody is wrong about an evolution from kinship fostering to female household work and apprenticeship.

In a study that appeared the year after Goody stated her conclusions, Robertson (1983) examined slavery in Accra from its formal outlawing by the British in 1874 to the last recorded slave transaction she was able to find in 1939. During this period the numbers of male slaves shrunk rapidly, but that of females did not. Between 1886 and 1918, 78.8 percent of the slaves mentioned in court cases Robertson reviewed were female, and most were children purchased between the ages of 5 and 10. "Female slaves were still needed by women to help with their labor-intensive tasks" (1983:223).[3]

Only 19 percent of the Accra slaves were indigenous Gã, and many of these were pawns, whose treatment was the same as that of slaves. The rest of the slave population originated in other regions of what is today Ghana. Some slaves, at least, were used in trading, and turned over their profits to their mistresses, as did junior relatives. In some cases where girls sought their freedom—and many did not—the court turned the girl over to her mistress as an unpaid apprentice.

Kin ties were also used to recruit urban female child workers during these same years, as Robertson's biography of Naa Kowa, born in 1892, makes evident (1984:124–132). Little seems to differentiate the roles girl slaves and kin played in assisting urban women in income-producing work and household tasks. If both slave and kin girl household workers coexisted 80 years ago, and both nonkin and kin ties are used to recruit girl household workers today, then Goody's structural approach is insufficient. A refocusing from relationships to roles is needed. We know what the girls did, both then and now, but why were they needed?

The growth of wage labor in Accra and other African cities over the last 100 years (at least) has intensified the demand for female labor in petty trade, prepared food production, and sewing. In this urban "informal sector," women who are successful, as well as those who are barren, have desired to recruit girls beyond their own daughters. Kin ties, slave purchase, local apprenticeship contracts, and recruitment of girls from poor, rural families have all been used. As their own daughters were increasingly sent to school—and few urban daughters were not by the 1970s—labor demand for girl workers increased, for household tasks as well as for commodity production and trade. As Robertson (1984:148–149) shows, schoolgirls *help* their mothers in the market, and may do some trading; girl apprentices *work* for their employers, doing more demanding tasks. Goody recognizes the point that girl household worker labor compensates for that lost when daughters are schoolgirls (1982:171), but this point is not central to her analysis, nor is the work of "housemaids" placed within a broader analysis of changing labor demands.

In fact, there are only a few references to "housemaids" in Goody's book (1982:143, 163, 170–171, 183–184, 256). In terms of roles (rather than relationships), she has much more to say about apprenticeship. There are more sources in the literature on apprentices than on maids, and her structural argument about a kin to nonkin transition is no doubt historically accurate for male apprenticeship. However, the issue of gender is not given its due; her data on types of training given fostered southern Ghanaian children are not differentiated fully by gender (1982:174, 175), and the bulk of her discussion of apprenticeship concerns male apprentices (1982: ch. 8). In my Accra fieldwork experience and from my knowledge of the West African literature, the "freeing" ceremony that ends male apprenticeship in Ghana and Nigeria (Goody 1982:200; Smutylo 1973) has no analog for female market women's apprentices.[4]

It is doubly unfortunate that Goody slights gender differences in her analysis of fostering, and that scholars attuned to gender in African studies (Hansen and Strobel 1985; Strobel 1982) pay little attention to work on female child household workers, and do not mention Goody's work on fostering. I will attempt to tie these strands together in my conclusion. But first I shall turn to the ethnographic setting from which my understanding of child fostering begins, and report my findings about child "maid servants" and apprentice market women in Adabraka.

Adabraka

Adabraka is a residential neighborhood within easy walking distance of the markets, government offices, and private firms of the central business district of Accra, Ghana's capital city. It was first settled in the early 1900s as old Accra overflowed its boundaries and people moved north, away from the sea coast. Since the late 1940s, Adabraka has become a neighborhood of large multi-household buildings. The typical Adabraka building is two stories, with the landlord and his or her family living upstairs, and the downstairs rooms rented to tenants. Most Adabraka buildings have electricity. Shared latrines, water taps, and kitchens are located in the paved courtyard areas around and behind the buildings, and are enclosed by a compound wall. Neighborhood life revolves around the courtyard, the areas fronting the streets, the streets themselves off the major traffic arteries, and the many shops, streetside sellers, bars, churches, and schools. By 1970, some 44,000 persons lived in Adabraka.

Adabraka life is comfortable compared with the poorer sections in old Accra and in the peripheral suburbs, but it is crowded and cramped when compared with the elite residential areas. Most Adabraka residents occupy middle rungs on the Accra occupational ladder. In the 11 buildings along the Adabraka street where Lani Sanjek and I lived in 1970–71, and returned in 1974, 31 percent of the adults were manual workers, 29 percent clerical workers, 18 percent self-employed traders, and 11 percent self-employed artisans. The highest income earners in the neighborhood, comprising 11 percent of the adults, were business men and women employing others, middle managers, a lawyer, and an architect. Along this street, more than 20 ethnic identities were represented in a population of 423, with Kwawus (26 percent), Gãs (17 percent), and Ewes (16 percent), the most numerous. Most were southern Ghanaians—Christian, literate, modern in every sense.

Fostering

Child fostering is as common, or more so, among Adabraka people as among other southern Ghanaians, according to our ethnographic reports. Of the 40 Adabraka adults in our network study (Sanjek 1978), 21, or 55 percent, had been fostered during their childhood. No ethnic differences were evident: 6 of the 10 Gã subjects had been fostered; 6 of the 10 Kwawus; 6 of the 10 Ewes; and 3 of the 10 others, of diverse ethnic identities. Some differences by gender emerged—13 of the 20 women had been fostered, but only 8 of the 20 men. We suspect however, our data on childhood residence for a few individuals may be incomplete. Certainly more than half, perhaps as many as two-thirds, of these 40 adults had been fostered during portions of their childhoods.[5]

The Adabraka adults of the 11 buildings studied were parents of at least 238 children under age 18 in 1970. (Some men probably had more "outside children" than we learned about.) Of these 238 children, 42 (18 percent) were fostered out. Nine resided in other parts of Accra, 15 in Kwawu towns, and the rest in southern Ghana (Akropong, Keta, Cape Coast, Tarkwa, Somanya), Togo, and Nigeria. All of these children were living with relatives. To my knowledge, all attended school, many of them having been sent expressly for that purpose. Most of them, therefore, could be assigned to Goody's "student" role.

A few of these fostered-out children, however, had been asked for by a grandparent, or were sent to live with an older person as a helper and companion, Goody's "older person's caretaker" role. This fostering role I believe to be primarily a rural one, involving either a rural-to-rural or urban-to-rural residence shift by the child (compare Brydon 1983:325–326; Dinan 1983:347). The "student" role turned up in Adabraka in urban-to-rural, and rural-to-urban forms, and has its rural-to-rural counterparts in Ghana as well.

Goody's other two foster child roles—"housemaid" and "apprentice"—are primarily rural-to-urban, and secondarily urban-to-urban, with much of the intraurban movement involving circulation by "maid servants" (the Ghanaian English term used in Adabraka) from one employer to another, a process well described by Oppong (1974).

In addition to the 42 out-fostered Adabraka children, another 14 were residing away from their parents in boarding schools. Such institutionally domiciled children do not meet Goody's definition of fostering; only those Adabraka children actually residing with a nonparental adult, and going to school there, may be considered fostered children (Goody 1982:168). However, if we include these 14 boarders with the fostered children, the total number of children living apart from their Adabraka parents is 56, or 24 percent of their 238 children.

It is against this outflow of 56 children that the inflow of 48 children fostered by Adabraka adults must be set. These in-fostered children account for 24 percent of the 200 children resident on the Adabraka street during the 1970–71 period of our fieldwork. In terms of relationships, 79 percent of these fostered children were kin of their "parent surrogates," or sponsors. Among the nonkin cases, half were of ethnic identities, or "tribes" in Ghanaian English, different from that of their sponsors. (And so was one of the kin-fostered children.)

Cutting across the kin/nonkin division are differences in roles. These differences, as Table 1 illustrates, were most striking between boys and girls. All of the 17 in-fostered boys were in the "student" role. Only a handful, 4 of the 31 in-fostered girls, were students. Most of these female foster child migrants to Accra were workers.

Maid Servants and Market Women's Apprentices

These girl workers, 27 of them between the ages of 7 and 17, worked in Adabraka households as maid servants, or assisted female market traders in their work. Half the maids were related by kinship to their mistresses. Half were not, and several of these girls were of ethnic identities different from their employer. Unrelated maids may be secured through making a cash payment to the parents of the girl, after which she becomes the full responsibility of the employer. Pay-

Table 1
Adabraka Fostering

	student	apprentice	maid servant	total
boys	17	—	—	17
girls	4	9	18	31
				48

ments to the girl, or the promise of paying for a sewing apprenticeship and machine when her service terminates, are at the discretion of the employer.

Maid servants who are kin may be short-term helpers, often a younger sister, for a woman with young children.[6] Others are more distant relatives from rural areas. Harsh treatment of girls who are related to their mistress may be controlled through kin pressure, particularly where the relationship is close—sister or niece—and when other relatives reside in the same building or nearby. Often such girls are promised the sewing apprenticeship and machine, and perhaps a cash payment when they leave their employer. More distant relatives, particularly those from poor, rural families, are more exposed to scolding, long, unbroken work hours, and physical disciplining—treatment that is most common among nonkin maid servants.

Not all girls are involved in the care of young children. Almost half (8 of the 18 in Adabraka), resided in households of women in their fifties and sixties, or of childless working women in their thirties. Many of these girls were sent out hawking items like biscuits, rubber sandals, or tinned foods, or tended a sales table with bread, or palm fans and brooms, in front of their employer's building. All maid servants assist their employer in cooking and housecleaning tasks. They also carry water to the bathing room for the woman, and may heat the water on a charcoal fire in cooler weather.

Only 1 of the maid servants—an Asante girl "given" by her parents to her Nzima employer—was sent to school. Most of the others had not attended primary school before joining their employers. The same was true of the 9 girls, aged 8 to 16, who were assistants to women traders of cloth, cooking utensils, beads, and cooked food. Only 7 of the 27 maid servants and apprentices had attended school at all before joining the Adabraka women.

The market women's assistants helped their employers transport goods, watched the trade location when the market woman was off on business or shopping, carried messages and ran errands in the marketplace, and learned to handle money and make sales. The girls acquired knowledge of trading the particular item their employer sold, but they also learned about trading and market activities in general. Often girls were started selling ice water—walking through the market while carrying on their head a water container in which a block of ice floats and calling out in search of customers. Such hawking is as much for education as for the modest profit: 15 to 30 new pesewas on a 10 to 15 new pesewa ice block. They might later be sent out hawking more valuable items. Girls working for cooked-food sellers learned the technology of cooking in commercial quantities, how to order supplies, and selling techniques.

Though we came across one case of a girl who lived with her family, and worked for a cooked-food seller living in the same building, all the apprentices considered here lived with their employers. Like the maid servants, apprentices also helped their employers with cooking and courtyard domestic work. Only two of the apprentices, however, worked for women who had small children. Unlike the maid servants, who may receive a sewing apprenticeship in the future, the market women's assistants were involved in an educational process day-to-day.

Conflict between Foster Child and Sponsor

Cases of conflict between female child workers and their employers certainly arise, and such cases were topics of street and courtyard gossip. The sources of such conflict are two: money and sex. Girls may be reprimanded for failure to conduct their hawking more productively; they may be scolded for claiming to have "lost" money; they may be accused of keeping trading profits for themselves. They may also be punished if found "lavishing" free goods or money on boyfriends. In some cases, gossip about such indiscretions circulated in the neighborhood widely before the woman was herself aware of it. A case in point: the young girl assistant whom everyone but her employer knew gave free cigarettes to a boyfriend, straight from the woman's trading stock.

Sexual relationships were problematic for many of the Adabraka fostered girls. According to Fiawoo's data, southern Ghanaian girls achieve their greatest spurt of physical growth between age 10 and 11; by 15, "growth declines appreciably" (Fiawoo 1976:82). They reach puberty at age 13, two years ahead of boys (ibid.:82, 85). Ofosu-Amaah (1969) found that 95 percent of the students at Aburi Girls Secondary School had begun menstruation between ages 12.5 and 13.5. Maid servants and apprentices then can be expected to be sexually mature by age 13 or 14 (compare Dinan 1983:346–347).

In Addo and Goody's survey of Ghanaian women, they found the mean age of marriage for uneducated women was 16.9 years (1976:17–18). The form of marriage they refer to is in almost all cases the customary "engagement" or "knocking fee," which usually occurs after the woman has delivered her first child. We may conclude that the period from age 14 to 16 in Ghanaian society is one in which the uneducated urban maid servants and apprentices are likely to become sexually active, or to feel societal pressures to do so from the young men and women around them.

This is certainly the case in Adabraka. But such sexual activity on the part of maid servants and apprentices is neither encouraged nor condoned by their employers. So the girls flirt when the woman is not around. They arrange sexual encounters when and where they can. Since they are always on call, and usually sleep in their employer's room, this is no easy task. Such encounters are easier to arrange for those maid servants who remain in the house, or should be out hawking on their own, during the daytime while the employer is off at work. For other girls, visits to the man's room occur when the maid servant or apprentice is able to steal away.

Employers object to sexual encounters not only because they lose the girls' time while she is off on dates, or because the girl may become lackadaisical about her duties while she is thinking about being with her boyfriend. Perhaps more important to them are their doubts that the boy will marry the girl should she become pregnant, and assume responsibility for her and the baby. They worry, therefore, that the costs of delivery and confinement may have to borne by the employers themselves. Depending upon the terms of the agreement between the woman and the girl's parents, she may bear complete economic responsibility for the girl, and for launching her into adulthood. At very least, she bears responsibility for the girl's behavior. Some women may be successful in sacking a pregnant maid servant, avoiding any further costs, but I believe it is most often the case that some economic outlay on the employer's part will be involved, to say nothing of the cost of replacing the girl's labor, either by herself, or with another girl.

Now, from the maid servant's point of view, the situation is different. There is no future in being a maid servant, and for most, no training or even the promise of learning a skill like sewing, or the cloth, bead, or cooked-food business. When she begins to work on her own, the ex-maid servant will most likely enter the urban informal sector at its lowest rungs—pounding fufu in a chop bar, or hawking low capital items "one-one."

Although a girl may believe her particular boyfriend is Prince Charming, and only unexpectedly find herself pregnant, we need not interpret her behavior as merely blinded by love, or even as economically irrational. Becoming a mother may offer the woman a source of income from the father—at least in terms of money for the child—even if the man does not marry her, but only acknowledges paternity by "naming" the child (compare Brydon 1983:326). If he does marry her, the husband may provide trading capital, allowing her to enter the market independently at a higher level, and also assume the cost of rent. In the worst case the man may deny responsibility, the employer may sack the girl, and parents back home may be furious. But even here the girl has lost little, and has gained a child. In the best case, she is certainly better off as a wife than as a maid servant. In the intermediate case, she gains some economic hold on the child's father, and begins the inevitable process of establishing a place in the informal sector.

It is my argument that maid servant-employer conflict over sexuality is almost a property of the maid servant role. On the basis of my admittedly few Adabraka cases, I will push the argument a bit further. I suggest that most maid servants becoming sexually active in the 14-to-16 age range will not be promiscuous. Rather they will attempt to form an enduring relationship with one man, and if they become pregnant, quietly let gossip circulate about the identity of the father. In many cases, they circulate the man's name in early phases of the relationship, telling a few girlfriends who will tell others, but not the employer. The gossip strategically creates a climate of neighborhood public opinion that makes it difficult for the man to deny paternity. The girls' pattern of behavior can be interpreted as a rational attempt to achieve an enduring—hopefully marital—relationship with one man.

My argument has been phrased in terms of maid servants, and not market women's apprentices. This is based upon my small, but patterned number of Adabraka cases. I will further suggest that apprentice market women, and also maid servants who are close kin to their employers, especially those promised machine and sewing training, will be less likely to have sexual relationships during the 14-to-16 age period. They have more to lose if they are discovered by their employer. They may also be more likely to seek abortions if they do become pregnant (compare Dinan 1983:347–348). But I suggest they in fact delay their active entrance into the sexual arena, as do the educated daughters of Adabraka parents.

The mean age of marriage for female primary and Arabic school attenders in Ghana is 18.5 years, suggesting they postpone sexual activity and pregnancy a year and a half later than do uneducated Ghanaian girls. Age of marriage increases with education level in Ghana. For middle school graduates it is 18.8 years, and for secondary school and more advanced levels, 21.2 years (Addo and Goody 1976).

One more suggestion: of all fostered girls, those who are sponsored by wealthy female traders, and who are incorporated into their employers' household and business, are probably most likely to avoid behavior leading to conflict over sexuality or money. Unlike big men, big women in Ghana cannot add children by taking wives.[7] Fostered girls, however, can be deployed to expand business activities where true daughters are few. Such girls who prove their abilities, and can expect an adult position in their sponsor's operations, have more to gain economically by remaining with their employer than by establishing a relationship with a man. Women in such cases may in fact arrange or assist their fostered girls in marriages to men whom they approve.

A negative case from Adabraka reinforces my point. The fostered "daughter" of a wealthy female market trader, a girl being groomed for a place in her sponsor's import trade became pregnant and married an artisan living nearby. The trader cut her off. She eventually entered the informal trading sector at a position far below what she might have, had she stayed with her "mother." The story was widely known, and perhaps served as a cautionary tale to younger apprentice traders.

How Common is It?

Maid servants and market women's assistants are mentioned in all substantial accounts of urban Ghanaian life. They are found among the people of the Zongo in Kumasi (Schildkrout 1972, 1978:117, 149–150); and in the households of the Akan elite civil servants of Accra (Oppong 1974). Other citations—including several in popular Ghanaian fiction (cf. Goody 1966, 1982:143)—could be mentioned (Azu 1974; Clark 1984:259–261, 1985; Kumekpor 1974; Pellow 1977:140–141, 226–227; Robertson 1974, 1984). Maid servants and market women's apprentices appear to be ubiquitous in urban Ghana.

If we turn to the 1970 census of Ghana, some interesting discrepancies in sex ratios begin to make sense in light of this pattern of female childhood urbanization. Although slightly more girls than boys are born in Ghana, and slightly more girls were recorded in the under 1 and 1-to-4 age cohorts in 1970 (see Table 2), as many boys as girls were enumerated in the 5-to-9 cohort, and 105 boys to each 100 girls in the 10-to-14 cohort, the prime maid servant years.

These sex ratios for the 5-to-9 and 10-to-14 age groups are the opposite of what we should expect. Mortality rates for boys in Ghana are higher than those for girls. Kpedekpo's study (1970) of death registration data showed ratios of infant deaths between 1955 and 1960 averaging 119 dead male infants to 100 female. Addo and Goody (1976) found that 87.6 percent of the deceased children of urban Ghanaian women had died before age 10; and 92.8 percent of those of rural Ghanaian women. The sex ratio among these dead children was 117 boys to 100 girls. Giasie's (1969) 1960 life tables for Ghana indicated that of every 100 boys born, 68.6 could be expected to reach age 10 to

Table 2
Sex Ratios (Males/100 Females) by Region, 1970

	under 1	1–4	5–9	10–14	15–24	25–44	45–64	65+
GHANA	99	99	100	105	93	92	110	102
Region:								
Upper	98	100	114	140	70	63	109	112
Northern	100	100	114	136	83	86	140	132
Brong-Ahafo	99	99	98	106	98	108	130	130
Ashanti	100	99	97	98	96	99	110	105
Volta	99	98	98	106	95	74	95	89
Eastern	99	100	99	105	100	91	100	91
Accra	100	100	91	81	98	135	128	84
Central	98	98	102	112	95	78	90	90
Western	100	98	97	102	99	108	134	120

14, but of every 100 girls born, 71.4 could be expected to reach that age. Gaisie's figures would yield an expected sex ratio for age 10 to 14 of 96 boys to 100 girls, yet the 1970 Census reported 105 boys to 100 girls.

If, then, more girls than boys are born, and if more boys than girls die, why do we find more boys age 10 to 14 in the 1970 Ghanaian population than girls? One possibility raised by the demographer Gaisie is that girls in the 10-to-14 age range who are pregnant or have delivered may report or be recorded by enumerators as older than their chronological age. Gaisie claims that 49 percent of these 10-to-14-year-old girls up-reported their ages in the 1960 census (Gaisie 1969:8). Gaisie does not present any evidence of such up-reporting actually happening. And such a claim assumes that all girls have in fact been enumerated, a situation my ethnographic experience makes me inclined to doubt. I suggest this assumption of female up-reporting of age is a post facto demographer's conceit to normalize discrepant age and sex numbers. Everything then works out neatly—too neatly.

I cannot claim that no girls in fact up-reported their age, or were enumerated by census workers as older than their true chronological age. But what I can show is that if this did occur, it varied considerably by region, and was in fact reversed in the cities. If we look at the 1970 census sex ratios for the 10-to-14 age cohort by region (Table 2), which I have computed, and which have not to my knowledge been examined by demographers, it is striking that some regions diverge markedly from the figure of 105 boys to 100 girls for Ghana as a whole. In Ashanti and Accra, the two regions that contain Ghana's two largest cities, the supposed up-reporting did not happen at all, and more girls than boys were enumerated—only 98 boys to every 100 girls in Ashanti, and 81 boys to every 100 girls in Accra. These are precisely the areas in which we would expect to find large numbers of female maid servants and market women's apprentices. The sex ratios for the three largest cities in Ghana—Accra, Kumasi, and Takoradi (see Table 3)— show even larger surpluses of girls in the 10-to-14 cohort, and also in the 5-to-9 age group (compare Clark 1985:140). The urban figures then are precisely the opposite of the general enumeration results, and also of the demographer's female up-reporting assumption.

My argument is that a substantial portion of the higher than expected national and selected regional male sex ratios in the 10-to-14 age cohort—which contradicts what we know about child mortality— is due to an outmigration from rural areas of female child workers, and to an under-enumeration of urban maid servants. If we look at regional rather than national age-sex ratios, we find that certain regions lose girls in these age groups, and others gain girls. Urban sex ratios, I suggest, in fact underrepresent maids and apprentices. Census enumerators do not ask about such categories.[8] Those who tell the enumerator who lives in the building—supposedly "household heads"— may easily forget some of the maids in the many tenant households in large urban buildings, or fail to remember those who have just recently arrived.

The maps, showing by region the actual numbers of girls versus boys in the 5-to-14 age range, give us an indication of regional flows and also of changes between 1960 and 1970. In 1960 only Accra, the most urbanized region, had a surplus of girls (+ 6033), and all other regions had deficits (Figure 1). In 1970 Accra had an even larger surplus of girls (+ 15,833), reflecting, I contend, an increase in numbers of maid servants and market women's apprentices during the 1960s at a rate greater than that of population increase (Figure 2). Ashanti and the western region, the locations of Kumasi and Takoradi, also showed surpluses of girls in 1970. All other regions showed deficits. The relatively more prosperous Eastern, Volta, and Brong-Ahafo regions were losing fewer girls, with larger populations, in 1970 than in

Table 3
Sex Ratios (Males/100 Females) in Three Largest Cities, 1970

City:	under 1	1–4	5–9	10–14	15–24	25–44	45–64	65 +
Accra (564,000)	100	99	89	73	92	136	134	77
Kumasi (260,000)	97	98	87	75	104	122	148	112
Takoradi (58,000)	98	99	87	77	100	140	185	115

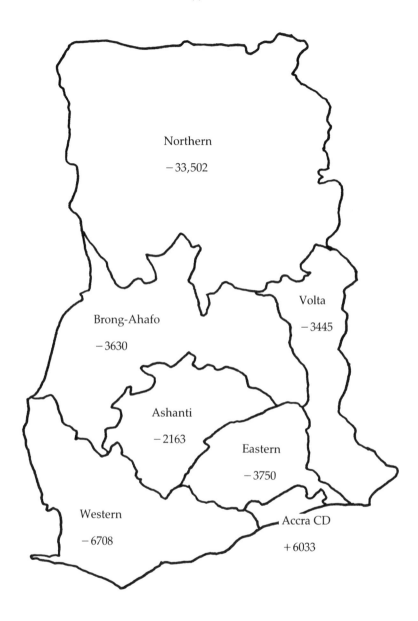

Figure 1
Number of girls age 5–14 in relation to number of boys
age 5–14, by region in 1960

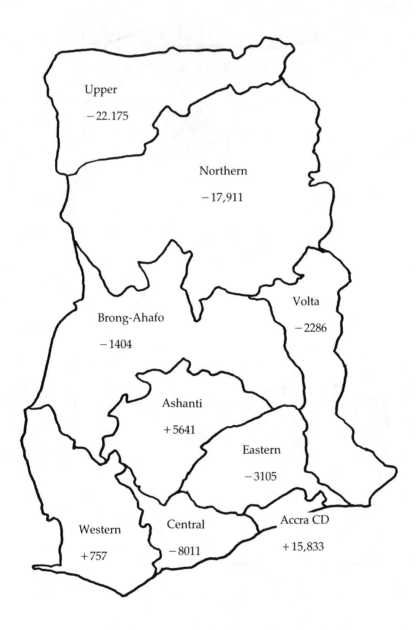

Figure 2
Number of girls age 5–14 in relation to number of
boys age 5–14, by region in 1970

1960. The relatively poorer Northern and Upper regions, and the Central region, had probably changed very little, given population growth. The most impressive change was in Ashanti—from a loser of girls in 1960 to an importer in 1970.

In Table 4 we see that Accra in 1970 had 14,399 more girls than boys in the 6-to-14 age range. We also see that more girls than boys attended school. Since the 1970 sex ratios for the under-age-5 populations of Accra are even (see Table 2), and since we know that all children living with their parents in Adabraka attend school (see also Azu 1974; Clark 1985:14; Pellow 1977:121), we may assume any discrepancies in the actual numbers of boys and girls in school reflect such minor considerations as boys finishing school earlier than girls, or the higher boy mortality rates here working themselves out.

The much larger number of girls (3,480) than boys (959) who attended school in the past, I suggest, consists primarily of maid servants and assistants. In Adabraka one-quarter of these girls had attended a few years of primary school before their urbanization. Of the numbers of Accra children in 1970 who had never attended school (shown in Table 4) the majority of boys I suggest are 6- and 7-year-olds who have not yet started. Only a small number of boys in Accra never attend school. With even sex ratios, the number of girls who have never attended school—given similar numbers in school—should approach the number for boys. Instead we find more than twice as many girls who never attended school (17,198) as boys (7,181). The 10,000 more girls than boys here represent maid servants and apprentices who did not begin school before coming to Accra. In Adabraka, those who never attended school account for three-quarters of the female child workers.

If my assumptions are correct, and I admit the room for counter argument is ample, then the 1970 census data indicate roughly 13,500 maid servants and apprentices between the ages of 6 and 14 in Accra. If the Adabraka street I studied were a microcosm, a perfect sample, of the city, there would be 36,000 maids and female apprentices under age 18 in the 1970 Accra population. While certainly not an elite neighborhood, Adabraka is toward the higher end of the economic scale

Table 4
Accra Children Age 6 to 14, 1970

	in school	past	never	total	difference
boys	47,423	959	7,181	55,563	
girls	49,284	3,480	17,198	69,962	+14,399

among Accra neighborhoods. It thus probably has more maid servants and apprentices than poorer areas of the city.

That said, I suggest the number of maid servants and market women's apprentices lies somewhere between the census number of 13,500 (probably too low, due to underenumeration of girls) and the Adabraka projection of 36,000 (certainly too high) for Accra as a whole. If we split the difference between these estimates, then roughly one in every three or four girls in Accra in 1970 was an in-fostered maid servant or market women's apprentice.

Other Issues

Questions of relationships, roles, magnitude, and regional variation by no means exhaust the issues around which survey and ethnographic case study data on in-fostered female child workers needs to be collected. Rather than more exercises in inference, projection, and ethnographically-informed guesswork, however, I will merely list some of these questions, and urge that further research in many disciplines be conducted to answer them. The entire phenomenon of female child labor migration has been neglected; ethnographic pieces and clues are the best that we have.

1. *Where Do the Girls Come From?* The Adabraka maid servants come primarily from the Eastern and Central regions, with smaller numbers from the Accra district itself, and from the Volta-Togo area (Table 5). Other data for Accra (Azu 1974; Oppong 1974) are consistent with these points of origin. I encountered no cases of northerner girls as maid servants or apprentices in Accra. Schildkrout's data (1972, 1978) on Kumasi Zongo indicate northern Togo as a source of Zongo market women's nonkin assistants, with a few northern Ghanaian Banda girls. I suspect that some households in Kumasi might employ northern girls as maids,[9] as might urban and rural households in the Ashanti, Brong-Ahafo, and western regions, prime destinations of northern migrants (Caldwell 1967, 1969; Hill 1970; Van Hear 1982), but I have no evidence for this. I can offer no other guesses about the ex-

Table 5
Region of Origin, Adabraka Maids and Apprentices

	Ashanti 1	
Western 1	Eastern 11	Togo 1
Central 8	Accra 3	Volta 2

ceedingly high boy sex ratios in the Northern and Upper regions (see Table 2, and Maps), where in 1970 some 136 and 140 boys were enumerated for each 100 girls in the 10 to 14 age range. I am reluctant to accept female up-reporting as the sole explanation of this marked discrepancy from what we should expect—more girls than boys.[10]

The northern Ghanaian sex ratio discrepancies first appear in the 5 to 9 age range, when migration of female child workers begins, and they increase in the 10 to 14 age range, when the phenomenon becomes even more numerically salient. I prefer to suggest that a social process which we already understand, if imperfectly, in southern Ghana also obtains in northern Ghana. The hard ethnographic work of tracing the destinations of female child migrants from northern Ghana remains to be done.

2. *At What Age Do They Come?* Table 6 shows that half the girls in Adabraka joined their employers before the age of 10, and half later. In fact, the data are not continuous. Some 13 of the 27 maids and apprentices left their natal households between the ages of 2 and 8. The relationships between these girls and their employers were extremely close, much more so than those between employers and girls who joined them at later ages. Adabraka people spoke of the employers of the early arrived child workers as the "mothers" of the girls, using "mother" in conversation as they did in referring to women whose own children resided with them in Adabraka. Such women referred to the girls as "daughter." As one woman put it: "I am making this girl."

The rest of the girls had joined the women at ages 12 to 15, either as maid servants for women with small children, or expressly to learn trading. Here the relationship may have less emotional bonding. Some of these girls stayed only a short time before the women "sacked" them or they ran away. I know of no systematic data on the ages at which maid servants and apprentices joined their employers.

Table 6
Adabraka Maids and Apprentices (N = 27)

	age 1970	age join mistress
2–4	—	2
5–9	6	11
10–14	15	11
15–17	6	2
no data	—	1
	27	27

3.   *What Are the Social Characteristics of the Sending Families?* Most Adabraka people told me that the rural families of the girls were poor—as compared with the Adabraka households they joined. Beyond that I can only raise questions deserving research. Within rural areas are poor families more likely to send children than wealthier ones? Are some rural areas or villages overrepresented by urban maid servants and apprentices, having established sending networks or migration channels? Does the number of siblings (see Caldwell 1969:73), and their sex ratios, influence parents' decisions to foster-out a daughter as a maid servant or apprentice?

4.   *How Do They Get to Accra?* Okediji (1978) has described a Nigerian pattern by which women specialize in recruiting and training female household workers. I learned of nothing comparable in Adabraka, though I never asked directly if such patterns exist. What data I have on recruitment suggest that poor rural relatives may ask urban kin to take a child, or that Adabraka women may return to their home village or town to attempt to locate a girl. Within Adabraka, people looking for a maid servant will tell friends, and the circulation of girls within the city appears to depend upon adult informal communication of such information. To my knowledge there is no printed advertising of the need for maid servants.

5.   *What Are the Social Characteristics of the Employers?* Even when women reside with husbands, maid servants are employed by women, not men. In terms of class, those Adabraka women of Ghanaian upper middle-class standing were more likely to have maid servants than were lower middle-class or working-class women. Housewives were far more likely than working women to have maid servants, but this is because "housewives" in Adabraka were working women temporarily at home taking care of newborns. Several of the maid servants were employed to help in infant care. Otherwise, women of all occupations, and of all ages, might have maid servants or trading assistants. Many who did not were actively looking for them. Most women in their fifties and sixties have a maid servant or assistant living with them. Those older women who did not all had a younger coresident daughter or female relative in their household.

Significance

Maid servants and apprentice market women present a distinct pattern of female childhood urbanization. Boys too may come from rural areas or smaller towns to Accra and Ghana's other cities, but they come as students, and they come at later ages than do girls. And they come in much smaller numbers (Isiugo-Abanihe 1985:65). Women in their twenties also migrate in increasing numbers to Ghana's towns along with men (see Caldwell 1969), but an important movement of their younger sisters occurs as well.

It is remarkable that this movement of girls to urban employment as maid servants and apprentices has eluded the attention of demographers. Caldwell's extensive survey of urban migration in Ghana (1969) missed the phenomenon entirely, although he noted, "In the villages one frequently hears stories of town relatives exploiting migrants, especially young females, by working them hard as unpaid domestic labour" (1969:134). Following an introduction and a discussion of the age discrepancies between his data and that of the 1960 census, a problem of numerical "validity" (1969:35), the analysis is limited to migrants over age 20 (1969:57ff). A brief inquest into why female child migration was missed in Caldwell's work suggests insights into the rural sending situation.

Caldwell's survey, which asked rural households about absentee members, turned up less than half as many such migrants under age 15 as did the 1960 census (1969:27, 38). Caldwell's explanation, that most of those others for whom no age was reported can be assumed to be under 15 (1969:27), is questionable in my judgment. More telling are his hints that young female migrants may no longer be considered part of their rural families of origin (1969:36–39). Why should this be so? Some may now have children, and be considered members of their husbands' families, Caldwell surmises (1969:37). Yet, other of his survey results point in a different direction.

Rural Ghanaians, Caldwell found, strongly believe young women to be in "moral danger" in the cities. "There is very definitely stronger emotional pressure exerted on girls to stay in the villages than there is on boys" (1969:103). Yet the rural respondents also agreed that women prefer to find husbands in cities, where life is more attractive (1969:109). Finally, few rural respondents would admit that needs for cash income pushed family members into urban migration (1969:114).

My interpretation is that many poor, rural families who send daughters to towns as maid servants, and may indeed accept cash payments for them, prefer not to remember or speak about it. Those who marry may well be remembered, but the many who do not, and assume independent careers as informal sector traders or commodity producers, are "forgotten." Additionally, the survey methods, which relied on older male household heads for information, would not maximize recall of missing young female relatives. They are more likely to be counted in cities, where they work and reside, then remembered in villages, and this is what Caldwell's survey demonstrates.

The childhood migration of maid servants and female apprentices continues to be a blind spot for demographers. In a recent summary paper on gender and migration in West Africa, Adepoju (1983) cites research showing that women outnumber men among younger migrants, and quotes demographers' guesses that early marriage is the primary explanation for the sex ratio discrepancies. In a face-saving argument, Paige (1986), a demographer familiar with the ethnographic literature on child fostering, attributes the blindness of demographers to the movements of female child workers to the absence of large-scale data sets confirming ethnographic microstudies of child fostering patterns. I doubt this. The numbers, I hope I have demonstrated, have been there all along in the census. What has been missing both in demographers' own surveys, and their use of census data, is the right questions. Paige's analysis of large-scale survey data from seven African countries confirms that nonparental residence of young girls is widespread, and especially so in Ghana, and that "demand for housemaids" is "probably largely" a factor in this (Paige 1986:15–16; see also Isiugo-Abanihe 1985:61).

Two modes of explanation of the Ghanaian situation can be offered. A functional or adaptive explanation would show how rural families benefit by securing cash payments and opportunities for daughters they cannot match. The girls benefit by learning urban skills, or by at least having a chance at marriage and employment in more favorable urban circumstances. Urban women benefit by utilizing child labor in raising their own children, thereby being able to work full time. They also benefit economically by sending their maid servants, or apprentices out selling. Urban daughters benefit through education, made possible in part because the labor of the maid servant replaces their own domestic labor contributions (compare Isiugo-Abanihe 1985:66).

While Goody says relatively little about girl household workers or market women's apprenticeship, she presents a forceful argument that fostering in general is "adaptive," a word she herself uses (1982:4, 67). She finds, "[I]n a society where fostering is positively valued by adults and viewed by fostered children with at least mixed feelings, it does not produce adults who are at a disadvantage with respect to success either in their marriage or in their career" (1982:53).

Goody's subjective approach to fostering is explicit. "[T]he model must reflect transactions from the point of view of the parent, the child and the pro-parent" (1982:22). Everyone benefits. "The proliferation of forms of delegation of parent roles in these complex systems allows maximum mobility; it does not restrict the children to the skills and resources controlled directly by their parents" (1982:5). The "Invisible Hand" of fostering at work?

Here the limitations of Goody's approach must be assessed. Counterposed to her focus on relationships, kinship and social organization, structure, and function, I suggest a viewpoint beginning with roles, work and labor systems, history, and inequality. One should be suspicious of analyses in which everyone benefits. I favor an analysis which sets Ghana in its world systematic context as a peripheral capitalist commodity state.

The general argument, though not specifically applied to maid servants and market apprentices, is spelled out by Sandbrook and Arn in *The Laboring Poor in Greater Accra* (1977). In peripheral capitalist states, the social reproduction of the external estate and the local upper bourgeoisie (political, administrative, military elites; upper level importers, manufacturers, and professionals) requires that formal sector workers be waged at very low levels. The social reproduction of the waged labor force requires in turn that artisans and workers in the vast informal sector:

> produce, under conditions of extreme competition, inexpensive and essential goods and services for (mainly) the poorer employees of large enterprises and the State. . . . [T]he availability of these cheap goods and services, themselves often a function of super-exploitation, . . . permit wages to be lower than they would otherwise be. In this way a larger portion of the economic surplus is transferred to the large firms [Sandbrook and Arn 1977:24]

The informal sector mobilizes masses of women who distribute and produce these goods and services. They also socially reproduce the male formal sector work force at home (Sanjek 1982). While women traders, artisans, and commodity producers figure into the more sophisticated analyses of the informal sector (Hart 1976), the specific place of female child workers receives no attention (see Sanjek 1982:64–65). Yet, urban Ghanaian women, in turn, mobilize female child labor in their informal sector activities, in day-to-day social provisioning tasks, and in transgenerational social reproduction. Through the labor of maid servants and apprentices, women are able to raise and educate their own daughters to replace themselves.

The process is longstanding in coastal Ghana, going back at least to the days of late 19th-century domestic girl slavery. In Ghana, as elsewhere, "child labour remains a seriously neglected area of labour studies" (Goddard and White 1982:466), an orientation surely as relevant for understanding fostering as that of kinship and social organization. Goddard and White point out, that where child labour occurs in capitalist production it is often recruited and controlled by what might be considered pre-capitalistic, personal relationships of kinship, friendship and parental or quasi-parental authority (or at least by relationships cast in that idiom). [1982:467]

While the girl workers of Adabraka cannot be considered to work in capitalist production, their reproductive labor is the basement supporting capitalist investment and surplus realization in the upper stories of the Ghanaian economy.

As one traces the links in the world economic chain further and further downward, through international inequalities, through class inequalities, through urban/rural inequalities, through waged/unwaged inequalities, and through male/female inequalities, one comes at root in urban Ghana to inequalities among women. We find middle and higher level working-class women exploiting in turn, for the relative advantage of themselves and their daughters, the rural-born, illiterate, female, child working class. It is a reality of the capitalist world in which we live that the life chances of many Ghanaian girls have been used up by the time they are 8 or 9 years old.

Notes

1. Earlier versions of this paper were presented at meetings of the African Studies Association in 1980, and the American Anthropological Association in 1985. I would like to thank Enid Schildkrout, Shellee Colen, Lani Sanjek, Gracia Clark, Hill Gates, Barbara Miller, Aidan Southall, and Rubie Watson for their comments. The research in Ghana during 1970–71 and 1974 was conducted with Lani Sanjek, and supported by an SSRC-ACLS Foreign Area Fellowship, a New York State Lehman Fellowship, and a City University of New York Faculty Research Award.

2. Gracia Clark (1984:122) has also remarked on the greater numbers of girls than boys in the 1960 and 1970 census data for Kumasi.

3. Slave recruitment of child domestic workers also occurred in early 20th-century urban Cameroon and Senegambia; see Austen (1977:326) and Klein (1977:348).

4. For a study of Ghanaian apprenticeship as work pattern rather than as social relationship, and one not cited by Goody, see Aryee (1978).

5. These figures of more than 50 percent are matched by Goody's for Gonja adults (1982:39). In a personal communication, Rubie Watson raised the question of whether fostering in the past, in these adults' childhoods, was then an avenue of upward mobility now less effective.

6. Barbara Miller and Aidan Southall both raised the question of how long a child must reside with a sponsor to be considered fostered. Goody gives no

time period, nor could she, as the agreement that the sponsor takes over some of the parental obligations is the hallmark of the relationship. Some relatives who come to stay with a new mother remain a few months; some maid servants leave after a few days.

7. Woman marriage is not practiced in Ghana.

8. Neither do demographers. Caldwell's book (1969) on rural-urban migration in Ghana contains no data on maids or market women's apprentices.

9. Clark (1984:259–261) does not report maids' ethnic identities for Asante women traders in Kumasi. In a personal communication, she wrote, "I rarely found Northern maids in Asante families, because of the language problem, for one thing."

10. Some anthropologists might suggest that female infanticide or dietary deprivation could be an explanation for these northern figures. Similar juvenile sex ratio discrepancies, and the cultural factors of boy preference underlying them, have been discussed for India by Miller (1980). I know of no ethnographic evidence to support a similar argument for northern Ghana. Jack Goody, who has conducted fieldwork in two northern Ghanaian societies, asserts that several bodies of evidence point away from any differential treatment of children by sex in Africa, unlike the situation in many Asian societies (1982:68; compare Ware 1983:9–10). Moreover, the census data show even sex ratios in the under-age-5 cohorts (see Table 2). In the absence of ethnographic evidence, an hypothesis of female neglect, like that of female up-reporting of age, would be something imposed on the numbers to smooth out discrepancies.

11. Limited data consistent with that for Adabraka is found in Clark (1985:17), Goody (1982:158), Robertson (1984), and Schildkrout (1972).

References Cited

Addo, N. O., and J. R. Goody
   1976 Siblings in Ghana. Legon: The Population Dynamics Programme, University of Ghana.
Adepoju, Aderanti
   1983 Patterns of Migration by Sex. *In* Female and Male in West Africa. Christine Oppong, ed. Pp. 54–66. London: George Allen & Unwin.
Aryee, George
   1978 Education and Training and Informal Sector Employment in Kumasi, Ghana. *In* Human Resources and African Development. Ukandi Damachi and Victor Diejomaoh, ed. Pp. 288–319. New York: Praeger.
Austen, Ralph
   1977 Slavery among Coastal Middlemen: The Duala of Cameroon. *In* Slavery in Africa: Historical and Anthropological Perspectives. Suzanne Miers and Igor Kopytoff, ed. Pp. 305–333. Madison: University of Wisconsin Press.
Azu, Diana
   1974 The Ga Family and Social Change. Leiden: African Research Centre.

Brydon, Lynn
  1979   Women at Work: Some Changes in Family Structure in Amedzofe-
    Avatime, Ghana. Africa 49:97–110.
  1983   Avatime Women and Men, 1900–80. *In* Female and Male in West Af-
    rica. Christine Oppong, ed. Pp. 320–329. London: George Allen & Un-
    win.
Caldwell, John C.
  1967   Migration and Urbanization. *In* A Study of Contemporary Ghana,
    Volume II: Some Aspects of Social Structure. Walter Birmingham, I.
    Neustadt, and E. N. Omaboe, ed. Pp. 111–146. Evanston: Northwestern
    University Press.
  1969   African Rural-Urban Migration: The Movement to Ghana's Towns.
    New York: Columbia University Press.
Clark, Gracia
  1984   The Position of Asante Women Traders in Kumasi Central Market,
    Ghana. PhD thesis, Cambridge University.
  1985   Domestic Work and Trading: Pressures on Asante Wives and Moth-
    ers. Paper presented at American Anthropological Association annual
    meeting, Washington, DC.
Cooper, Frederick
  1979   The Problem of Slavery in African Societies. Journal of African His-
    tory 20:103–125.
Dinan, Carmel
  1983   Sugar Daddies and Gold-Diggers: the White-Collar Single Women in
    Accra. *In* Female and Male in West Africa. Christine Oppong, ed. Pp.
    344–366. London: George Allen & Unwin.
Fiawoo, Dzigbodi
  1976   Physical Growth and the Social Environment: A West African Ex-
    ample. *In* Youth in a Changing World: Cross-Cultural Perspectives on
    Adolescence. Estelle Fuchs, ed. Pp. 79–92. The Hague: Mouton.
Gaisie, S. K.
  1969   Dynamics of Population Growth in Ghana. Legon: Demographic
    Unit, Department of Sociology, University of Ghana.
Goddard, Victoria, and Benjamin White
  1982   Child Workers and Capitalist Development: An Introductory Note
    and Bibliography. Development and Change 13:465–477.
Goody, Esther N.
  1966   Fostering of Children in Ghana: A Preliminary Report. Ghanaian
    Journal of Sociology 2(1):26–33.
  1970   Kinship Fostering in Gonja: Deprivation or Advantage? *In* Socializa-
    tion: The Approach from Social Anthropology. Philip Mayer, ed. Pp. 51–
    74. London: Tavistock.
  1973   Contexts of Kinship: An Essay in the Family Sociology of the Gonja
    of Northern Ghana. Cambridge: Cambridge University Press.
  1982   Parenthood and Social Reproduction: Fostering and Occupational
    Roles in West Africa. Cambridge: Cambridge University Press.
Goody, Jack
  1982   Cooking, Cuisine and Class: A Study in Comparative Sociology.
    Cambridge: Cambridge University Press.
Hansen, Karen Tranberg, and Margaret Strobel
  1985   Family History in Africa. Trends in History 3:127–149.

Hart, Keith
    1976   The Politics of Unemployment. African Affairs 75:488–497.
Hill, Polly
    1970   The Occupations of Migrants in Ghana. Ann Arbor: Museum of An-
    thropology, University of Michigan.
Isiugo-Abanihe, Uche C.
    1985   Child Fosterage in West Africa. Population and Development Review
    11:53–73.
Klein, Martin
    1977   Servitude among the Wolof and Sereer of Senegambia. *In* Slavery in
    Africa: Historical and Anthropological Perspectives. Suzanne Miers and
    Igor Kopytoff, ed. Pp. 335–363. Madison: University of Wisconsin Press.
    1978   The Study of Slavery in Africa. Journal of African History 19:599–609.
Kpedekpo, G. M. K.
    1970   Some Statistical Aspects of the Compulsory Registration of Births and
    Deaths in Ghana. *In* Symposium on Population and Socio-Economic De-
    velopment in Ghana. N. O. Addo, G. Benneh, S. K. Gaisie, and G. M. K.
    Kpedekpo, eds. Legon: The Demographic Unit, Department of Sociology,
    University of Ghana.
Kumekpor, Tom
    1974   Mothers and Wage Labour Employment (Some Aspects of Problems
    of the Working Mother in Accra). Ghana Journal of Sociology 7(2):68–91.
Lovejoy, Paul
    1983   Transformations in Slavery: A History of Slavery in Africa. Cam-
    bridge: Cambridge University Press.
Lovejoy, Paul, ed.
    1981   The Ideology of Slavery. Beverly Hills: Sage.
Miers, Suzanne, and Igor Kopytoff, ed.
    1977   Slavery in Africa: Historical and Anthropological Perspectives. Mad-
    ison: University of Wisconsin Press.
Miller, Barbara
    1980   Female Neglect and the Costs of Marriage in Rural India. Contribu-
    tions to Indian Sociology 14:95–129.
Ofosu-Amaah, S. O.
    1969   The Menarche at Aburi Girls' School. Ghana Journal of Child Devel-
    opment 2(2):48–52.
Okediji, Oladejo O.
    1978   On Voluntary Associations as an Adaptive Mechanism in West Af-
    rican Urbanization: Another Perspective. *In* The Processes of Urbaniza-
    tion: A Multidisciplinary View. Joyce Aschenbrenner and Lloyd Collins,
    ed. Pp. 195–221. The Hague: Mouton.
Oppong, Christine
    1969   Education of Relative's Children by Senior Civil Servants in Accra.
    Ghana Journal of Child Development 2(2):43–47.
    1974   Marriage among a Matrilineal Elite: A Family Study of Ghanaian Sen-
    ior Civil Servants. Cambridge: Cambridge University Press.
Paige, Hilary
    1986   Child-Bearing Versus Child-Rearing: Co-Residence of Mothers and
    Children in Sub-Saharan Africa. Brussels: Interuniversity Program in De-
    mography.

Pellow, Deborah
    1977   Women in Accra: Options for Autonomy. Algonac, MI: Reference
    Publications Inc.
Robertson, Claire
    1974   Economic Woman in Africa: Profit-making Techniques of Accra Mar-
    ket Women. Journal of Modern African Studies 12:657–664.
    1983   Post-Proclamation Slavery in Accra: A Female Affair? *In* Women and
    Slavery in Africa. Claire Robertson and Martin Klein, ed. Pp. 220–245.
    Madison: University of Wisconsin Press.
    1984   Sharing the Same Bowl: A Socioeconomic History of Women and
    Class in Accra, Ghana. Bloomington: University of Indiana Press.
Robertson, Claire, and Martin Klein
    1983   Women's Importance in African Slave Systems. *In* Women and Slav-
    ery in Africa. Claire Robertson and Martin Klein, ed. Pp. 3–25. Madison:
    University of Wisconsin Press.
Sandbrook, Richard, and Jack Arn
    1977   The Labouring Poor and Urban Class Formation: The Case of Greater
    Accra. McGill Centre for Developing Area Studies.
Sanjek, Roger
    1978   A Network Method and Its Uses in Urban Ethnography. Human Or-
    ganization 37:257–268.
    1982   The Organization of Households in Adabraka: Toward a Wider Com-
    parative Perspective. Comparative Studies in Society and History 23:57–
    103.
Schildkrout, Enid
    1972   The Fostering of Children in Urban Ghana: Ethnographic Analysis in
    a Multicultural Setting. Urban Anthropology 2:48–73.
    1978   People of the Zongo: The Transformation of Ethnic Identities in
    Ghana. Cambridge: Cambridge University Press.
Smutylo, T. S.
    1973   The Freeing of Yaw Asare. Institute of African Studies Research Re-
    view 9(2):39–43.
Strobel, Margaret
    1982   African Women. Signs 8:109–131.
Van Hear, Nick
    1982   Child Labour and the Development of Capitalist Agriculture in
    Ghana. Development and Change 13:499–514.
Ware, Helen
    1983   Female and Male Life-Cycles. *In* Female and Male in West Africa.
    Christine Oppong, ed. Pp. 6–31. London: George Allen & Unwin.
Watson, James L., ed.
    1980   Asian and African Systems of Slavery. Berkeley: University of Cali-
    fornia Press.

4

Household Workers in Nyishang, Nepal

M. T. Cooke

The Nyishang people (or Nyishangte) are an ethnically bounded group whose homeland is the Nyishang valley, an isolated locality bordering Tibet in Manang District, Gandaki Zone, in west-central Nepal. The valley comprises six major villages, ranging in elevation from 3,000 to 3,500 meters, with a total population of approximately 5,000. This figure includes a large number of absent villagers who have relocated on either a temporary or permanent basis to urban trade centers, primarily Kathmandu, Nepal's capital and center for international transportation. These migrants are generally unmarried or married males between the ages of 14 and 60 who establish residence in Kathmandu in order to pursue international itinerant trade in India, Southeast Asia, and points beyond. The relatively low incidence of outmigration by intact households is reflected in survey data which show a 3-to-1 ratio of male to female absenteeism in the 21- to 30-year-old age group and a 4-to-1 ratio in the 30- to 60-year-old age group.

These demographic data provide an introduction to the subjects of this essay, the role of non-Nyishangte household workers in the valley, and their relevance to the social organization of Nyishang identity. The presence of a large number of household workers in the valley is a modern response to the loss of household labor occasioned by the trading activities of able-bodied Nyishangte males.

While the practice of international itinerant trade by the people of Nyishang is documented for a period of 200 years, the hiring of household workers to replace the labor of absent family members is a recent development. It is only with the community's rise to affluence over the past 25 years that cash income has reached a level able to support wage labor. The extent of the Nyishang community's recent enrichment is apparent in levels of household cash income significantly higher than those reported for either the Sherpa, a group which has profited enormously from the tourist industry, or the Thakali, a group whose unusual success in trade has been widely noted. The unprecedented level of cash income to Nyishang village households helps explain why the scale of employment of household workers in Nyishang surpasses that in other regions of rural Nepal.[1]

Ethnic and social organization in Nyishang is complex and, for that reason, it is important to specify the various categories of household workers with some precision. The social category of household worker (literally "work doing person") is distinguished in Nyishang from other categories of non-Nyishangte resident workers by criteria of ethnic origin and type of work. Government personnel, for instance, may be members of those ethnic groups which supply Nyishang with a large number of its household workers but government workers posted in Nyishang stand apart from household workers on the basis of their duties and on the basis of educational level, wealth, and patterns of residence and interaction. Conversely, ethnic Tibetans who perform many of the same tasks as household workers are jurally and interactionally distinguished from them. Fundamentally, the basis for this distinction lies in the relative permanence of residence by Tibetan workers. Families of Tibetan workers who have in fact resided in the valley for several generations and who have applied to a village council for formal resident status are known as "new people" (*sarma sermi*) while Tibetan workers who have taken up residence more recently are known simply as "resident workers" (*tsu-ri Tuba mi*). While household workers are seasonally employed and reside under the direct care of their employers, Tibetan workers are generally year-round caretakers for the houses of absent Nyishangte families.

The social distinctiveness of seasonal household workers as compared to their more permanent Tibetan counterparts highlights an important pattern of ethnic dichotomization in the valley. From the emic perspective of Nyishang villagers, the ethnic/caste hierarchy of the country at large is collapsed locally into three basic categories: (1) *mwee*, or "lowlanders" (comprising various high caste groups such as Brahmin, Chetri, and Marwari); (2) *phwee*, or ethnic Tibetans; and (3) *mwee a-yin phwee a-yin* (literally, "neither lowlanders nor Tibetans"), a category which includes groups of close linguistic affinity but widely varying lifestyle such as the Nyishang people, Gurungs, Tamangs, Magar, and Thakali.

Whereas permanent workers and "new people" are, without exception, of Tibetan highland origins, seasonal household workers are recruited among both lowlanders and the "neither lowland nor Tibetan" peoples. This ethnic patterning of employment is consistent with the responsibilities of permanent employees acting as caretakers in the homes of absentee owners; they must possess the full range of skills required in highland locales like Nyishang. They are familiar, for instance, with high-altitude crops such as buckwheat and with the special requirements of yak herding.

Seasonal household workers, on the other hand, perform less complex tasks such as wood collecting and clothes washing and are under the day-to-day supervision of their employers. In contrast to the exclusively Tibetan origins of permanent workers and "new people," household workers may be either *mwee* or *mwee a-yin phwee a-yin* (with the exception, for the latter category, that it would be untenable for a Nyishang person to serve in such a capacity). As a practical matter, the majority of domestic workers are drawn predominantly from Gurung regions within a few days' walk of Nyishang.

Household workers, as distinguished from resident workers, generally arrive in the village prior to planting and then depart en masse immediately following the harvest. With one or two exceptions they are male and unaccompanied by wives or children. Apart from interim tasks connected with the peak periods of planting and harvest (transporting manure, weeding, irrigating, etc.), their main activity during these months is collecting firewood.

Household workers to perform these tasks are recruited locally from among porters arriving in the valley and from contract workers unemployed following the completion of local development projects. Others are recruited in Kathmandu by urban-based traders who send them to their village households loaded with packaged foods and other supplies. In many cases, however, recruitment is not necessary. News of labor opportunities to be found in Nyishang travels by word of mouth in the villages of workers returning home each winter, attracting other workers who will accompany veterans back to Nyishang the following spring. It is this practice which accounts for the fact that over 90 percent of the household workers in one village in lower Nyishang came from a tight network of villages in a neighboring district.

The activity in which household workers have the greatest impact is firewood collection. With the deterioration of local forest resources, the one-way distance to travel to procure firewood in the upper valley has increased from one to three hours over the past decade. Cutting with a simple scythe or ax and transporting a full 30 kilo load by means of a flat rope or back harness, a worker is able to deliver only a single load of wood in the course of a day. This only slightly exceeds the average wood requirement of an average-size household, roughly three-quarters of a load per day. Since the majority of village households do not have a mature male family member in residence and since wood chopping and portering is considered unsuitable work for females, the importance of hired household workers is quite evident.

It is worth pointing out that both household workers and resident workers frequently become involved in disputes over alleged infractions of regulations governing wood collection. These disputes arise, in part, because forest lands are collectively owned by village and supra-village units and because regulations concerning the regulation of these resources are complex.[2] Employed workers have only restricted access to the meetings of the local councils responsible for the administration of these areas. Accordingly, there are constraints on their ability to acquaint themselves with the details of regulation prior to committing an infraction or to mobilize support for their defense following an infraction.

Other tasks performed by household workers include such chores as fetching water from village taps, doing laundry, feeding household livestock, and representing the household in community-wide labor conscription projects. This range of tasks needs only be performed during the six months of the growing season due to the practice of seasonal migration by the Nyishang people. With the exception of the elderly and the infirm, almost all village residents of Nyishang quit the valley for warmer areas during the winter months, either for purposes of trade or for relaxation. The only domestic tasks which require attention in the village during the winter are the regular feeding of household livestock and the occasional clearing of snow from rooftops. As these tasks do not demand much time, a few year-round residents can provide these services for a large number of absent householders. As a matter of strict general custom, Nyishangte will perform such services for kinsmen or friends without direct compensation whereas the services of permanent Tibetan residents are secured only on a paid basis.

The labor demands of village households coupled with practices of male outmigration account for the high number of seasonal household workers found in Nyishang households without an able-bodied male. However, household workers are not found only in households lacking an able-bodied male. Two less common patterns of employment are the sharing of a single worker among several poor households and the hiring of several workers by individual households involved in the local tourist trade.

Although mechanisms of social support and economic redistribution keep wide disparities of wealth from occurring in the village locale, varying involvement and success in urban-based trade has recently led to the emergence of ranked categories of wealth there. The category of relative poverty termed *tuuba* is limited to those households which lack the labor resources to allow even a single household member to leave the village for urban-based trade or which lack the cash resources to free a household member for those pursuits through the hiring of a household worker. Widows, who are not permitted to remarry in the community, frequently head households which are in this unenviable position.

It is through mechanisms of social support that poor families are able to circumvent the need for hiring household workers for a full season. Poor households obtain firewood through outright donations by kinsmen and covillagers and through the services of workers loaned temporarily and free of charge by kinsmen and friends. With the exception of plowing and harvesting, members of poor households generally themselves take on other chores which are assigned to household workers in more affluent households. It is primarily during the intensive labor demands of harvest, a time when kinsmen and friends are preoccupied with their own fields and unable to offer assistance, that poor households must rely on hired labor. Although the standard monthly wage for hired labor is less than what an urban-based trader might spend on a single meal in Hong Kong or Kathmandu, poor village households may economize on this expense by sharing a single worker among several households.

The circumstances of hotel proprietors illustrate a different variation on the standard pattern whereby households without an able-bodied resident male hire a single worker on a seasonal basis. Proprietors of hotels, representing only about one percent of village households, belong uniformly to the ranked category of relative wealth termed *ploba* and, in the upper valley at least, all include an able-bodied resident male. Although the income from hotel proprietorship is no more than a "neither rich nor poor" household receives from the trading activities of an urban-based family member, the investment requirements of hotel proprietorship limit participation in this form of business to a small number of households. In the initial phase of establishing a hotel, household workers are used to relieve the proprietor's family of nontourist-related responsibilities. As the hotel becomes more profitable, additional workers are hired to relieve the proprietor and his family of repetitious duties such as food preparation. It is not unusual for a well established hotel to employ five or more household workers simultaneously.

Whether employed by a single family, shared by a pool of households, or hired for hotel duties, household workers receive a standard monthly wage. Although the cash component of this salary is modest (approximately US$15 per month in 1985), household workers also receive all their food and clothing from their employer. Nyishangte generally take pride in these terms of employment and take pains to point out that workers "get fat" *(mreeba)* from the meals they are given in Nyishang.

Nyishangte also point out that the wages which they give should be sufficient for thrifty workers to start themselves in business or to buy land in their own villages. They attribute the failure of most workers to achieve this as due to their propensity to squander money on gambling and liquor. For their part, household workers view these terms of employment as more advantageous than available elsewhere but as somewhat less than generous on the part of their employers.[3] Household workers point out that the supply of clothes they receive only represents what they wear out in the course of employment in Nyishang and does not include extra clothes to take back to their village. Also, the clothing of workers is of manifestly lesser quality than that worn by Nyishang villagers. Efforts by workers to emulate the standards of dress of Nyishang people, especially young urban-based traders, are condemned by villagers as extravagant and inappropriate for village work. Such divergent perceptions of the value of items of exchange in the employer/servant relationship have been noted elsewhere in this volume by Rollins, Armstrong, and Colen.

Surveying a wider spectrum of social arrangements, it is apparent that lowland household workers are rigorously differentiated from their Nyishang employers, with Tibetan resident workers occupying an intermediate position. In matters of residence, household workers depend directly on their employers for housing and sleeping accommodations while resident workers, as caretakers in "empty houses" *(thin thee)*, have more autonomy in this respect. Household workers sleep separately, invariably on bedding on the floor (though this is not uncommon for the Nyishang family members either), and are rarely given enough blankets to satisfy their aversion to cold. While employers point out that they invite workers to their hearth and feed them the same food as the family eats, they nonetheless insist that workers wash and store their utensils separately. This provides a contrast with both the service caste of resident blacksmiths who are forbidden entry into the hearthrooms and nonkin Nyishangte who freely share utensils. Also, household workers, like Tibetan resident workers, tend to be referred to by nonpersonalized terms of reference. Whereas Nyishangte are invariably referred to in their absence by name or by kin terms, workers are generally referred to by various undifferentiated terms such as "worker," "lowlander," or "Tibetan."

Objective economic disparities clearly underlie many of the social distinctions imposed on local workers, but perceptions of economic disparity are also important. While it is true that even a poor Nyishang household has greater economic resources than that of a successful seasonal worker, household workers are conscious of the Nyishang people's reputation as international traders and tend to suppose greater wealth on the part of individual households than may actually be the case. If a level of wealth commensurate with their expectations is not readily apparent, household workers are apt to explain away the discrepancy by claiming that wealth is hidden in the house in the form of coral and turquoise necklaces or other jewelry.

Such divergent attitudes help explain why small-scale thievery is sometimes regarded by employees as an emolument of their employment in Nyishang and why any act of theft occasions strong resentment in Nyishang employers. One example of this conflict involved workers temporarily involved in a community-wide development project. In the course of their employment in this project, several household workers were caught stealing from a community orchard and from the private garden of a Nyishangte custodian of that orchard. During an appearance by the workers at a Nyishang council meeting called to settle the dispute, it became clear that the laborers felt themselves in some sense justified in taking the produce. They protested that they were so poor and the Nyishang people so rich that no harm could be done by their taking a few apples and potatoes.

The attitudes of Nyishang employers regarding theft by their workers betrays a comparable degree of stereotyping. While it is true that the local practices of recruitment of household workers limit an employer's ability to check on worker trustworthiness or to seek recourse in the event of theft, reports of theft by workers are frequently unfounded. One example of this is seen in the community's handling of an instance of intracommunal theft. While it eventually became known privately that the person responsible for the theft of a porterload of supplies from Kathmandu was a Nyishang villager, publicly the non-Nyishang porter continued to be identified as the culprit.

In a larger sense, the issue of theft, alleged and otherwise, by workers in Nyishang is revealing of the ways in which relations with outsiders shape and reflect the identity of the Nyishang people. Nyishang employers pride themselves in the supposed generosity of their terms of employment. They point to the large number of workers present in the valley to validate this pride and stress that it is only the workers' tendency to squander their salaries which prevents them from buying their own fields or starting themselves in business (which is to say, becoming like their Nyishang employers). Given these pretensions of their own generosity, Nyishangte are deeply offended when workers engage in even minor theft in the community. Especially when thefts are committed against the household which has taken the thieving laborer in, these actions are seen as a challenge to the community's values of generosity and as something that only outsiders (*mi shen*, "other people") do.

Like the stereotyped views of employer wealth held by household workers, there are elements of both truth and distortion in this atti-

tude. The three public thefts which occurred in my village of residence
during the fieldwork period were all committed by non-Nyishang
workers, two by lowland household workers and one by a Tibetan
permanent resident.[4] While such occurrences serve to confirm attitudes held by Nyishang employers, there is little accompanying sense
of the factors accounting for the problem, other than the basic unscru-
pulousness (*a-sebba*, "badness") of such people.

To complete a balanced treatment of this issue, it is important to
point out that local workers and their Nyishang employers face different types of constraint with regard to theft in Nyishang. The lack of
any check on the trustworthiness of workers, the lack of recourse in
cases of theft, and the relative affluence of employers set the conditions for what Nyishangte view as a high incidence of theft by local
workers. This, in turn, has led to the creation of a formal responsibility
system whereby every employing household is obligated to register
and assume responsibility for their laborers. Specifically, each house-
holder must sign his name to village council records when a laborer
begins working for him, and withdraw the registration at the end of
employment. In the event that, during this period of registration, a
worker is involved in a theft or other dispute judged by the village
council to be a punishable offense, the sponsoring household must
pay of fine of 10,000 rupees (approximately US$650). The degree to
which Nyishang employers are held financially responsible for wrong-
doings by their workers tends to heighten their distrust of workers.
Moreover, they feel vulnerable to victimization by workers in their
own homes. Over the course of a year or more of employment, a laborer acquires intimate familiarity with a household, learning where
keys are hidden and wealth stored. It is easy for a household worker
to forfeit the last installment of his salary and vanish prematurely,
helping himself to more valuable household goods instead.

While the watchfulness of a sponsoring employer is the only effective constraint on a household worker's possible impulse to steal,
there is every constraint for a Nyishang villager. The closeness of village life makes well-informed suspicion, if not certain detection, of the
responsible party highly likely. Once responsibility for a serious theft
is publicly agreed on, the thief's standing is irreparably impaired. Under such circumstances, there is little possibility of ameliorating the
burden of guilt short of severing all ties with the community, a course
of action more appropriate to guilt in cases of wrongful death.

These generalizations are borne out by the handling of the case or
porterage theft alluded to earlier. Faced with a choice between divisive
public accusation of the known Nyishangte thief or the insinuations
of gossip and slander against workers, the victim chose the latter

course. While he might have recovered some of his loss by doing otherwise, it would have been at the cost of lasting hostility in future relations with the accused and his entire network of support. It might even have provoked wide censure on account of the accuser's perceived selfishness in disrupting the community over a matter of material loss, a loss to which entrepreneurial traders are not unaccustomed.

The different ways in which thefts are handled within and outside the ethnic community illustrates how interactional dichotomization reinforces ethnic boundaries for the Nyishangte. Household workers are subject not only to such interactional discrimination but they represent, more abstractly, a conceptual antithesis to Nyishangte ideals of autonomy and self-assertion. In this sense, local workers are important in symbolic constructions of Nyishang identity, as models of behavior antithetical to intracommunal norms. In the case of thefts alleged to involve household workers, the opposition is between Nyishangte's self-conception of their indiscriminate generosity as employers and their stereotype of workers' abuse of that generosity.

An equally important aspect of the role of workers in Nyishang has to do with a dynamic and tension involving changing relationships within the community. In this aspect, household workers are symbolically important as a model for increasingly commodified relationships and, more generally, for a perceived breakdown of group values. This tension is especially acute between urban- and village-resident segments of the Nyishang community. The village focus of my field research prevents me from treating the urban side of this issue in equal depth, but a few observations may suffice to indicate its importance.

One typical manifestation of this tension occurs when villagers spend the winter in the urban residence of a relative. When, as frequently happens, the villager comes to feel that his presence is merely tolerated rather than welcomed, he may break social relations and solicit support from other Nyishangte on the grounds that he has been treated by his kinsmen "like a household worker."

Another manifestation of this same tension is apparent in the formation of trade groups in Kathmandu for the conduct of international itinerant trade. A young boy newly arrived in Kathmandu from the village may find himself in a relationship of obligation to an urban-resident kinsmen who has provided him with start-up capital and initial exposure in trade. The discomfiture of this relationship is such that new traders frequently terminate their unequal participation in the trade groups of wealthy sponsors once minimal training and capital resources have been secured. They then form new trade groups with partners with whom they share a more equal standing in terms of capital resources. Young traders who choose to endure as subordinates in unequal trading relationships are criticized for acting more like the workers of Nyishangte than like the Nyishangte who employ them.

These observations suggest a general dynamic of social change which is clearly in play within the Nyishang community. As Nyishang traders have realized unprecedented profits over the last generation and as continued success in trading has become more capital intensive, traditional norms of generosity have lost effectiveness as a route to prestige within the urban-resident segment of the community. Nyishangte in the village locale, however, are less comfortable with the commodification of relationships introduced by the new modes of participation in international trade. Their ambivalence to these changes accounts for both their stress on ethnic exclusiveness as a strategy to press traditional norms of prestige and their own growing tendency to commodify relations within and outside the group. Household workers in Nyishang represent an important element of this dynamic because their social position in Nyishang clearly reveals both sides of this ambivalence.

Notes

1. The best documented case of widespread employment of laborers in Nepal concerns the Thakali people. See Furer-Haimendorf (1966) and Parker (1985).

2. For further information on household workers and their role in firewood collection, see Cooke (n.d.).

3. It is a clear failing of my treatment of this and related issues that I am not able to provide a better sense of the workers' perspectives as opposed to those of their patrons. Since my research focused on Nyishangte ethnicity, I included non-Nyishangte groups in my research only to the extent that they contributed to a relational understanding of ethnic boundaries involving the Nyishangte. Although I have considerable interest in the issue, I feel unqualified to comment on subjective aspects of the experience of non-Nyishangte household workers in Nyishang.

4. For other considerations of workplace theft, see Liebow (1967) and Mars (1982).

References Cited

Cooke, M. T.
  n.d.   The Social Organization of Forest Resources in the Manang Valley.
    Presented at First Annual Conference on South and Southeast Asia, Uni-
    versity of California, Berkeley.
Furer-Haimendorf, Christoph von
  1966   Caste Concepts and Status Distinctions in Buddhist Communities of
    Western Nepal. *In* Caste and Kin in Nepal, India and Ceylon: Anthro-
    pological Studies in Hindu-Buddhist Contact Zones. C. von Furer-Hai-
    mendorf, ed. Pp. 140–160. New Delhi: Sterling Publishers.
Liebow, Elliot
  1967   Talley's Corner: A Study of Negro Streetcorner Men. Boston: Little,
    Brown & Company.
Mars, Gerald
  1982   Cheats at Work: An Anthropology of Workplace Crime. London:
    George Allen & Unwin.
Parker, Barbara
  1985   The Spirit of Wealth: Entrepreneurship among the Thakali of Nepal.
    Ph.D. dissertation, University of Michigan.

Euroamerican Forms of Household Work

5
Ideology and Servitude

Judith Rollins
Simmons College

In this paper I examine the social psychology of the relationship between household workers and their employers by focusing on the African-American worker-white employer relationship in contemporary Boston. I preface my discussion of the relationship between the women with a brief overview of household work in the United States during the 20th century and of the position of African-American women within that labor group.[1]

The U.S. Labor Department includes these workers in the "private household workers" category: housekeepers, cooks, child-care workers, launderers, maids, servants, and cleaners. Household workers constituted the largest single occupational group of all employed American women during the 19th century. The percentage of working women in the occupation peaked in 1870 when household workers were 52 percent of all employed women. Since 1900, this sector has consistently shrunk in relation to the size of the total female labor force. Absolute numbers, however, continued to increase until the Second World War. At the turn of the century, the U.S. Census reported 1.5 million household workers in the United States; by 1940, the official count peaked at 2,277,000; by 1970, the total was back to 1.5 million; and in 1979, there were 1,062,000. But while the total numbers in 1900 and 1970 were similar, the figures represent quite different proportions of the female labor force. Household workers constituted 28.7 percent of all working women in 1900, but only 5.1 percent of employed women in 1970. And the one million reported in 1979 represents just 2.6 percent of all women workers (Grossman 1980:18; U.S. Department of Labor 1980:9).

Government figures, however, are highly problematic because of the gross underreporting which has been characteristic of this occupation and which, indications suggest, has become more extensive in recent years. It is easier for live-out workers to avoid detection than it was for the live-in workers who were more numerous in the past. And the motivations for doing so are many. It is commonplace for Social Security, which has covered most categories of household work since 1951, not to be paid. (The employer saves the 5.85 percent of the employee's salary that would be her share; the worker gains immediate cash.) Such workers would, of course, not want to reveal their employment. Also, some household workers are working while receiving government support (e.g., old age benefits or disability payments). And, of course, there are the foreign-born who are working illegally or are in the country illegally and who cannot reveal their employment.

As the number of women in these situations continues to increase, it may be expected that household workers will become more and more invisible in this country. The obsolescence of full-time workers in this occupation is hardly as imminent as Coser (1973) has suggested. There are even indicators—for example, the new household employment agencies and new divisions of existing agencies that have come into being in the Boston area in the last decade—that the demand is now on the increase.

Household work has always been a significant occupation for African-American, Native American, Hispanic, and some groups of Asian women. For example, from 1905 to 1970, it was the largest occupational category for Japanese immigrant women and their daughters (Glenn 1980:1). Even during the 19th century, when it was the main occupation of white women, women of color represented almost 30 percent of all household workers, though they were less than 10 percent of the total female population (Katzman 1978:62–63). As white women moved into factory, sales, and clerical jobs in the early 20th century, women of color came to account for 45.8 percent of household workers by 1920 (Stigler 1946:6–9). Women of color were locked into the occupation over generations because of the deliberate exclusion of these women from other kinds of jobs, because of the wage hierarchy within the occupation based on race, and because of obstacles to men of color in obtaining a family wage. In this case, rather than household work functioning as a gateway into the mainstream as it had for economically marginal white women, the occupation instead functioned to maintain women of color in a social and economic underclass.

Throughout the 20th century, until the 1970 census, household work has been the largest occupational category for African-American women. But since 1940, the percentage of employed African-American women reported by the census as "private household workers" has been decreasing dramatically: in 1940, nearly 60 percent of all African-American women workers were household workers; in 1970, 18 percent were; and by 1980, only 5 percent of employed African-American women were still doing household work (Treiman and Terrell 1975:160; U.S. Department of Commerce 1983). They are, of course, being replaced by women from Latin America, the Caribbean, and Asia. Why? As the director of an employment agency in Newton Center (a middle-class suburb of Boston) told me:

> Right now, I'm getting a lot of calls from people who have heard about the boat people—the people from Vietnam, Cambodia, Haiti, Cuba, and anybody that's coming in—Chinese people. The living over there and the living here—they don't understand what's going on. They'll do anything. I just had one women come in who requested a Cambodian or Vietnamese. Why? Because she can get them cheap!

Women from less developed parts of the world are not only cheaper to employ and more willing to work hard and long, they are also more deferential in manner and, because of their economic and social precariousness, more docile. The director of a social service program for household workers in Boston during the late 1960s and early 1970s said:

> At one time, [employers] would stipulate, "I want a Southern girl." They like that "Yes, Ma'am" and the "Yes, Sir." They *loved* that. But, later on, they'd say, "I want a West Indian girl." Now the reason for that was when they got on that job, they'd do anything, they'd work any number of hours—because here's an opportunity to come to this country. And they would work for less money. So everybody wanted a West Indian. No one ever asked for a Northern girl. They felt they'd get more loyalties from people from other places.

The status of women of color in household work has never been and is not now equal to that of white women in the occupation. Historically, the most difficult kind of household work was laundering and its job force was made up almost exclusively of African-American women. Today, while 60.2 percent of white household workers are child-care workers and 30.3 percent are cleaners, 10 percent of women of color are child-care workers and 73 percent are cleaners (Grossman 1980:20).

Within each job specialty, there is additionally a wage hierarchy and women of color are on the bottom of it. The salaries of the African-American women I interviewed in Boston ranged from $3.50 to $6 an hour but employers interviewed reported paying white household workers from $6 to $10 an hour. All of these Boston salaries, it should be noted, are well above the national average. The 1982 mean income for year-round, full-time female household workers over 18 years of age was $5,883 or the equivalent of $2.83 an hour (U.S. Department of Commerce 1984). The widespread disregard for the minimum wage law, particularly in the South where household workers are predominantly African Americans, in the Southwest and far West where they are predominantly Latinas, and among immigrant workers everywhere, accounts for the low national average.

Clearly, the objective for most American employers, like that of employers all over the world, has been to extract as much work as possible while paying as little as possible. The arrangement between employer and worker is, as Dill (1979) has stated, first and foremost a class relationship. Though the remainder of this essay focuses on the psychodynamics of the relationship between employer and employee, that focus does not indicate a belief that the material aspects of the relationship and the social structure in which it exists are of less importance than the ideational. Rather, the emphasis emanates from my belief that an understanding of the interplay between the material and the nonmaterial is of critical importance to those concerned with structures of inequality. Worldwide, the employer-household worker arrangement is grounded in class stratification. The following exploration of the thoughts and behavior of the women involved in this arrangement assumes, builds on, and should not distract from, that basic reality.

Methods

The research for this study was conducted during 1981 and 1982 in greater Boston. There were three sources of data: (1) I read narratives and articles written by household workers and employers as well as studies by historians and social scientists; (2) I interviewed 20 workers, 20 employers, and various personnel of agencies dealing with household work; and (3) I worked as a household worker for ten employers for various periods of time (typically, one month; for two, six months). Though my original focus was on the white employer-African-American worker relationship in contemporary Boston, information about other kinds of relationships, other times, and other places was plentiful. Thus, my interviews yielded a rich and textured portrait of what the employer-household worker relationship has been since the 1920s in the eastern and southern parts of the United States (Rollins 1985).

The Relationship

The relationships within employer-worker dyads vary dramatically with the diverse personalities involved. Yet, there are patterns that emerged from my research, patterns which led me to the conclusion that the relationship is essentially one of psychological as well as material exploitation. What is unique about this labor arrangement—the personal, sometimes intimate relationship between employer and employee—is precisely what allows for a level of psychological exploitation unknown in even other low-paid occupations. Employer interviewees repeatedly emphasized the importance of the personality of the household worker and the kind of relationship they were able to establish with her. Many explicitly stated that work performance was not their highest priority. The comments of these four employers were typical:

> I wouldn't feel comfortable with someone coming in on a regular basis unless they were warm. I think of help as a friend helping more than I do a more formal relationship.

> I look for someone trustworthy and friendly, someone I'm comfortable with.

> They didn't last long if they came in and it was obviously just a job.

> She doesn't clean very well, you know, but I would never think of letting her go. . . . She never comes to work on time but that's all right. We have a great relationship. . . . It's worth much more to me to have her loyalty and her trust. . . . That's more important than the cleaning.

Why are these nonmaterial aspects of the work arrangement as or more important to employers than the worker's job performances? Precisely what personality characteristics and what kind of relationship are employers seeking? A personality type and a relationship which, I will argue, (1) afford the employer the ego enhancement that emanates from having an "inferior" present and (2) validate the employer's lifestyle, her class and racial privilege, her entire social world. Most important, the performance and relationship demanded function to provide the employer with ideological justification for the economically and racially stratified system in which she lives and from which she derives benefit.

These ego and system supporting psychological functions of the employer/household worker relationship may partially explain the ubiquitous world history of household work and its tenacious presence in contemporary American life. And it is through the exploration of the interpersonal dynamics that we can glimpse the ideological role this occupation has played in the myriad kinds of hierarchical societies in which it has existed—a role, I submit, fundamentally conservative and reproductive of inegalitarian social systems.

The psychological exploitation of household workers takes many forms. Some are obvious, like the demanding of deference and the treatment of workers as nonpersons. Others are more subtle, like maternalism, gift-giving, and the tolerance of irresponsibility. It is the belief system that generates and is reinforced by these dynamics that makes them ideologically beneficial to the employers and to the maintenance of inequality in the larger society at the expense of the workers. Let us look at some of the behaviors I have come to consider the foundations of the psychological exploitation in the employer-household worker relationship.

First, many forms of deference are expected of household workers. And deference behaviors are, in Goffman's (1956:479) words, "something a subordinate owes his superordinate." Deference confirms the inequality of the relationship and the deference giver's acceptance of that inequality. In household work, there are forms of *linguistic deference,* such as the use of worker's first names while the employers expect to be called by their last names, the use of the term "girl" for workers no matter what their age, and the encouraged use of terms like "Ma'am" by workers. There may be deference related to the *structure of communication,* as when household workers do not initiate unnecessary conversation and employers exercise more rights of familiarity, frequently asking very personal questions in order to use workers as "windows to exotica." Encountering this latter phenomenon in his 1953 study of domestics in a western Massachusetts town, David Chaplin stated that female household workers found themselves:

> drawn into a peculiar relationship involving self-abasing exposés of the most intimate details of their private lives as part of a quite unconscious bargain with paternalistic employers. Female domestics were subject to a sort of verbal voyeurism on the part of their mistresses. [1964:540]

Beyond giving the employer the opportunity to assert her superior position, this "verbal voyeurism" may also be an effort to confirm negative stereotypes about the personal lives of African-American people/household workers/the lower classes and, thereby, provide another justification for a system which keeps such people in a disadvantaged position.

There were also examples of *spatial deference,* related to both body and house space. The worker does not initiate touching her employer and maintains appropriate distance to show respect for the private

space around the employer's body. This distancing suggests to the
employer that the worker recognizes that the employer's mental and
physical privacy are more valuable than her own and should therefore
not be intruded upon. Within the house, except when cleaning other
rooms, the worker's "space" is in the kitchen. The significance of this
is explained by Trudier Harris:

> The most comfortable realm of [the domestic's] existence is the kitchen;
> it becomes the black town, the nigger room, of the white house. The black
> woman cleans the living room or the dining room or the bedroom or the
> bathroom and retires to the kitchen. . . . The kitchen is . . . the one room
> in the house where the white woman can give up spatial ownership with-
> out compromising herself. Kitchens have connotations of hard work and
> meniality—sweat, grime, broken fingernails and other things from which
> the mistress wishes to dissociate herself. Passing *that particular* space on
> to the domestic is a royal decree of her subservience and inferiority.
> [1982:15–16]

Eating arrangements, too, confirm the low status of the household workers in relation to members of the employing family. While
live-in and all-day workers may have lunch with the wife and children
at the kitchen table, it is almost unknown for household workers to eat
in the dining room and/or with the husband, the person highest in the
intrafamilial hierarchy. The various kinds of spatial deference, like the
deferential use of language, serve to reinforce the inferior position of
the household worker.

And the deference may also be *gestural*—the subservient, obsequious performance associated particularly with this occupation and
called, in the case of African-American household workers, the "Uncle
Tom" performance. How popular is this type of act? This worker's
statement is typical: "Sure, they still like the Uncle Tom performance,
the grinning maid. They eat that up." The one time I decided to try
out such a performance I was shocked at how pleased and totally un-
suspicious my employer was of my obsequious behavior, especially
since she had seen me the previous week without it. But my performance confirmed for her my acceptance of my own inferiority and her
desire for that confirmation from me was apparently strong enough to
remove from her memory the contradiction of my previous behavior.
Acting subservient, to some degree, is still encouraged in this occupation; those women who so perform are more successful in manip-
ulating employers and holding jobs.

Thus, deference behaviors are very much a part of household
work and it should be kept in mind that the basic function of such behaviors is the affirmation of a relationship between unequals and the
apparent acceptance of one's inferior position. But deference rituals

are only one part of the essential dynamic of the employer-worker relationship. The other major dynamic is maternalism.

Most writers describe the employer-household worker relationship as paternalistic. But since middle- and upper-class women have taken responsibility for the hiring and deportment of household workers at least since the 19th century in the West, the dynamic is properly called maternalism. And this is more than just a change in the gender of the word. Women employers are in a different position in the familial and social structure than are male employers and, because of socialization, operate with a distinct value system (see Gilligan 1982; Chodorow 1978).

Paternalism is grounded in the tradition of patriarchal authority, a system of male power emanating from the political economy and reflected in all major institutions, including the family. In the West, there is, of course, no comparable matriarchal authority in which maternalism might be based. And our conceptual definitions of the words differ. Paternalism refers to the giving of protection by the more powerful male in exchange for loyalty; it is one element that interrelates with a complex social structure dominated by males and the masculine ethos. Maternalism, on the other hand, refers to a woman's intrafamilial role of giving support, caring, and nurturance. The different connotations of these ostensibly parallel words reflect the different gender positions in Western society.

The similarity of the two words, however, is that both suggest a parent/child relationship. Maternalism of employer toward employee has the same purpose as deference demands: it affirms the superiority of the employer. The employers I interviewed demonstrated their view of their household workers as children both in explicit language ("I regarded her as an ignorant child. [She was] about 22 going on ten.") and in their behavior. I encountered many forms of maternalistic behavior: treating workers as children, loaning money, explaining bills, demanding to meet friends, replacing the household worker's last name with that of the employer, making business calls and travel arrangements, interceding with the legal system (in the South), and, most common, giving gifts. Because the giving of gifts has been and is so prevalent in this occupation, it merits further discussion.

The giving of old clothes, old furniture, and leftover food to household workers with no expectation of return is another statement that the relationship is one of inequality. For, as Marcel Mauss wrote:

> To give is to show one's superiority, to show that one is something more and higher. . . . To accept without returning or repaying more is to face subordination, to become a client and subservient. [1925:72]

And Whisson and Weil, writing of this practice in South Africa, are even more explicit:

> The giving of unreciprocated gifts places the recipient in the position of a child or a beggar, being too poor, too young or too low in status to be able to participate in the system of exchanges which mark the social boundaries of the donor's group. . . . [Employers] give in order to assert their dominance and their possession of their servant. [1971:41, 43]

It is noteworthy that items are given rather than wages raised, for higher pay could threaten the employer's belief in the inferiority of the worker. For the employer, the household worker's acceptance of low wages is further evidence of that person's inferior worth. It is also noteworthy that *old* items are given. If, indeed, "gifts are one of the ways in which the pictures that others have of us in their minds are transmitted" (Schwartz 1967:1), the employer, in giving used and discarded items, is acting on her perception of the worker as unable to provide adequately for herself and willing to accept others' devalued goods. All the household workers I spoke with said they always accepted any item offered and they always appeared grateful. Both forms of thanks were expected. As these two workers put it:

> This woman was always giving me her size 5½ shoes. I wear an 8! . . . And I dragged those damned 5½ *double A* shoes home! I'd give them to somebody else or throw them away. [Another employer] was always offering me bags of stuff. But if it was something I didn't want, I'd thank her, walk out of there, go around that corner, and the first trash can I got to, I'd throw it in. But you take it, whatever they give.

> I didn't want most of that junk. But you have to take it. It's part of the job, makes them feel like they're being so kind to you. And you have to *appear* grateful. That makes them feel good too.

Workers must appear to be what their employers want them to be: needy and grateful. The giving of old clothes to household workers, then, an apparently innocuous and even benevolent practice, is another aspect of the interpersonal dynamic designed to affirm the worker's inferiority in relation to the employer.

Another aspect of this dynamic is the requirement of evidence of inferiority from the worker to justify the maternalistic treatment. Behaving deferentially is not enough: the worker is asked to demonstrate inferiority in her material conditions, her intelligence, her appearance, and sometimes even her character. The household workers I interviewed said that they had to hide evidence of improved material conditions. Some who have bought cars park them a few blocks away from their jobs. One woman who bought a home with her husband said she would never let her employers know about it. And another whose son attends an Ivy League school in New England hides this fact from her employers. Why? The explanations of these two workers are representative:

> Some whites feel very threatened by you. They just don't want you up on their level; they want you lower. This is mainly true of the middle- and lower-income-bracket whites. The people with real high incomes don't care what you got or what you're doing. But someone just making it, just across that border in Brookline, just barely got there, they don't want to know you've got a home, a car, and don't let them know you've got kids in college.

> You've got to stay down here and act like you're down here. They might say they have nothing against Black people but they still want you in your place. When you tell them where you're coming from, they can hinder you. And they will. When you keep it to yourself, you're puzzling them. If I said my son was entering college next year, and if I'm working for three women who know one another, they're going to gang up on me. When they get together for bridge or tea, they'll say, "Well, she's doing pretty good, she's putting her son through college. We got to cut her hours. We got to let her go." I always say: don't let them know anything.

Similarly, household workers felt that less intelligent workers were preferred. During my work as a household worker I was frequently spoken to as if I were close to retarded. It was impossible for me to discern how many of these assumptions about my intellect were racism and how many were class prejudice. In any case, low intelligence was expected and, according to household workers, desired. Their interpretation of this preference was that such workers are more easily taken advantage of. For example, two women said:

> They prefer uninformed workers. They can take advantage of you more. . . . A lot of them want to take advantage. That's why they like to hire a lot of foreigners.

> They definitely want less educated servants. They want you to be able to read and write; they might want you to answer the phone and take a message right. But they don't want you to know *too* much.

I would add to this explanation that it also helps employers feel superior in yet another way—as does the preference for less attractive household workers.

In this society where women are evaluated on the basis of appearance more than men, it is not surprising that appearance is an issue in this female-female labor arrangement. A number of my worker interviewees became far more attractive for our talks in their homes than I had seen them on their jobs or on public transportation to and from work. They knew, as I did when working, that the worse they looked, the more the female employer liked it. To appear too attractive, too pretty, or too glamourous was to risk disapproval and, perhaps, the job. Employers want household workers whose appearances, as well as intelligence and material conditions, are clearly inferior to their own. As Trudier Harris observed:

> No maid could expect to keep a job if she appeared for it in her Sunday-go-to-meeting dress or if she arrived for an interview with luscious curls, lipstick, and beautifully manicured nails. The message conveyed by that personal fastidiousness would be that the black woman was stepping out of her predetermined place. [1982:13]

Tolerance for unprofessional behavior was the way employers expressed their desire for evidence of weak characters in household workers. Although this pattern was the least prevalent of those discussed, to be sure, the fact that it exists at all suggests that it serves the interests of the more powerful member of the dyad. I heard an employer speak jokingly about her employee who regularly arrived late and who cleaned poorly. Another employer told of a worker who was stealing the employer's underwear and was never questioned about it or dismissed for it. I heard many descriptions of household workers who drank on the job. This employer, for example, was not only tolerant, she was amused by it:

> [She] drank all the time. I don't think she drank my stuff. Sometimes she was so funny. Even when we'd have guests for dinner, she'd come sailing in. She'd put the vegetable dishes on the table and fly out! (Laughter) And you knew that she'd had six shots of vodka. She was just great. Everybody was hysterical about it. Nobody cared about that.

This tolerance for indications of weak character may be interpreted as another part of the employer's desire for evidence of the inferiority of the worker as a total human being. Such behavior confirms class and racial stereotypes further justifying the disadvantaged position of household workers and the social system which permits such exploitive arrangements to exist.

Demanding evidence of inferiority in ability to cope with one's material conditions, in intelligence, in appearance, and in character— like demanding deference and acceptance of maternalism—is another way the employer enhances her own psyche by forcing the worker to *act* as if she is less than she is. This mistress, by reason of her position as employer, her higher class and often caste, her greater education and sophistication, holds the power in this relationship. And she uses the power to benefit herself at the expense of the worker. Though household workers derive some satisfaction out of fooling their employers (see Powdermaker 1943) and those whom I interviewed had retained their self-respect and dignity amazingly well, the behaviors and attitudes they must exhibit on their jobs are, nevertheless, degrading. Rituals of deference and expressions of maternalism, then, are the two clusters of behavior that form the foundation of the psychological exploitation that permeates the relationship between female employers and female workers. But they do not, by any means, tell the whole story.

Household workers are hired to do the "dirtywork" of the female employer. Household chores are the most devalued work of the employer's "woman's work." Passing on her dirtywork to a woman who is also lower class, often of a subordinate racial/ethnic group, a woman who is asked to demonstrate various kinds of inferiority, further allows the employer to devalue the person of the worker. This overall "inferiority" of the household worker (an inferiority which is, in fact, created by the employer) not only justifies paying her low wages. More important, it suggests to the employer and her family that entire categories of people (the lower classes, people of color, etc.) may indeed be inferior. And if that is true, a social structure that maintains such people at a disadvantage may be a justifiable and legitimate structure. It is in this way that the historical allocation of this dirtywork to certain categories within the population, and the kind of performance and relationship employers prefer with the people who do the work, provide employers with ideological support for a society stratified by class and race.

And the hiring of a household worker also supports gender subordination. The middle- or upper-class female employer is able to purchase her freedom from the least rewarding, least prestigious aspects of her socially defined gender obligations. But she solves the problem of having the main responsibility for such drudgery work (and increasingly from having the double burden of a job and full responsibility for the housework) in a way that does not challenge patriarchal ideas about appropriate gender roles. She thus circumvents some of the most oppressive aspects of her woman's role—as defined by the patriarchy—and, in doing so, leaves the patriarchy intact and contributes to the continuation of gender inequality.

By bringing in a lower-class and often Third World woman to serve and help maintain the employer's family, the employer implicitly teaches her children lessons that will foster their continued support of inequality. The children learn that it is appropriate that they be served, that such dirtywork is appropriate for the lower classes and darker people, that housework and child care are women's work. The critical role of modeling (Bandura 1973) was evident from my findings: *all* of the mothers of my employer interviewees had themselves employed household workers. Interviewees' comments indicated that they had grown up not only expecting to become employers ("I had been raised in a home where my mother had always had household help. And I think it was something I just anticipated.") but that they had come to identify themselves as employers long before they were in a position to employ anyone. Note this identification in the language of a 22-year-old describing the situation that existed for him from age six to ten:

> She was live-in. *We gave her weekends off.* . . . She also played games with me; the only maid I had that ever did that. . . . And eventually it got to the point apparently that she spent more time with me than she did on her housework. *And we eventually had to get rid of her* for that reason. [Emphasis mine]

The relationship between employer and household worker—with its rituals of deference, its maternalism, its demands of performances of inferiority—is a relationship which is not only *based* in stratification, but also *reinforces* and *reproduces* class, racial, and gender stratification. The employer wants the worker to exist as the employer has defined her in order to enhance her own ego, to strengthen her own class and racial identities and, most important, to provide justification for the inegalitarian social structure. The findings of my research illustrate the fundamentally conservative ideological role the occupation of household work plays in this hierarchical social system.

Notes

1. This paper draws on material from the author's 1985 book, *Between Women: Domestics and Their Employers*, published by Temple University Press.

References Cited

Bandura, Albert
  1973   Social Learning Theory. Englewood Cliffs, NJ: Prentice Hall.
Chaplin, David
  1964   Domestic Service and the Negro. *In* Blue Collar World. Arthur Shostak and William Gomberg, eds. Pp. 535–544. Englewood Cliffs, NJ: Prentice Hall.

Chodorow, Nancy
   1978   The Reproduction of Mothering: Psychoanalysis and the Sociology of Gender. Berkeley: University of California Press.
Coser, Lewis
   1973   Servants: The Obsolescence of an Occupational Role. Social Forces 52:31–40.
Dill, Bonnie Thornton
   1979   Across the Boundaries of Race and Class: An Exploration of the Relationship Between Work and Family among Black Female Domestic Servants. Ph.D. dissertation. New York University.
Gilligan, Carol
   1982   In a Different Voice: Psychological Theory and Women's Development. Cambridge, MA: Harvard University Press.
Glenn, Evelyn Nakano
   1980   Occupational Ghettoization: Japanese American Women and Domestic Service, 1905–1970. Manuscript, files of the author.
Goffman, Erving
   1956   The Nature of Deference and Demeanor. American Anthropologist 58:473–502.
Grossman, Allyson Sherman
   1980   Women in Domestic Work: Yesterday and Today. Monthly Labor Review 103(8):17–21.
Harris, Trudier
   1982   From Mammies to Militants. Philadelphia: Temple University Press.
Katzman, David
   1978   Seven Days a Week: Women and Domestic Service in Industrializing America. New York: Oxford University Press.
Mauss, Marcel
   1925   The Gift. Glencoe, IL: Free Press.
Powdermaker, Hortense
   1943   The Channeling of Negro Aggression by the Cultural Process. American Journal of Sociology 48:750–758.
Rollins, Judith
   1985   Between Women: Domestics and Their Employers. Philadelphia: Temple University Press.
Schwartz, Barry
   1967   The Social Psychology of the Gift. American Journal of Sociology 73:1–11.
Stigler, George
   1946   Domestic Servants in the United States, 1900–1940. Occasional Paper No. 24. New York: National Bureau of Economic Research.
Treiman, Donald, and Kermit Terrell
   1975   Women, Work and Wages: Trends in the Female Occupation Structure. *In* Social Indicator Models. Kenneth Land and Seymour Spilerman, eds. Pp. 157–199. New York: Russell Sage Foundation.
U.S. Department of Commerce, Bureau of the Census
   1983   1980 Census of Population: General Social and Economic Characteristics. Washington, DC: U.S. Government Printing Office.
   1984   Money Incomes of Households, Families and Persons in the United States, 1982. Washington, DC: U.S. Government Printing Office.

U.S. Department of Labor, Bureau of Labor Statistics
   1980   Perspectives on Working Women: A Databook. Washington, DC:
   U.S. Government Printing Office.
Whisson, Michael, and William Weil
   1971   Domestic Servants: A Microcosm of "The Race Problem." Johannesburg: South African Institute of Race Relations.

6

"Housekeeping" for the Green Card: West Indian Household Workers, the State, and Stratified Reproduction in New York

Shellee Colen

Is slavery really abolished? There is not much difference between working in this situation and slavery. The working hours are the same, the exploitation is the same. There is no human recognition. We eat the same food, live together in the same house, but we don't mingle. I am in it but not part of it. . . . I thought slavery was abolished 150 years ago [as it was in the English-speaking Caribbean].

> —Marguerite Andrews,[1] a Vincentian mother of four, speaking of conditions of her live-in child-care and housekeeping job on Park Avenue. She hoped it would lead to sponsorship for legal residence in the United States.

Marguerite Andrews is one of many undocumented West Indian women "housekeeping" in New York City to support families in the Caribbean and to become legal permanent residents of the United States—"green card" holders—through employer sponsorship. The conditions of employer sponsorship in household work trouble most West Indian women. Several compared living in others' homes in this clearly unequal status to slavery. In actuality, the situation faced by women like Ms. Andrews approximates legally sanctioned indentured servitude.

Private household work figures centrally in the experiences of many West Indian women in New York with and without legal permanent resident status. Through immigration procedures, the state directs undocumented West Indian women without other means to legal status to perform the reproductive work of others' households in order to achieve it. The state thereby addresses a domestic labor shortage, tensions within changing middle-class households, and demands for state or private support for child care by ensuring a large pool of increasingly vulnerable potential workers. A highly stratified system of reproduction operates in which households accomplish their reproductive tasks differentially according to the class, race, place in a global economy, and migration status of their members (on reproduction see Edholm, Harris, and Young 1977).

Ms. Andrews's experiences resemble those of other, especially live-in, household workers in various cultural and historical contexts. Globally, household work emerges from, reflects, and reinforces some combination of hierarchical relations of class, gender, race/ethnicity, migration and/or age. In the United States, inequalities of class, race, ethnicity, gender, and migration status are central to the asymmetrical relations of household work.[2] With wages paid to household workers, employers purchase aspects of their class position and lifestyle. Household workers' labor frees employers from many of their own reproductive tasks. This enables employers to pursue more remunerative, highly valued, or pleasurable activities. Workers support their own households with their relatively meager wages. The tension between household work as wage labor under capitalism on the one hand, and its location in the household and highly personalized relations on the other, contributes to this asymmetrical relationship. Unlike most hierarchical relations of work in the United States, those between private household workers and their employers are most often between women (see Rollins 1985). The configuration of familiar features of household work and the labor needs and related legal structures of the contemporary global economic system creates distinct patterns of household employment for many West Indian women in New York.

This essay is a narrow slice of a wider study which examines the highly stratified system of reproduction represented by West Indian household workers and their employers in New York (Colen 1986, 1987, 1989). West Indian women's experiences of private household work and family as they are textured by class, gender, migration, and race/ethnicity form the basis of this study. They are compared to white employers' experiences of parenting, working, and employing West Indian child-care workers. The experiences of both sets of workers/ mothers illuminate the continuous interpenetration of the falsely dichotomized public and private realms. Moreover, they point to the increasingly commoditized, contested, and class-stratified nature of many reproductive activities in the contemporary urban United States. The larger project explores meanings of child care and household maintenance as they are performed by mothers and by others for love and for money.[3]

Here, I focus on only one aspect of West Indian women's private household work experiences in New York: performing household maintenance and child-care work to obtain employer sponsorship for permanent resident status with an immigrant visa, the "green card."[4] I examine the process and implications of labor migration and household work in the Caribbean and in New York and then describe the sponsorship process and West Indian household workers' experiences in sponsor jobs. After touching on the asymmetrical relations of household work, examples of the special impacts of the sponsor job for West Indian women are considered. A glimpse of life after the green card follows.

The Interviewees

At the outset, I want to establish several points. First, the West Indian women discussed here emigrated from the English-speaking Caribbean to New York since 1965. All are mothers. Most are between 30 and 50 years old. Most initially spoke to me after obtaining their green cards; a few spoke with me soon after arrival or in the early stages of their migration process. A few others spoke with me near the end of their sponsorship. All have done or do private household work in the New York area.[5]

Second, these women are among the large numbers of West Indian women that census and Immigration and Naturalization Service (INS) data indicate have immigrated to New York since 1965. The 1980 U.S. Census shows that 7,460 West Indian women in New York City were employed as servants, cleaners, maids, or housekeepers—a figure exceeded for West Indian women only by combining the categories of nurses' aides and nurses in first place and combining those of secretarial and clerical workers in second place (Bogen 1985a:7). However, neither census data nor INS data represent the full realities of this phenomenon, on several counts: (1) the census figures do not account for arrivals after 1980; (2) many documented and most undocumented immigrants are not counted in the census; (3) INS data provide information on those who become legal permanent residents in any given year and therefore reveal little about the undocumented; and (4) it has been speculated that the ratio of illegal to legal Caribbeans in New York is as great as 1:1 (Bogen 1985a:2; 1985b:2). Since undocumented most often means uncounted, the official figures do not truly reflect the immigrant population. Given these factors and the availability of private household work to undocumented women, the actual number of household workers in the West Indian immigrant population must exceed the official one. Moreover, some of the West Indian women counted in the census in other occupations, especially nursing aide and a variety of clerical jobs, have done household work earlier in their migration careers either with green cards or in order to obtain them. Therefore, one can infer that a significant number of West Indian women work in private households in New York at some point in their migration careers.

According to the provisions of the 1965 Immigration Act and subsequent revisions, legal permanent resident status is primarily available to those West Indian women who are sponsored by either legally specified kin or spouses, or by employers in specified occupations and conditions.[6] While a few of the women interviewed entered the country illegally, most of the women traveled to New York alone with three- or six-month visitors' (non-immigrant) visas which they overstayed, thereby becoming undocumented.[7] A few lucky women were sponsored by kin either prior to migration or after entering with visitors' visas. While their New York community of kin and friends provided housing and various kinds of support, it was often unable to provide legal status. For West Indian women without appropriate kin or professions, household work is one of the few routes to the green card. Without a green card, household work is also one of the few jobs available.[8]

The Immigration Reform and Control Act (IRCA), passed November 6, 1986, established sanctions against hiring or recruiting workers without verification of their legal eligibility to work (e.g., proof of citizenship, permanent resident status, temporary worker's or other visa permitting work granted by the INS) at any time after November 6, 1986. Sanctions, which took effect six months after the law passed, ranged from initial warnings to fines of $250 to $10,000 per each undocumented worker hired after November 6, 1986, as well as possible civil or criminal actions. Technically these provisions apply in all cases, however the INS indicated that their primary targets would be employers with large numbers of workers and repeat offenders. While there have been a few scattered reports of sanctions imposed on employers of household workers, employer sponsorship of household workers continues in spite of IRCA. As other job opportunities for undocumented workers tighten, more women look to household work for sponsorship for legal residence. However, the added level of illegality multiplies the potential for exploitation of undocumented workers on sponsor jobs.

Although almost all of the employers of the West Indian women discussed were male/female couples, most of the women spoke primarily of the relationship with their female employers. The boss was generally referred to as "she." This is congruent with the sexual division of labor in most upper- and middle-class households for more than 100 years in the West.

Finally, in this highly personalized relationship, employers' behavior toward workers falls on a continuum from that which is fair and helpful to that which is exploitive and disrespectful. Some amount of ambivalence surfaced in all workers' discussions of their employers. Variability in treatment of workers and in workers' perceptions of their situations are influenced by the variable conditions of the household work situation and broad cultural factors.

Labor Migration and Household Work: Process and Implications in the Caribbean and in New York

Much has been written on labor migration that is relevant here (see Piore 1979; Portes 1978a, 1978b). The centuries-old phenomenon of Caribbean internal, regional, and international migration has received increasing attention with a focus on the post-1965 migration to the United States (see Chaney 1985; Cross 1979; Foner 1978, 1979, 1983; A. Marshall 1983; D. Marshall 1982, 1984; Sassen-Koob 1981, 1984a, 1984b; and edited volumes by Bryce-Laporte and Mortimer 1976, 1981, 1983). The significant representation of the English-speaking Caribbean in the female-dominated migration since 1965 has motivated studies of that process (see Chaney 1982; Foner 1975, 1976; Mortimer and Bryce-Laporte 1981; and others). In addition, there is a well documented relationship between migration and household work for areas around the globe (e.g., see Introduction, Conclusion, and the rest of this volume).

In the complex dynamics of current Caribbean migration, West Indians confront and leave conditions of underdevelopment, especially limited educational and occupational opportunities and low standards of living, which are the legacies of Caribbean articulation in the world capitalist system. As economic conditions worsen, due in part to multinational domination and the vagaries of capital investment, more West Indians, representing different classes, migrate to centers of the system. Emigrants form a large percentage of the sending country's population (Chaney 1985:14–16). Their economic role is crucial through their remittances of money and goods which support households and influence consumption values and patterns in the home communities. While emigration may alleviate certain tensions born out of unmet needs for jobs, goods, and services in the sending countries, it can mean the loss of motivated and/or trained workers which can have a negative effect on development (for overviews see Brana-Shute and Brana-Shute 1982; Rubinstein 1982). Many migrants to New York find work in occupations (often in the expanding service sector) with relative shortages of native-born workers (see A. Marshall 1983; Sassen-Koob 1981). For nonelite West Indian women, most of whom bear the major responsibility for their own and their children's welfare, emigration constitutes, as Bolles (1981:62) states, an "alternative employment strategy." In recent times, due to the labor market conditions (e.g., the availability of private household and other service employment) and due to immigration procedures (e.g., employer sponsorship for legal status), women have often been the first links in West Indian chain migration.[9]

The women I interviewed perceived migration as a means to fulfill economic and other responsibilities for themselves, their children, and other kin which became increasingly difficult to shoulder at home. Most women interviewed had relatively "good" jobs by West Indian standards. They were teachers, policewomen, and clerical and service workers in the public and private sectors. One ran a dressmaking business employing a few workers and another did factory work at one time. Prior to migration, few had done paid household work, while some employed household workers themselves.[10] For most, upward occupational mobility was limited and pay was low relative to the inflated costs of basic consumer goods. Under- and unemployment were constant threats. Several women had occupational goals requiring education unobtainable in their own countries. The desire to educate and facilitate future employment of their children motivated many mothers to migrate. The major impetus for migration among a few solidly middle-class West Indian women was the prediction that however well educated their children became, they were likely to face unemployment and a lower standard of living than that in which they were raised. Migrating for expanded opportunities, better pay, education, and access to consumer goods for members of their own households, they sought the prior condition of legal resident status (for themselves and their children) through household work in New York.

Labor shortages in private household work have been noted in urban areas of the northeastern United States since the 1960s.[11] At that time, many older workers retired from or abandoned the field and many younger women avoided it, moving into higher status and often better paying occupations in the expanding service and clerical sectors. For native-born African-American women, who constituted a large proportion of the household work force in the region since at least 1920 (see Hamburger 1977:23; Katzman 1978:93–94), this process was aided by the gains won in the Civil Rights movement. By the mid-1960s, studies were conducted and plans were discussed to rectify the shortage (see Noble 1967 for study of Harlem household workers). These included schemes for the recruitment of West Indian women for household employment (household employment agency owner, personal communication), though none were as formal as the Canadian one begun in 1955 (see Henry 1968, 1982; Silvera 1983).

In the context of these shortages, the socioeconomic conditions confronting nonelite West Indian women, and the immigration legislation of the second half of the 1960s, it is not surprising that large numbers of green cards have been granted to West Indian women since 1967 in the private household category, according to the provisions of the immigration legislation. Dominguez (1975:13–14) found that since 1967 "an inordinately high percentage" of immigrant visas issued to "citizens of Barbados, Jamaica, and Trinidad and Tobago has gone to private household workers." Between 1960 and 1970, A. Marshall (1983:23) found a decline of native-born black women and an increase in non-Hispanic Caribbean women in household work in the New York area.

I assume that more precise statistics would show that West Indian women's labor has ameliorated a household worker shortage in the 1970s and 1980s in the New York area. New York's expanding service economy, changes in women's labor force participation patterns, a shrinking labor pool of local native-born workers willing to perform household work, a growing pool of immigrant workers whose choices are constrained by immigration regulations and other social and economic conditions all factor into this phenomenon. The proliferation of advanced services and professions which provide high incomes on one pole and the concommitant expansion of the low-waged service sector (providing such increasingly commoditized services as housekeeping, child care, and food preparation) at the other pole outlines the context for this situation (Sassen-Koob 1984a). The increase in labor force participation rates of women, especially mothers of pre-school children, and the so-called baby boomlet represented by the offspring of the baby boom generation and those who followed, set in the context of a sexual division of labor which assigns most household reproductive work to women, contributes to the rising demand for the services of household workers. Adult household members in the middle- and upper-income gentrified urban and suburban areas of New York hire West Indian (and other) workers to care for their homes and children while they work or are engaged in other activities. Household worker agencies flourish and "household help" advertisements abound in large New York daily newspapers as well as in the specialty papers like the *Irish Echo*. Advertisements and agencies represent seekers both of employment and of labor.

Household workers' labor allows their employers to maintain a class position and lifestyle unattainable otherwise. This is clear in the case of the Brooklyn couple desiring individualized in-home care for their children who hire a child-care worker to cover for them during working hours. If one parent made caring for their children and home a full-time job, their $60,000 household income would be halved. The working couple with a combined household income of $150,000 acknowledges that without a worker to tend their house and three-year-old daughter, one of them would have to give up employment and the income and prestige it provides. This would reduce their household income sufficiently to necessitate selling their large, centrally located Manhattan condominium and moving elsewhere to reduce their mortage costs. Without the services of the live-in household worker whom she is sponsoring, the suburban New Jersey mother whose husband earns $200,000 a year could not maintain her active schedule of participation in a variety of organizations, decorating her home (in difficult-to-maintain white), and ferrying her children to lessons and other activities; without either of their services her husband could not devote his time to his lucrative medical practice. Most employers acknowledge their dependence on workers, but many seem to have difficulty letting workers know that their labor is appreciated and not taken for granted.

West Indian women's labor, then, underwrites the labor force participation, the leisure pursuits, and in some cases the child rearing, of their middle- and upper-class employers. Of profound importance is that it does so without challenging either the sexual division of reproductive labor or the prevalent notion of private responsibility for child care. Child care and household maintenance, assigned to women within the dominant sexual division of labor, remain "women's work" when they are passed from "wife" to waged worker across class and race lines. While hiring household workers may strain current ideologies of the privatized nuclear family, it keeps the responsibility for child care and other household tasks a private one and thus eases the demand on the state for quality child care accessible to all households.[12]

At the same time this situation structures a stratified system of child raising and places additional hardships on the worker in her household and family relations. The workers' children are often forced to remain in the sending countries for years during the sponsorship process, thereby reducing the responsibility of the state for their reproduction while placing additional strains on immigrant workers and their kin at home to educate and care for their children. While the undocumented live-in worker provides the wealthy suburban mother with the time to devote to her children's activities, legal structures and oceans often separate the worker from her own children, and class position constrains child-care options for workers with children in New York.

Sponsorship for the Green Card

Jennifer Miller expressed the feelings of most of the women in this study: "You come from a good job back home and end up here being a housekeeper. . . . And only because you need the job and only because you need a sponsor. And the worst part of it is you have to live in."

Employer sponsorship for legal status is minimally a two-year process from first filing to green card for West Indian women household workers. The process requires obtaining Department of Labor certification that there are no documented workers available in the area to perform the same work at the "prevailing wage," petitioning the Immigration and Naturalization Service, and providing evidence that applicants have at least one year of experience at similar work. While their actual wages are frequently less than either the required current minimum wage or that which is stipulated to be paid at the granting of the card, they must pay income taxes based on those figures covering the duration of their sponsorship, and pay immigration lawyers' fees ranging from $500 (for church-subsidized legal services) to $3,000. Migrants are rarely able to start the process immediately as they must find willing and tolerable sponsors. Two to five or more years often pass between their arrival in New York and the acquisition of green cards. This means an equivalent or longer separation from kin left behind.

Although a shift to day work rendered live-in work uncommon in many areas of the United States since 1920 (see Clark-Lewis 1985; Katzman 1978:51, 87–91, 177), most West Indian women must live in while being sponsored. While living in facilitates saving money, it also increases the worker's isolation, potential exploitation, and loss of autonomy. Those who can avoid living in do so, and those who cannot face a difficult adjustment.

Experiences on the Sponsor Job

West Indian women's experiences of the sponsor job are varied. Those who can bypass the live-in requirement report more positive experiences as do those whose employers show concern and respect for them. After a short-lived live-in situation in the suburbs, Dawn Adams found a sponsor job in Manhattan which did not require living in. This, combined with a caring and generally thoughtful employer, made her sponsor job experience the best reported to me. While all workers expressed gratitude for being sponsored, many women experience a range of problems on their sponsor jobs from material exploitation to more subtle indignities and disrespect which make for less tolerable, more problematic sponsor experiences than that of Ms. Adams.

While some sponsor employers are fair, helpful, and supportive, and many are merely thoughtless about workers needs and feelings, some manipulate the workers' undocumented status and dependence to their advantage. Workers quit intolerable jobs both before and after initiating sponsorship, but most only reluctantly forfeit their investment of time and legal fees by quitting once the process has begun. Seeking to extend the period of employment, some employers take advantage of the worker's reluctance to quit by holding up the sponsorship process.

Unlike legal permanent resident household workers who have a greater choice of jobs and more control in defining their responsibilities, undocumented sponsored workers must often take over the majority of the reproductive tasks of the employing household. A familiar pattern is one in which sponsoring employers steadily lengthen the list of assigned tasks. Whether employers do this consciously or not, few workers feel comfortable refusing to perform the additional work once involved in the sponsorship process.

Yvette Phillips began her live-in sponsor job in New Jersey after having worked for several years in Toronto on the West Indian "domestic workers scheme" (on this program see Henry 1968, 1982; D. Marshall 1984; Silvera 1983). Although initially she was clear about not performing several tasks such as cooking, her employers changed that. As Ms. Phillips said,

> First when we talked about the job, I didn't want to do any cooking because I had done a lot of cooking in Canada. So I was told, "You won't have to do any cooking, just maybe set the table, make a salad." But as the months and years go by, it became, "Help me. Do this. Do that." And . . . she start and then she'll have to go out, and then I'll finish it. And eventually it ended up that I'm doing all the cooking.

Material exploitation characterizes many, especially live-in, sponsor jobs. Monica Cooper's responsibilities during her four-and-one-
half years on the job consisted of all housework, cooking, cleaning,
child care, and laundry. As she put it,

> Everything. Meals, cooking, everything. And at that point [1976] I was
> making $80 a week for five and a half days, they call it . . . [My] day off
> was Sunday and I had to be back by noon on Monday. I decided to do it
> to get my sponsorship.

Remembering her suburban sponsor job at which she worked
from 1977 to 1981 Jennifer Miller said, "I work sometimes till 11 o'clock
at night . . . I get up early in the morning and I get up at night to tend
the baby." Full-time care of the newborn third child meant that Ms.
Miller was truly on call 24 hours a day. She was responsible for all
cooking, cleaning, washing, and child care seven days a week for $90
a week. Her wages, like those of most others, stretched to support kin
left behind.

Christine Williams experienced a similar situation:

> For the first two weeks [after the employer returned from delivering her
> third baby], she had a nurse. . . . After that it was I to do all the caring,
> the cooking, the housekeeping, the laundry, the shopping. Everything
> was I. So it wasn't too sweet and easy for me. [She laughed.]

The material exploitation takes on added dimensions because the
worker, especially when she lives in, is often performing many of the
tasks assigned to wives and mothers within middle-class homes.
While compensation for this already undervalued work is difficult
when done for love or for money, undocumented status often pro-
motes low wages and large workloads as if the promise of the green
card should be enough compensation.

Judith Thomas described her feelings on her live-in sponsor job:

> They just somehow figure because they're sponsoring you, they own
> you. And if they say jump, you should jump. And if they say sit, you
> should sit. When you start in at the beginning they tell you certain
> amount of . . . work, and then as you go on, they just keep on adding
> more and more. It was really a dedication. . . . I felt as if I wouldn't hold
> out. I couldn't make it. But then . . . I just think . . . that . . . I'd be better
> off staying here now and continuing, knowing that one day I'll get it over
> with. . . . And I think about my kids and just say regardless to what, I
> just have to do this. But I tell you it wasn't easy. There were some nights
> when I would just cry and cry and cry myself to sleep and say, "God,
> how long it's going to be?"

Ms. Thomas, a Vincentian mother of four, like many others, was
motivated by both the desire for reunification with her children and

her aspirations for herself and for them. Both were predicated on the green card.

Yvette Phillips said, "There were times there were things I didn't want to do but I did it. I know what I wanted, so I did it." Like Ms. Phillips, many undocumented women kept their eyes on the green card, tolerating more than they would otherwise as they persevered on sponsor jobs. As Christine Williams expressed it,

> I just wanted to know I would achieve the card. The green card was the most important thing on my mind. I *wanted* to get it. Because it was like I was living in a fear in the country without it. When I hadn't it, I was always in a fear, thinking well probably someday police could just hold me and send me back home, you know because I was illegal all that time. I wanted to know that I *had* it and I had a right to remain in the country. So that's why I really put up with what I did put up with to get it. I managed to and I was so happy and thankful to God when I did get it.

Under the Immigration Reform and Control Act (IRCA) of 1986, the potential for exploitation on sponsor jobs has intensified. The added level of illegality heightens pressure on undocumented workers to conform to the demands of their employers. Immigration attorneys and staff at immigrants' rights organizations with whom I spoke have received more reports of employer abuses of undocumented household workers on sponsor jobs since IRCA. Some employers pay less or extract an extra day's work from undocumented workers who feel trapped in their jobs by fears of not finding other employment (due to eligibility verification requirements) and by the need for green cards. As the pressure to obtain green cards intensifies, sponsor jobs become more problematic.

The Asymmetrical Relations

Beyond the exhausting physical work, the expanding household duties, the hours, and the pay, most troubling to all of the women was the nonreciprocal nature of respect at work. Jennifer Miller expressed this central concern:

> I'm not looking for them to shower us down with money, with clothes, but with a little respect and feelings. You know because they want full respect from us and at the same time they want to treat us like nothing. . . . A lot of West Indians are very insulted, but we do it because we have no choice.

This nonreciprocal respect characterizes much of the asymmetrical social relations of household work in the United States. In spite of different values placed on various household activities (e.g., child care is more highly valued than housecleaning), the social relations reflect a general devaluation of household work in North American culture. Assigned to women as an extension of childbearing capacity, household work is naturalized, trivialized, and considered unskilled. It is further devalued as it passes across class, race, ethnic, or migration lines from women who choose not to do it to other women who perform it in employers' households. Furthermore, due to Western ideological constructs of the last 150 years, work performed in the home is often not recognized as work, which further obscures the value of household work. This devaluation is aggravated by the current North American strain of disdain for domesticity and for those who are "housewives," and by the growing expectation that working-, middle-, and upper-class mothers should be engaged in activities outside the home. Currently, when female employers work outside the home, they look not across gender lines to the men in their own households (when relevant), but across class, racial, or ethnic lines to West Indian and other women to perform their household labor. West Indian household workers are thus heir to a system of household work in the United States which both reflects and reinforces a set of hierarchical relations in which they and their work are devalued (see Colen 1986; 1989).

West Indian workers and their employers enter into social relations that are fraught with tensions. Primary is the tension between the status of household work as low-paid wage labor in the framework of the capitalist cash nexus and its highly personalized relations and location in the household. Paid household labor strains the ideological constructs of separate public and private realms and of motherhood that have been dominant (but in flux) recently. When child care is done in the home for money by "others" instead of for "love" by mothers, the discord between ideological construct and reality results in stressed relations. The relations are characterized by contradictions between the worker's intimate involvement in the household, the employer's dependence on her, and her poor pay and the varieties of employers' distancing, depersonalizing, and thoughtless behaviors.

West Indian household workers' experience of these asymmetrical social relations takes many forms (see Colen 1986, 1989 on these experiences). Aside from the material conditions, West Indian women described employer behavior which left them feeling held in low esteem, taken for granted, and denied their adult humanity. The social geography of household spaces means that some employers force live-in workers to share rooms with children or pets or that the workers do not have access to certain "public" rooms except to clean them. Rituals of eating symbolically express inequalities when some employers ask live-in workers to serve meals in the dining room then insist that workers eat the leftovers in the kitchen. Several workers have been expected to pick up and launder trails of clothing dropped on the floor. Some workers describe being taken into employers' confidences and treated "like friends" only to be called "the maid" and kept at a distance when guests arrive moments later. Live-in workers who become second class members of employers' households are clearly not "one of the family" as employers sometimes suggest (perhaps to ease discomfort with the level of dependence and intimacy in the context of waged workers living in their homes). Workers read that phrase as an attempt to extract more labor from them (Colen 1986, 1989). These relations, while structural to much household work in the United States and elsewhere, have particular meaning to West Indian women in the context of a live-in sponsor job.

Identity and Respect: Special Impacts of Sponsor Jobs for West Indian Women

Judith Thomas's reaction to her sponsor job exemplifies the confrontation between West Indian women's notions of social behavior and their experiences on some sponsor jobs. For her, as for most others, living in, and the often concommitant isolation and loss of autonomy made the depersonalization, trivialization, and lack of respect all the more stinging.

> It was another hard thing that as a woman, a mother, responsible for a home, with a husband . . . to come here to New York City and have to be living with people. . . . It was definitely hard for me. You know at times they would talk to you as though you were just some little piece of a girl. It was really humiliating at times. . . . Most of the time they wouldn't see me as that [fully adult] person. . . . A couple of times I really had to tell them that. I really had to say, "Well, I want to be treated as a full adult. You know, you all must remember that. . . . once I had a husband and kids and had the same responsibility as you all but because people go through different stages in life, here I am now in this situation. So, you know, don't forget that . . . remember, I was once this responsible person. And don't treat me like a child or some little girl."

Being treated "like a girl," being related to as if they are invisible, or being asked to wear uniforms (to mark their status), further exemplify behaviors in which employers withhold respect and deny workers' adult humanity and personhood. While these are rooted in prevalent relations of class, race, and gender, they contrast starkly with the cultural values and assumptions about social relations through which West Indians experience their sponsor jobs.

As many anthropologists have noted, respect is a central concept in West Indian social relations (Barrow 1976; Durant-Gonzalez 1976, 1982; Foner 1973, 1978; Makiesky-Barrow 1976; Sutton 1969, 1976; Sutton and Makiesky-Barrow 1977; and others). Dominant cultural notions of stratification based on such factors as education, occupation, and income structure relations of status in West Indian communities. This system is crosscut by another more egalitarian system of social relations based on concepts of respect which guide an individual's interactions with others which form the basis of reputations. According to Barrow, respect is rooted in "appearance, manner, behaviour, and conduct in social relationships" (1976:108). For example, according to Barrow, a man's self-respect hinges in part on public "authoritative," "assertive" behavior, while a woman's depends in part on public "modesty, restraint, and discretion" (1976:109–110). She states that "a villager's reputation depends largely on the way in which he conducts himself according to the idiom of 'respect.' 'Respect' is a fundamental moral concept, central to one's existence as a human being and a member of the locality" (1976:108). Respect so conceived is "the key concept according to which individuals judge each other and the cornerstone of a system of ranking based on these reputations" (1976:113).

Almost every woman in this study has expressed the expectation that "if I respect myself and give respect to my employers, they should respect me." This notion of giving and getting respect is a central tenet of West Indian social interactions as reported by Barrow (1976) and others. Individuals behave in a manner which indicates self-respect, which gains the respect of others, and which gives respect where it is due.

Thus, when Ms. Miller states that West Indian women are insulted by the nonreciprocal relations of respect (which new migrants may endure in order to get their green cards ["because we have no choice"]), she points to a crucial clash in cultural values and expectations. On the other hand, Janet Taylor was in the hospital after an appendectomy and her sponsor employer laundered and brought her fresh underwear and nightclothes. The reciprocity involved in this act carried significant weight as Ms. Taylor discussed the relations of respect on her sponsor job.

Within their home communities the women in this study were accorded a high degree of respect deriving from these patterns of ranking and reputation. Teachers, civil servants, or clerical workers are highly regarded. But even women for whom these avenues are closed are respected in the community's indigenous value system centered on such things as motherhood, raising children, age, marriage, and various aspects of behavior. Durant-Gonzalez (1976, 1982) and others have noted that motherhood is highly valued across class lines (Kerns 1983; my observations; see Powell 1984:97–122 for an overview). Bearing, raising, and being responsible for children and for a home or "yard" earns a woman the respect of her community. Age and raising more than one generation of children adds to this; those who, having raised their own children, "care" their grandchildren and other children, kin or nonkin, including those of migrant mothers, are held in high esteem in their communities. Thus when Ms. Thomas, a mother with a home and a legal marriage (not to mention a white collar job) was treated "like a girl" she expressed her protest in West Indian cultural terms.

For most of the West Indian women interviewed, their communities provide a degree of continuity in their social relations and are the source of reaffirmation of their personhood.[13] Foner's research (1986) corroborates my own findings that many of the patterns of respect and identity forged in West Indian social relations are reconstituted in West Indian communities in New York. While respect may be lacking on the job, participation in the everyday informal social life of the community as well as in clubs, churches, lodges, associations, and community organizations from home, reinforces these West Indian women's identities and provides them with respect. A worker may be first named or referred to as "the girl" on the job, but may then attend a gathering of the Vincentian Teacher's Association, and be addressed as "Mrs.," to which she is accustomed. She may devote hours to her church where the pastor and the congregation with whom she worshipped at home respectfully know her as "Sister Thomas." A worker may squeeze in hours to share pleasure with close friends who give her the love and support of "sisters."

However, while these reconstituted West Indian communities are important in resisting the disempowerment and depletion of emotional resources possible on the job, living in cuts a woman off from them and this separation intensifies any assaults or her humanity. Suburban jobs heighten the isolation. While Monica Cooper did whatever she could to get away on her day off to avoid being constantly "on call," Jennifer Miller could not leave for a day without a deduction from her wages. Beyond reducing the material exploitation, getting away allows the worker to distance herself from the social relations of the job. Remaining on the job not only means that five work days become six or seven, but that the worker engages in few social interactions outside of the job. Those who have the opportunity to renew themselves in relation to their community, kin, and friends fare better. Those, like Dawn Adams, who return nightly to their own communities suffer the least in this respect.

Child Care on the Sponsor Job

Child care constitutes a central component of most of the sponsor jobs I have discussed. For many West Indian women in sponsor jobs, child care responsibilities are replete with contradictions and conflict. We know that meanings of child care activity and motherhood are redefined in each social and historical context and that they vary across historical moments and cultures and across class and ethnic lines within them (see e.g., Badinter 1981; Margolis 1984). In this situation, different cultural values and meanings of child-care activity operate at the same time as behaviors and ideologies are undergoing change.

West Indian workers' cultural values and codes concerning motherhood, child-care activity, and adult social behavior do not prepare them for the attitudes and behaviors surrounding child-care work in New York. Motherhood, highly esteemed, is a mark of adult status for West Indian women. Caring for children is valued and care givers are admired in West Indian culture. Raising other mothers' children is commonplace in a culture in which child fostering is a deeply embedded pattern (see Durant-Gonzalez 1976, 1982; Powell 1984). In fact, several of those interviewed had been fostered at some point during their childhood and most of their children were being fostered, primarily by female kin, during the mothers' sponsorship. While the cultural values about motherhood and child care might facilitate West Indian women's entry into child-care work, they quickly learn that in New York, this work commands low wages and little respect for the care givers. Their encounters with children and with employers on the job often surprise and disturb them.

Ambiguity, affection, and emotion work (Hochschild 1983) suffuse child care in the live-in sponsor job. Caring for children blurs the distinctions between physical work and affect. Beyond "loving children" in general, which some workers report, child-care responsibilities of long duration often produces affective ties and "parental" feelings such as love, pride, and embarassment toward the particular children in their care. Especially prone to developing deep attachments were those who had virtual 24-hour responsibility, including night feedings, for children from infancy. These attachments, possible to some degree in any child care situation, may assume more importance in the isolation of the live-in sponsor job and separation from the worker's own children. While all child care involves at least minimal levels of emotion work (e.g., showing lively interest whether or not one is truly interested; Hochschild 1983), enduring legally imposed separations from their own children leads many women to pour more of themselves into relationships with their charges. In this situation some "give them [employer's children] more because I just think of them as my own. Just because I was lonely I gave them all I have."

For some workers, child care is the most rewarding aspect of their sponsor jobs and relationships with the children provide them with emotional satisfaction unavailable otherwise on the job. However, when children are rude and disrespectful to them and to other adults, workers are troubled and deeply offended. Workers tend to disapprove of codes of behavior which, unlike their own, permit this behavior. For some workers, poorly behaved children are a major source of discontent on sponsor jobs.

Relationships with employers are more complex. In part, this stems from contradictory values about motherhood and child care in the dominant culture of employers. On one hand, more middle- and upper-class mothers are joining working-class women in the paid labor force. The "career" activities of middle- and upper-class women are generally more highly valued than their "housewife" and "mothering" activities. On the other hand, women generally are expected to and expect to become mothers. While an employer's law practice or her volunteer work earns her more prestige than her mothering work, in dominant white "middle-class" culture, there is a persistent underlying assumption that motherhood involves biological mothers as primary caretakers of their own children at home. These messages and other feelings leave some employers feeling conflicted and uncertain about their behavior.

Child-care workers, especially in live-in sponsor jobs, act as surrogate parents for employers' children. Employers desire that workers provide the physical care, nurturance, and socialization that this entails. With full-time responsibility for children, a worker becomes, as Grace Ellis from Guyana stated, "like a mother to them." But this does not ensure that a worker is treated as a valued adult who contributes substantially to the well-being of the employing household. As Danielle Alleyne from Barbados said, some employers expect you to "give extra to these children," and yet they "treat you as if you were part of the furniture." The development of close mutual affection between worker and child may threaten employers' claims to the primacy of parent/child relations, provoke parental jealousy, and challenge their notions of motherhood. According to June Morris, employers "get very jealous. They feel their kids are too much attached to you."

Although North American ideologies around motherhood and child care are in flux and generally stretch to accommodate contradictory realities, the meaning of motherhood in the employers' culture may be called into question when child care is divorced from biological motherhood, mothers leave the home for most of the waking hours, and the privatized realm is penetrated by waged relations. As contradictions surface, they may add tension in employer/worker relations.

For West Indian workers, neither mothering nor child care activity are quite so anchored in biology. Their caring for employer's children does not challenge their concepts of motherhood. While some workers, like Danielle Alleyne, question employers with other choices who spend so little time with their own children (e.g., those who go out every night after working all day), they know that their own responsibilities as mothers bring them to work on sponsor jobs. Immigration procedures and not choice determine the nature and duration of the separation from their own children.

Paid child-care work, although enormously transformed by wages and cross-class and race relations, may have at least some of the value associated with child rearing in their own homes for the new migrant. Negative employer behavior toward workers not only defies cultural codes which accord them respect as adults, but it contrasts with the respect conferred on child-care activity in West Indian communities. "Why," as Grace Ellis and other women ask, "would an employer behave disrespectfully toward the person to whom she entrusts her children?"

Life with the Green Card

The years of household work leading to the last stage of the sponsorship process do not always guarantee obtaining a green card. Most women are called to the United States embassy serving their home country for their interviews. This means returning home (or to a neighboring island) and seeing long-missed children and other kin, but it also represents the financial burden of air fare and lost wages. During this last phase, some women's petitions for permanent resident status are delayed, pending further investigation, or denied for reasons that include inadequate proof of one year of paid household work experience prior to initiating the sponsorship process or non-payment of taxes during sponsorship (something many employers neglect to do, leaving workers with a large back tax debt from which deductions for their dependents are not allowed). When confronted with delay or denial after fulfilling the obligations of the indenture-like sponsor job, women feel betrayed in a kind of cruel hoax. The perception of some of the women interviewed is that this pattern was on the rise in the mid-1980s, however this could not be confirmed.

Most West Indian women completing the process do obtain legal permanent resident status. Those interviewed describe suddenly feeling "free." As the undercurrent of fear and the internalized insecurity associated with undocumented status dissipate, the character of their lives changes. Most who did not include their children in their own sponsor process file to sponsor them immediately (a process taking a minimum of about 18 months in 1986). Most stop living in on a full-time, year-round basis within a year of obtaining their green cards. Shifting to live-out jobs, they regain autonomy and control over their lives, strengthen the psychological boundaries between the social relations of their "work" lives and those of their "personal" lives, increase both their formal and informal participation in their communities, and begin to reunite with their own children (see Clark-Lewis 1985, 1987 on the shift to day work in a different period). Many initiate a return to school by taking high school equivalency examinations.

After obtaining green cards, most of the women interviewees stopped living in on the job and began "living in" in their own communities. Some of those who had good relationships with employers remained with sponsor employers longer than those who did not but all eventually left sponsoring employers. Most chose jobs they experienced as "better," within and outside of household work. With green cards, few workers live in and most who continue in household work shift to child care or home care (for the ill or elderly), jobs with limited housekeeping responsibilities, higher status, and perhaps more personal rewards. Living out with a green card lessens the potential for exploitation by reducing the level of personalization and offsetting work relations with residence in their own households and communities. Legal residents command higher wages and are better able to define their responsibilities and working conditions. As Judith Thomas said, "I paid my dues when I wasn't legally here and I just believe that since I became legal, then every right of a legal person should be mine."

Decisions to remain in household work are based on a combination of life cycle, migration career, and domestic cycle factors as well as job availability, the constraints of race, sex, and age discrimination, and what some women who have left the field call "ambition." Some West Indian women with green cards do household work (primarily child care and home care for the elderly) indefinitely with no alternate plans. Some of them take courses in neonatal or gerontological care which may increase their value and wages in the job market.[14] Valuing and enjoying care giving, and having good relations with employers, satisfactory schedules, acceptable pay, social networks created through the job, and the relative autonomy of day work in which employers are absent are frequently cited as benefits of the job. Although mobility and job security are lacking, some enjoy working in a home environment and feel secure in the assumption that they will keep their jobs until "their" children go to school.

Some legal workers who have "good" child-care jobs and "better" salaries (which in the low-wage world of women's service work means they may earn above the poverty line in New York) may have difficulty switching to jobs in clerical or health care fields (those which seem to be most readily available to them). While held in higher regard, more contractually secure, and offering better long-term benefits and conditions such as medical coverage for the worker and her children, sick leave, and, in some cases, pensions and job ladders for upward mobility, these jobs may pay lower starting salaries than some workers with green cards receive on child-care jobs, and, thus, initially reduce household income. A divorced woman with sole responsibility for four teenage children may feel that the relative merits of these benefits may be outweighed by her immediate need for the higher income. A mother of one with additional support from a husband's income might take the initial risk as might a single mother of two children with a commitment to advancing in a business career through education and job experience. A married woman with grown children and her husband's medical and other benefits may stay on the child-care job she enjoys. Some older women's decisions to remain in household work are influenced by fears about age discrimination (in addition to that of race and sex) as well as by insecurity about their educational backgrounds.

While some West Indian women leave household work immediately after obtaining their green cards, many plan to and actually do so after completion of education or training programs, reunion with children, or saving money. During and after the transition, many women live under the pressure of schedules laden with work, school, additional income-producing activity such as dressmaking, and their own household responsibilities. They often turn to occupations in health care (from nursing aides to registered nurses in private and institutional settings), clerical, banking, and other business-related fields (increasingly computer oriented), and other, often pink-collar, jobs. Some start their own businesses. They work toward some form of upward mobility for themselves and their children. Many reconstitute their larger kin networks in New York by becoming citizens and sponsoring family members. In whatever fields they work, they juggle the material and emotional worlds in which they work and live with those from which they came.

Conclusion

I have focused on experiences of West Indian women who perform household work for others in New York in order to obtain legal permanent resident status in the United States. In a process of labor migration in an international capitalist system, many West Indian women migrate to fulfill their household responsibilities. Seeking legal status, they are directed by immigration policies to enter an indenture-like period of private household work. They perform many of the reproductive tasks of employing households and fill jobs abandoned by both men and women in those households and by many native-born workers.

In a period of increasing female labor participation, increasing commoditization of reproductive activities, an expanding service sector, cultural stress on the ideology of family, and emphasis on individual rather than social responsibility, the state, through its immigration policies, engineers a "partial solution"[15] to pressures within middle- and upper-class families and on the state and industry to provide quality child care and other support services. It ensures a vulnerable immigrant household labor force. In the face of increasing demands for household labor, recent legislation, the 1986 IRCA, theoretically, cuts off this pool of workers. What it has really done is heighten the vulnerability of the current undocumented household work force.

A system of reproduction operates, encouraged by the state, which is highly stratified by class, race, place in a global political economy, and migration status. In it, West Indian women's household labor underwrites the labor force participation and the leisure pursuits as well as the lifestyle and class position of their middle- and upper-class employers. It does so without challenging either the sexual division of reproductive labor or the prevalent notion of private responsibility for child care. Employers look to the marketplace across class and race/ethnic lines to accomplish their reproductive tasks. That marketplace is populated by undocumented West Indian women, and others, who need the employer sponsorship for legal status and/or the wages to support their families.

At the same time, most undocumented West Indian women's children must remain in the sending countries for the duration of the mothers' and children's sponsorship processes. Supported by their migrant mothers' regular remittances, the children are cared for by kin or friends. The state reduces its responsibility for the children while placing additional strains on immigrant workers and their kin to raise and educate them.

Undocumented status leaves West Indian household workers vulnerable to material and other exploitation in live-in sponsor jobs. The status and the job may impose a difficult separation from children, kin, and communities. The asymmetrical relations with the employers with whom they most often must live, clash with West Indian identities, values, and concepts of social behavior in the key arenas of respect and valuation of child-care activity. Housekeeping for the green card, while sharing features with other forms of household work and of coerced labor, as Ms. Andrews pointed out, is its own peculiar institution.

Jennifer Miller, grateful to her employers for sponsoring her in spite of the exploitation involved, left her sponsor job, took a full-time day child-care and housekeeping job in Manhattan for a year, settled into an apartment in Brooklyn, sponsored her son and other family from Jamaica, and now works as a bookkeeper in a Manhattan office. Recalling the material and psychic costs of her indenture-like sponsor job, she spoke of getting her green card:

> People don't understand how hard it is to get here. And we try to explain it to them. It's terrible. And you think of all you go through. You go through all this paperwork and go through the lawyer and pay so much money and you get this blooming little piece of card, green paper. It's not even green. The day when I got it I said, "This is IT?" They should have a better system than this.

Notes

Acknowledgments. My deepest gratitude extends to the West Indian women who shared their lives with me through interviews and beyond. An earlier version of this article was presented at the American Anthropological Association Annual Meeting in 1985. I want to thank Roger Sanjek for conceiving the panel on household workers, sustaining the energy we needed to transform it into this volume, and making helpful suggestions on this essay. I am grateful to Deborah D'Amico-Samuels, Michael Landy, Mindie Lazarus-Black, and Constance Sutton for critical comments and suggestions on earlier drafts of this paper.

1. All names are pseudonyms.

2. Much of the growing literature on household work is relevant in here. For example Katzman (1978) presents historical material on household work

in the United States to 1920 (see also Dudden [1983], Palmer [1984, 1987], and Sutherland [1981]). Glenn (1980, 1986) on Japanese-American women, Clark-Lewis (1985, 1987), Dill (1979), and Rollins (1985, this volume) on African-American women, Romero (1987, 1988) on Chicanas in Denver, and Ruiz (1987) on Chicanas in Texas, all discuss the household work experiences of racial or ethnic minority women in the United States. Clark-Lewis's richly tex-tural oral histories about the meanings of the shift from live-in to day work and their relationship to migration and to community have some parallels in West Indian women's experiences. Rollins insightfully explores contemporary experiences of African-American domestic workers in relationship to their white female employers in Boston.

3. Fieldwork for the larger project involved participant observation and multiple, in-depth interviews with 25 West Indian women (who had migrated to New York since 1965) at their jobs, in their homes, and at various family, social, and community activities. In addition, I visited two Eastern Caribbean communities. In the first case, I accompanied a migrant and her children on a visit home to do research on return visits and on West Indian child care and child fostering and in the second to collect data on child fostering and immi-gration procedures. Interviews were conducted with 20 white, native-born employers (mostly female) of West Indian child-care workers in the New York area. I also consulted immigration lawyers, attorneys, and staff at immigrants' rights organizations, household employment agencies, service agencies in West Indian communities, and United States Embassy staff in the Eastern Car-ibbean.

4. Private household work encompasses the reproductive tasks of child care, housekeeping/household maintenance (including cleaning, laundry, cooking, etc.), and home health-care work (attending to the ill or frail elderly). Sponsorship for the green card is possible in all three of these categories of household work, although it is less frequent for home-care workers. West In-dian women are employed in all of them with and without green cards and for sponsorship. While my primary focus is private household child care and housekeeping work, many West Indian women in New York provide private home care to the elderly and infirm. Several women in the study obtained le-gal status and now work as home-care attendants. Those who are members of Local 1199 of the Hospital and Health Care Employees Union have some mea-sures of protection usually unavailable to other, especially undocumented, private household workers (see Dinkins 1987 on home health workers).

5. Child care has been the primary responsibility for most of the women in this study. Without green cards and/or in sponsor jobs, they performed most and generally all, of the housework of the employing households as well. Once legal residents, most of the women in the study who remained in house-hold work found child-care jobs in which they did such tasks as washing dishes, and possibly bedmaking or laundry in addition to their primary child-care responsibilities, but they rarely performed heavy household chores. Many households employing full-time, live-out child-care workers with green cards hire other West Indian women to perform the major cleaning and house-hold maintenance on a weekly or biweekly basis. It seems that many of these women who housekeep on a rotating daywork basis are awaiting either family sponsorship or an appropriate sponsor job. Some women with legal residence

take an extra weekly or biweekly weekend cleaning job to augment their regular incomes.

6. Employer sponsorship is prevalent for West Indian registered nurses (due to a declared nursing shortage in the New York area) and some other professionals.

7. Most women interviewed who arrived with visitors' visas intended to be sponsored by kin or (more often) by employers. A minority of those interviewed traveled with children and mates with visitors' visas. After the visas lapsed the family remained undocumented until the women were sponsored either by employers or by kin. Many West Indian women come to New York with visitors' visas, do household work during their stay, and leave within the stipulated period with earnings and basic goods (rice, oil, flour, soap, etc.) purchased in New York that ease a tight financial situation at home.

8. West Indian women who enter with green cards sometimes do household work, especially child care, because it is the easiest form of employment to secure (especially given the job information networks to which many West Indians have access). Others are motivated by confrontation with racist or anti-immigrant prejudice and demands for local experience when they apply for employment similar to what they had at home. Many view the jobs as temporary employment while they adjust to their new environment, save money, and perhaps acquire education, job training, connections, or the capital to find other jobs or start their own businesses. Very few live in on the job, generally only for a brief period, primarily to save money given New York's high-cost housing market.

9. While household work and employer sponsorship contribute to West Indian women's frequent position as the first link, as more women obtain green cards and become citizens, they increasingly sponsor their kin, male and female, sparing them the sponsor job experience. The next generation of West Indian women immigrants experiences arrival in New York quite differently.

10. Most of the women in this sample entered the labor force with somewhat higher educational levels and expanded occupational opportunities, as well as higher employment expectations than their mothers had. Many of their mothers, like many nonelite West Indian women in the 1940s, 1950s, and 1960s, had done household work at some point in their employment histories, often in conjunction with internal, rural-to-urban migration. A couple of women who had done household work in Trinidad were recruited there with the promise of sponsor jobs on their arrival in New York.

11. For overviews of different periods and workers in household work history in the United States see Almquist (1979), Dudden (1983), Katzman (1978). For a brief summary, see Colen (1989). Household work was central to the migration experiences of many earlier groups (e.g., Irish, Japanese, and others). Confronting racial discrimination similar to that faced by their African-American contemporaries, many West Indian women of earlier migrations did private household work.

12. Child-care expenses of working mothers (with or without working fathers present) are frequently discussed in relation to the mother's salary (e.g., she spends one-fourth of her salary on child care). Thus even the expenses of

child care are seen as women's responsibility rather than that of the family, the larger community, or the state.

13. Paule Marshall (1981, 1983) beautifully describes the way an earlier generation of Barbadian household workers in New York "reaffirm self-worth" in conversations in each other's kitchens (1983:6).

14. In 1985 some documented private household child-care workers commanded as much as $250 to $300 a week gross. While similar wages might be earned doing home care for the elderly, many home-care workers employed by agencies earned substantially less (closer to $140 to $200 a week gross) when they could get a full-time schedule.

15. I thank Saskia Sassen for our discussion of the "partial solution."

References Cited

Almquist, Elizabeth McTaggart
  1979   Minorities, Gender, and Work. Lexington, MA: Lexington Books.
Badinter, Elisabeth
  1981   Mother Love: Myth and Reality, Motherhood in Modern History. New York: Macmillan Publishing.
Barrow, Christine
  1976   Reputation and Ranking in a Barbadian Locality. Social and Economic Studies 25(2):106–121.
Bogen, Elizabeth
  1985a   Caribbean Immigrants in New York City, A Demographic Summary, October 1985, Office of Immigrant Affairs, New York Department of City Planning.
  1985b   Testimony at Hearings on Non-Hispanic Caribbeans in New York, called by Congressman Robert Garcia, 7 June 1985.
Bolles, A. Lynn
  1981   "Goin' Abroad": Working Class Jamaican Women and Migration. *In* Female Immigrants to the United States: Caribbean, Latin America, and African Experiences. RIIES Occasional Papers No. 2. Delores M. Mortimer and Roy S. Bryce-Laporte, eds. Pp. 56–84. Washington, DC: Research Institute on Immigration and Ethnic Studies, Smithsonian Institution.
Brana-Shute, Rosemary, and Gary Brana-Shute
  1982   The Magnitude and Impact of Remittances in the Eastern Caribbean: A Research Note. *In* Return Migration and Remittances: Developing a Caribbean Perspective. RIIES Occasional Papers No. 3. William F. Stinner, Klaus de Albuquerque, and Roy S. Bryce-Laporte, eds. Pp. 267–289. Washington, DC: Research Institute on Immigration and Ethnic Studies, Smithsonian Institution.
Bryce-Laporte, Roy S., and Delores M. Mortimer
  1983   Caribbean Immigration to the United States. RIIES Occasional Papers No. 1, Second printing. Washington, DC: Research Institute on Immigration and Ethnic Studies, Smithsonian Institution.
Chaney, Elsa M.
  1982   Women Who Go and the Women Who Stay Behind. Migration Today 10(3,4):6–13.

1985   Migration from the Caribbean Region: Determinants and Effects of Current Movements. Hemispheric Migration Project Occasional Paper Series. Washington, DC: Center For Immigration Policy and Refugee Assistance, Georgetown University.
Clark-Lewis, Elizabeth
1985   "This Work Had a' End": The Transition From Live-In to Day Work. Working Paper 2. Southern Women: The Intersection of Race, Class, and Gender. Memphis, Memphis State University: Center for Research on Women.
1987   "This Work Had a' End": African-American Domestic Workers in Washington, D.C., 1910–1940. *In* "To Toil the Livelong Day": America's Women at Work, 1780–1980. Carol Groneman and Mary Beth Norton, eds. Pp. 196–212. Ithaca: Cornell University Press.
Colen, Shellee
1986   "With Respect and Feelings": Voices of West Indian Child Care and Domestic Workers in New York City. *In* All American Women: Lines That Divide, Ties That Bind. Johnnetta B. Cole, ed. Pp. 46–70. New York: Free Press.
1987   ". . . Like a Mother to Them": Meanings of Child Care and Motherhood for West Indian Child Care Workers and Their Employers in New York. Paper presented at Session on the Caribbean Experience, Part Two: Ideology and Politics, American Anthropological Association Annual Meeting. Chicago, Illinois. November.
1989   "Just A Little Respect": West Indian Domestic Workers in New York City. *In* Muchachas No More: Household Workers in Latin America and the Caribbean. Elsa M. Chaney and Mary Garcia Castro, eds. Pp. 171–194. Philadelphia: Temple University Press.
Cross, Malcolm
1979   Urbanization and Urban Growth in the Caribbean: An Essay on Social Change in Dependent Societies. Cambridge: Cambridge University Press.
Dill, Bonnie Thornton
1979   Across the Boundaries of Race and Class: An Exploration of the Relationship Between Work and Family among Black Female Domestic Servants. Ph.D. dissertation. Department of Sociology, New York University.
Dinkins, David N.
1988   Plight of the Home Care Worker: Report of the Manhattan Borough President's Hearing on 29 April 1987. New York: Manhattan Borough President's Office.
Dominguez, Virginia
1975   From Neighbor to Stranger: The Dilemma of Caribbean Peoples in the United States. New Haven: Antilles Research Program, Yale University.
Dudden, Faye E.
1983   Serving Women: Household Service in Nineteenth Century America. Middletown, CT: Wesleyan University Press.
Durant-Gonzalez, Victoria
1976   Role and Status of Rural Jamaican Women: Higglering and Mothering. Ph.D. dissertation. Department of anthropology, University of California, Berkeley.

1982   The Realm of Female Familial Responsibility. *In* Women and Family. Joycelin Massiah, ed. Pp. 1–27. Women in the Caribbean Project, Vol. 2. Cave Hill, Barbados: Institute for Social and Economic Research, University of the West Indies.

Edholm, Felicity, Olivia Harris, and Kate Young
1977   Conceptualising Women: Critique of Anthropology 9–10:101–130.

Foner, Nancy
1973   Status and Power in Rural Jamaica: A Study of Educational and Political Change. New York: Teachers College Press.
1975   Women, Work, and Migration: Jamaicans in London. Urban Anthropology 4:229–249.
1976   Male and Female: Jamaican Migrants in London. Anthropological Quarterly 49:28–35.
1978   Jamaica Farewell: Jamaican Migrants in London. Berkeley: University of California Press.
1979   West Indians in New York City and London: A Comparative Analysis. International Migration Review 13(2):284–297.
1983   Jamaican Migrants: A Comparative Analysis of the New York and London Experience. Occasional Paper No. 36. New York Research Program in Inter-American Affairs. New York: New York University.
1986   Sex Roles and Sensibilities: Jamaican Women in New York and London. *In* International Immigration: The Female Experience. Caroline B. Brettell and Rita J. Simon, eds. Pp. 133–151. Totowa, NJ: Rowman and Allanheld.

Glenn, Evelyn Nakano
1980   The Dialectics of Wage Work: Japanese-American Women and Domestic Service, 1905–1940. Feminist Studies 6(3):432–471.
1986   Issei, Nisei, Warbride: Three Generations of Japanese American Women in Domestic Service. Philadelphia: Temple University Press.

Hamburger, Robert
1977   A Stranger in the House. Southern Exposure 5(1):22–31.

Henry, Frances
1968   The West Indian Domestic Scheme in Canada. Social and Economic Studies. 17(1):83–91.
1982   A Note on Caribbean Migration to Canada. Caribbean Review. 11(1):38–41.

Hochschild, Arlie Russell
1983   The Managed Heart: The Commercialization of Human Feeling. Berkeley: University of California Press.

Katzman, David M.
1978   Seven Days a Week: Women and Domestic Service in Industrializing America. New York: Oxford University Press.

Kelly, Joan
1979   The Doubled Vision of Feminist Theory: A Postscript to the Women and Power Conference. Feminist Studies 5(1):216–227.

Kerns, Virginia
1983   Women and the Ancestors: Black Carib Kinship and Ritual. Urbana: University of Illinois Press.

Makiesky-Barrow, Susan
1976   Class, Culture, and Politics in a Barbadian Community. Ph.D. dissertation. Department of Anthropology, Brandeis University.

Margolis, Maxine L.
   1984   Mothers and Such: Views of American Women and Why they Change. Berkeley: University of California Press.
Marshall, Adriana
   1983   Immigration in a Surplus-Worker Labor Market: The Case of New York. Occasional Paper No. 39. New York Research Program in Inter-American Affairs. New York: New York University.
Marshall, Dawn
   1982   The History of Caribbean Migrations: The Case of the West Indies. Caribbean Review 11(1):6–9, 52–53.
   1984   Report of the Eastern Caribbean Migration Project. Bridgetown, Barbados: Institute of Social and Economic Research (Eastern Caribbean).
Marshall, Paule
   1981   Brown Girl, Brownstones. Old Westbury, NY: Feminist Press.
   1983   From the Poets in the Kitchen. *In* Reena and Other Stories. Pp. 3–12. Old Westbury, NY: Feminist Press.
Mortimer, Delores M., and Roy S. Bryce-Laporte, eds.
   1981   Female Immigrants to the United States: Caribbean, Latin American, and African Experiences. RIIES Occasional Papers No. 2. Washington, DC: Research Institute on Immigration and Ethnic Studies, Smithsonian Institution.
Noble, Jeanne L.
   1967   An Exploratory Study of Domestics' View of their Working World (An Inquiry into the Methodology of a Research Design Formulated to Gather Information for a More Extensive Investigation). New York: New York University School of Education.
Palmer, Phyllis
   1984   Housework and Domestic Labor: Racial and Technological Change. *In* My Troubles are Going to Have Troubles with Me. Karen Brodkin Sacks and Dorothy Remy, eds. Pp. 80–91. New Brunswick, NJ. Rutgers University Press.
   1987   Housewife and Household Worker: Employer-Employee Relationships in the Home, 1928–1941. *In* "To Toil the Livelong Day": America's Women at Work, 1780–1980. Carol Groneman and Mary Beth Norton, eds. Pp. 179–195. Ithaca: Cornell University Press.
Piore, Michael J.
   1979   International Migration and the Dual Labor Market. Migration Today 7(1):7–12.
Portes, Alejandro
   1978a   Migration and Underdevelopment. Politics and Society 8(1):1–48.
   1978b   Toward a Structural Analysis of Illegal (Undocumented) Immigration. International Migration Review 12(4):469–484.
Powell, Dorian
   1984   The Role of Women in the Caribbean. Social and Economic Studies 3(2):97–122.
Rapp, Rayna
   1978   Family and Class in Contemporary America: Notes Toward an Understanding of Ideology. Science and Society 42:278–300.
Rollins, Judith
   1985   Between Women: Domestics and Their Employers. Philadelphia: Temple University Press.

Romero, Mary
  1987   Domestic Service in the Transition from Rural to Urban Life: The Case
         of La Chicana. Women's Studies 13:199–222.
  1988   Day Work in the Suburbs: The Work Experiences of Chicana Private
         Housekeepers. *In* The Worth of Women's Work: A Qualitative Synthesis.
         Anne Strathern, Eleanor M. Miller, Hans O. M. Mauksch, eds. Pp. 77–
         92. Albany, NY: State University of New York Press.
Rubenstein, Hymie
  1982   The Impact of Remittances in the Rural English-Speaking Caribbean:
         Notes on the Literature. *In* Return Migration and Remittances: Develop-
         ing a Caribbean Perspective. RIIES Occasional Papers No. 3. William F.
         Stinner, Klaus de Albuquerque, and Roy S. Bryce-Laporte, eds. Pp. 237–
         265. Washington, DC: Research Institute on Immigration and Ethnic
         Studies, Smithsonian Institution.
Ruiz, Vicki L.
  1987   By the Day or Week: Mexicana Domestic Workers in El Paso. *In* "To
         Toil the Livelong Day": America's Women at Work, 1780–1980. Carol
         Groneman and Mary Beth Norton, eds. Pp. 269–283. Ithaca: Cornell Uni-
         versity Press.
Sassen-Koob, Saskia
  1981   Exporting Capital and Importing Labor: The Role of Caribbean Mi-
         gration to New York City. Occasional Paper No. 28. New York Research
         Program in Inter-American Affairs. New York: New York University.
  1984a The New Labor Demand in Global Cities. *In* Cities in Transforma-
         tion. Michael P. Smith, ed. Pp. 139–171. Beverly Hills: Sage Publications.
  1984b Notes on the Incorporation of Third World Women into Wage-La-
         bor Through Immigration and Off-Shore Production. International Mi-
         gration Review 18(4):1144–1167.
Silvera, Makeda
  1983   Silenced. Toronto: Williams-Wallace Publishers.
Sutherland, Daniel E.
  1981   Americans and Their Servants: Domestic Service in the United States
         from 1800 to 1920. Baton Rouge, LA: Louisiana State University Press.
Sutton, Constance R.
  1969   The Scene of the Action: A Wildcat Strike in Barbados. Ph.D. disser-
         tation. Department of Anthropology, Columbia University.
  1976   Cultural Duality in the Caribbean. Caribbean Studies 14(2):96–101.
Sutton, Constance R., and Makiesky-Barrow, Susan
  1977   Social Inequality and Sexual Status in Barbados. *In* Sexual Stratifica-
         tion: A Cross-Cultural View. Alice Schlegel, ed. Pp. 293–325. New York:
         Columbia University Press.

Neocolonial Forms of Household Work

7

Part of the Household Inventory: Men Servants in Zambia

Karen Tranberg Hansen
Northwestern University

During the first half of the 1980s, several monographs written by historians and sociologists appeared on household work in different parts of Western Europe and North America (e.g., Dudden 1983; Fairchilds 1984; Glenn 1986; Maza 1983; Rollins 1985; Sutherland 1981). Anthropologists are expanding this field of study to include the developing countries (e.g., Bunster and Chaney 1985).[1] While these studies are providing a wealth of information on an occupational relationship that for a long time has been ignored, they do not analyze gender relations in household work sufficiently. With the exception of Maza's work on men servants in prerevolutionary France (1983), these studies overwhelmingly focus on women. Although some of them note the presence of men in household work at an earlier time,[2] they neither raise, nor answer, questions about the causes and consequences of the differential gender allocation of domestic tasks. Most of these studies emphasize, as do several recent articles (e.g., Glazer 1980; Grossman 1980; Palmer 1984), the central involvement of women in household work, paid and unpaid. They explain the subordination a servant experiences in private household employment as a result of women's subordination in patriarchally structured societies, thus making household work both cause and consequence of *women's* subordination. Although race or ethnicity sometimes complicates the explanation, it makes use of a biological metaphor that links women to household work because of their nature (Sacks 1982:24–64).

Household work is a gender role whose allocation is not biologically destined. Although all societies practice a division of labor by sex, the gender allocation of tasks differs widely. Factors additional to the directly economic are involved in the assignment of work to either sex and they depend more on culturally created practices than on biology (Ortner and Whitehead 1981:6–7). These culturally elaborated practices take socially and historically specific forms that are made and re-made as a result of men's and women's diverse experiences as members of their changing societies. Scholars who emphasize the central involvement of women in household work extrapolate from the 19th-century pattern in the West, use the gender relations characteristic of this pattern to make universal statements about its decline in the present situation, and thereby underestimate its singularity. This helps gloss over that household work persists, and appears to be on the rise in terms of the numbers of people employed, in the advanced capitalist systems of the West, in new labor forms undertaken by women *and* men. These forms are variations on the theme of live-in household work, which is very much alive and growing in many developing countries.

Today, household work is not everywhere women's work, nor was it so historically. The case of Zambia provides an interesting setting in which to explore how, when, and why jobs in household work became differentially allocated to African men and women. Similar questions could be pursued in much of the rest of Africa, for aside from scattered references in the context of other work and casual observations, we have amazingly little substantive knowledge about the gender dynamics in household work in other African countries. The existing studies concern almost exclusively southern Africa where they offer a kaleidoscopic trajectory of women of all races and African men passing through the occupation (Cock 1980). African men remained in household work on the Witwatersrand until the late 1930s (van Onselen 1982), but were replaced by "coloured" and African women in the Cape much earlier (Gaitskell et al. 1984). In the Republic of South Africa today, household workers are gender-typed as African and female; this appears also to be the case in Zimbabwe, where African women began to move into household work in the early 1950s (Clarke 1974; Weinrich 1976). But for the entire colonial period in Zambia, household work remained an almost exclusively male preserve. It continues to be so today in spite of the growing entry of African women into this occupation after independence in 1964. Today, as in the past, employers of servants in Zambia continue to prefer men workers. Although more African women than ever before take jobs in household work, men still outnumber them by far. This paper discusses the gender dynamics in Zambia. My chief concern is with gender relations between workers and their employers in the private household situation. Elsewhere, I have discussed servants' activities beyond the work locus (Hansen 1986b), as well as the question of low-income women's restricted wage labor opportunities historically and at the present time (Hansen 1980a; 1980b). Here, I seek both to raise and to answer questions of how and why race, gender, and skill factors over time have interacted differently with social and cultural practices as well as economic ups and downs to construe jobs in household work as fitting for one sex and not the other. I discuss these questions at a very general level, knowing full well that no two household arrangements are quite alike. For the colonial period, I rely on archival sources, life-history data, and interviews; my sources for the post-colonial period consist of the results of a large sample survey and participant observation.[3]

In this paper, I first discuss how a male gender role was created in household work during the colonial period. In the second section I problematize the question of gender, asking why household work remained a man's job, and how, why, and when the development of a colonial labor force came to exclude African women. I then examine postcolonial continuities and changes, focusing on one of these changes: the ongoing entry of women into household work. In conclusion, I return to the issue of how, when, and why gender roles are allotted to one sex rather than the other, emphasizing the need to tease out of lived and changing experiences the socially and historically specific forms gender roles in household work may take.

The Male Servant: A Fixture of Colonial Society

Personal service made up one of the earliest, and over time, numerically largest sectors of wage employment during the colonial period in what was then known as Northern Rhodesia. Together with porters, African men servants accompanied travelers and explorers who traversed this territory during the previous century in the days before any significant white settlement had taken place. These servants cooked and cleaned for the travelers and often served as intermediaries between them and the local populations (Simpson 1975). Some were taken on at the chief port towns leading into the interior, others at the major inland trading stations where caravans were resupplied and trade goods purchased. Considered part of the caravan inventory, servants were discussed alongside the supplies in many of this era's travel books (e.g., Becker 1887, I:457–490; Galton 1893:308–310). Some had received prior training in the arts of cooking, laundering, and ironing at mission stations, and some spoke a degree of English. When misbehaving en route, they were laid off, and a replacement from the staff of porters might be advanced to personal servant, receiving training on the job.

When a small but slowly growing white population gradually began to settle in Northern Rhodesia in the early 1900s, a pattern of live-in household worker developed. The job as a traveling servant became a sideline pursued from time to time by servants employed by officials on up-country tours. The white population lived scattered across the territory's small towns and tiny provincial and district headquarters and at rural outstations. It consisted of officials, missionaries, business people, and farmers. Until 1924, when the British South African Company ceded the administration of the territory to the Colonial Office in London, most officials were English-speaking South Africans.

The missionaries represented different European mission societies who had established a base in the territory prior to the advent of colonial rule (Rotberg 1965). The business people were a mixed lot, including Greeks and East European Jews. Their ranks were augmented, especially from the postwar years, by persons from the Indian subcontinent, who traded goods to Africans. The farmers were predominantly Afrikaans-speaking South Africans. When copper mining was developed on a commercial scale in the north in the late 1920s, more whites were attracted to the country, the majority of them of British and South African background. A large African labor force was attracted as well.

Initially, the sex ratio in the growing settler society was skewed in favor of men, and sexual relations between the largely bachelor white population and African women were quite common. In the postwar years the imbalance between the sexes evened out considerably, and the experience of the first generations of white men who had lived with African women in the bush became part of colonial folklore about the pioneers. Sexual relationships between white men and African women by no means disappeared with the arrival of more white women, but it became a practice about which it was not polite to speak.

Although the settled society that evolved was strongly hierarchical and had its urban and rural differences, its members shared one thing: keeping African servants to attend to their needs and comforts and to do the labor-intensive manual work of keeping house in the manner of their home country—a difficult task under tropical conditions, where such basic amenities as water, fuel, and electricity were lacking. This standard of replicating the urban British lifestyle, set by colonial administrators, represented an ideal that other segments of the settled population sought to emulate.

The servants whose labor maintained this lifestyle were predominantly male, and this trend toward male servants remained for the entire colonial period. To understand why this was so requires taking into account demographic and economic factors of the time along with ideological factors, particularly the role race played in structuring the evolving society and its social and cultural practices. These practices were informed partly by ideas that the diverse constituent population segments of Africans and whites brought to the new encounter and partly by ideas that arose from the nature of their interaction. These factors combined in different ways over time, reshaping arguments about the proper place for the two sexes and the different racial groups.

Whites who went out to Northern Rhodesia during the early decades of this century came from societies in which the era of the footman and butler had long gone (Hecht 1980). Many of the first generations of settlers, however, came from servant-keeping backgrounds and from a tradition of employing women household workers. In Western Europe men had exited from domestic service at the end of the 1700s, leaving the occupation as the main source of wage employment for women until about the 1920s (McBride 1976). Europeans brought with them to Northern Rhodesia class-based assumptions about the relationship of master to servant, which were reinterpreted in racial terms in the new society.

Like the servant class in Europe, Africans were viewed as inferior in the scale of civilization. Working on the white farms, in the small towns, and in the mines from the late 1920s, Africans were to do only manual and unskilled labor; they were to keep to their place, the village, and live in towns only as long as their labor power was needed. The towns were segregated by race, and legal rules and ordinances restricted their freedom to move within towns and between the rural and urban areas (Heissler 1974). Until the interwar years, there were few African women in the towns. Colonial authorities desired a migrant male labor force, one that after the completion of work contracts would return to the rural areas to join wives and dependents. Given this geographical and gender based division of labor, there are clear demographic reasons why European householders initially employed African men as household workers.

Influenced by an ideology of domination that required the upkeep of white civilized standards, the male gender role in household work gradually became institutionalized. The sharing and exchanging of advice, hints, and experiences among employers had the cumulative effect of producing patterns and conventions of management practices in household employment. In the process African men, no longer autonomous agents in their own villages, had to succumb to an everyday regime of wage labor under very special circumstances.

In the view of their employers, these African men servants were part of the household inventory. They were part and parcel of these households in the manner of pots and pets, but never as full-fledged members. As household commodities, ways of handling them, their price, and work capacity were discussed a great deal. They differed little from other African workers in terms of overall employment legislation yet were unlike other workers because of the privatized nature of their work. In contrast to other Africans many household workers lived in the white parts of town. Some of the household's workers were typically housed in quarters at the bottom end of their employers' gardens. Most households had a fair number of them, distributed across different domains that formed a hierarchy between kitchen, house, and grounds. As many as nine servants were typical in small towns and rural outstations in the 1920s and 1930s. In Lusaka in the 1950s persons of standing would often employ at least five men. Their number was influenced by the different level of amenities available in rural as compared to urban areas, and by the size and composition of the employing household and its place in the colonial hierarchy. The number was also influenced by the employers' view of their workers' capacity; Africans were considered simple-minded and unable to handle more than a very circumscribed job. In addition, their wages were low and even white artisans could afford to employ several.

The patterns and conventions that developed in household work helped lessen two contradictions within this employment relationship in the racially structured colonial situation: the shared space of the dominant and the subordinate in their physical proximity within the household; and the sexual confrontation between the African male household worker and his white female boss. White women's almost compulsive attention to the do's and don'ts of housekeeping may reflect an unconscious attempt to control a situation that was ripe with contradictions (Bradley 1939).[4] A properly managed colonial household was part of civilized society and as such, it was on permanent display. The labor behind the display was done by numerous male workers who from the employers' perspective were members of an otherwise invisible African mass and somehow had to be incorporated into the white household.

The hierarchical relationship between master and servant was evident in the architectural set-up of the colonial residence where the workers' quarters were built alongside the sanitary lanes from which nightsoil, in the days before flush toilets, and garbage were collected. Within the household and on the grounds, elaborate rules of etiquette governed the conduct of workers and employers. Regardless of age, all servants were referred to as "boys," as were all other African men except perhaps chiefs and headmen. Workers were rarely addressed by their own names but became known by place names, names of things, or names from the bible. They, on their part, did not always know the exact names of their employers, whom they referred to and addressed as Bwana or Master, and Madam, Missus, or Dona. Most households furnished servants with two types of uniforms: khaki for heavier work, and white when serving at table. Workers rarely wore shoes when in the house. Neither in the employer's presence or absence were they to use the facilities of the main house. Some areas were off-limits all the time in order to prevent pilfering: kitchen stores and liquor cabinets. But bedrooms seem not to have been considered private. Most Europeans had tea brought to their bedside in the early morning; "boys" made their beds and washed their sheets and every item of their clothing, including underwear. When on duty, household workers were not supposed to speak unless they were spoken to.

Work was carried out in a hierarchical communication situation especially in households where *kitchen Kaffir* was used. This hybrid language, a product of the contact situation in South Africa, was used to some extent in Northern Rhodesia but it never developed into a *lingua franca*.[5] Consisting mainly of command and obey expressions, *kitchen Kaffir* provided a language of subordination. In other households, workers learned the rudiments of English on the job or some had acquired a smattering of that language in schools.[6] Those who did not master English well were likely to be caught in all kinds of problems: mixing the wrong ingredients into recipes, not doing what they were told, or doing it very differently. Such mistakes were part of the stuff that servant stories were made of. Exchanged at women's teas, such stories helped construe the image of the male household worker as inferior to his white female employer in a way that accentuated the distance between the two on the otherwise shared space within the household. Not necessarily malevolent, the stories depicted workers as irresponsible, having no sense of time, lazy, lacking understanding, and therefore in need of constant supervision and coaching.

White women employers also observed rules of decorum. When speaking to workers in English, they were recommended to "talk slowly, simply, and distinctly" and to treat them with "tolerance and understanding, but not with familiarity. Discipline should be firm, but fair" (Northern Rhodesia 1950:78). Revealing clothing should not be worn in the presence of household workers. The matter of dressing properly was of great concern. Some dressed in evening garb for dinner at home and at formal events, hats, gloves, and pumps were *de rigueur* for women. Men dressed in formal wear as well. The habit of keeping up appearances may have helped reassure the employers' sense of the familiar, and bolstered their belief in their own civilized standards.

The contradictions inherent in the space and place allocations in the colonial household involved both male workers and their women employers in ways that play havoc with the gender demarcation of public and private, or domestic, domains (e.g., Rosaldo 1974:17–42).[7] Because it was on permanent display, the mistress's household was hardly her private domain. It was open to inspection as to its upkeep of standards to other whites and most certainly to workers whose work it was to do the toil of the upkeep. Although the household was the employers' territory and they set the terms that governed the coming and going of workers, it was also the household workers' place of employment and they knew every nook and cranny, as well as what went on. To them, it was a very public place, and the conventions that structured their work did not differ much from those at other places of employment. There was subordination everywhere and all men were considered "boys." What differed was the inclusion of the worker's household in the overall space. Household workers domiciled on their employers' premises were on constant call. If their actual work chores were done, they were still considered available. Employers set the rules for whether wives and dependents were allowed to live with them in the quarters, when and which visitors could call, and what sort of leisure activity servants might pursue. Both worker and mistress were adversely affected by their unequal incorporation: the women employers as subsidiary actors to their husbands' work in the colony,[8] and workers as laboring commodities in the colonial household. For both, the private domain was one of time, and it existed mainly when workers were off duty and not on call.

The conventions, patterns, etiquette, and decorum that developed in colonial household employment accentuated the social difference between the African household worker and his white boss, but did not disguise that one was a man and the other a woman. Undoubtedly, sexual phobias were bandied around at white women's teas as were beer-hall stories told by Africans of workers seducing their white housemistresses, whether true or false. But collective sexual hysterias, such as those directed against men household workers in South Africa in several waves between 1890 and 1911 (van Onselen 1982:45–54) and in Southern Rhodesia prior to World War One, were not experienced in Northern Rhodesia. The women employers of servants are likely to have been considered whites first, and women second. What mattered for this side of the relationship was perhaps not so much the sex of the person as the question of who had the power to hire, fire, and to report misdemeanors. African men household workers were merely paid hands, distinguished from the surrounding society by clothing, speech, and demeanor. Called by classificatory labels rather than names, their personal circumstances were made irrelevant to the work regime. They were set off from fellow Africans by their uniforms and the nonuse of shoes when inside. The *kitchen Kaffir* spoken in some homes crudely exemplified a language of subordination. The demeanor of not talking unless spoken to, of being present without being seen reduced the African person to an object. As paid hands, reduced to a kind of invisible presence, these African workers were first and foremost part of the colonial household inventory.

Sex and Gender in Colonial Household Work

Household work remained almost exclusively a job for African men during the entire colonial period in Northern Rhodesia. Some white women were engaged as governesses and ladies' helpers by persons of means; they were rare, for as one visitor to Northern Rhodesia observed in the late 1930s: "European nannies were about as scarce as ice in the Sahara—and about as expensive" (Bigland 1939:191). For nursemaids, meaning caretakers of children, other whites employed "coloured" women, that is, women of mixed racial background, and still others took on young African girls to watch their babies. Even in this field, young girls were outnumbered by "juveniles," meaning young boys who pushed the prams and washed the nappies.

While demography helps us understand why household work initially was assigned to African men, it does not provide the explanation for why that employment tradition persisted. In spite of attempts by colonial officials and rural native authorities to restrict them to the rural areas, African women migrated to towns from the earliest years. Long before the colonial authorities in the late 1940s began to pursue a policy of stabilizing part of the African labor force in the towns and thus allowing urban African family life to begin, some of the mining companies had encouraged workers to bring their wives to towns (Chauncey 1981). This promoted labor productivity, and that indeed is what the authorities had in mind with the stabilization policy. For the mining industry experienced an economic boom during the postwar years which lasted until the mid-1950s. Labor was scarce across all sectors of the economy. The urban populations, African and European, grew rapidly, and among both, the skewed sex ratios evened out.

Needing additional labor, colonial authorities singled out employment of African men in household work as wasteful. In 1949, when this argument was made several times, 23,000 African men were employed in the occupation compared to 37,220 in mining and 20,300 in agriculture (Northern Rhodesia 1949:21). They should be released, it was suggested, for more "productive" work elsewhere, and African women should take their place. This idea had initially been voiced during the labor shortages of the Second World War, when many able-bodied African men participated in active war service inside and outside the African continent. The campaign for African womanpower produced a long-winded debate about the possibility of recruiting African women to work in white households.[9] It had little to do with demography, but ostensibly revolved around supply and demand factors in the labor market. The discussion about these factors was shot through with contradictions that embodied complex ideological assumptions about sex and the gender division of labor in the late colonial situation. As I shall show below, these assumptions were not shared but differed among authorities, white women employers and their men, and African women and their men. The debate masked the underlying issue; at stake was sexual anxiety, expressed not in words, but in action. This anxiety, a product of white men's sexual involvement with African women in the previous decades, was a delicate issue, to be avoided in public. At the same time, as everyone knew, it still could and did happen. The private actions of women, African and white, were taken against the background of that knowledge.

When labor shortages had become critical, colonial authorities and the segment hardest hit, namely farmers, wished to tap the available labor supply. Assuming that units of labor were mutually interchangeable, they argued that African women should replace men in household work to release the latter for labor elsewhere. But sex was not an irrelevant factor in the labor market and one occupation, household work, was construed in gender terms as male. There were, in the view of the men administrators and white women, three chief "problems" that made the prospective employment of African women household workers difficult: there was no housing for them; they were not trained; and their men would object.

The contorted discussion about the need for hostels and training for African women camouflaged the sexuality issue. It was suggested that African women could not work as servants in white households until hostels were built to accommodate them away from white residential areas. Under the watchful eye of a white supervisor, African women living in such a fashion would be less likely to become involved with African men. It would also limit their exposure to white men, although this was not spelled out. The reverse had never been argued, namely the need to house African men household workers away from the employers' homes in order to reduce their possible sexual involvement with the white mistress of the house. It seems that white women in Northern Rhodesia had been used to having African men living in their backyards without problems for decades. But the idea of building hostels to house urban African women workers, sometimes coupled with suggestions about training them in domestic skills, never materialized, as neither government, local authority, or missionary societies were willing to, or interested in, assuming the responsibility.

White women argued over and over again that African women needed education before they were able to go into service. In their view, African women were not domestic "by nature." White women appear to have been unwilling to socialize African women into household work on the job as they had done with previous generations of African men. In the past, men's work in homes had not been deemed problematic because they had little education. On the contrary, and in the early days, many employers avoided "mission boys" with a rudiment of education, and several white women had preferred what they called "raw natives," that is, men fresh from the bush whom they had trained themselves. But when it came to considering the possible entry of African women into household work, their lack of education was held against them. Making this argument, white women chose to disregard that the curriculum in African girls' schools, such as they were at this point in time, was heavy on domestic science subjects with the intention of making African women good mothers and proud housewives (Northern Rhodesia 1948).

These mutually contradictory attitudes did not cancel each other out. In the view of white women employers, African women were less controllable than men; they were less tractable and caused more problems in the running of the white households. The debate showed how white women almost unanimously declared that African women were nowhere near capable of taking over from men in household work, and they themselves made little or no effect to see to it that they were. In the final analysis, white women appear to have been unwilling to take on African women and domesticate them into household service for fear, I suggest, of their sexuality. Their presence in the white household was too close for comfort.

Colonial authorities described African men as reluctant to allow their women to work away from home on the assumption that African women would involve themselves sexually with other men. A previous official in the colonial service from 1944 to independence elaborated this as follows: "the idea of employing [African] female servants in European households, other than on certain mission stations, was treated with grave suspicion by many Africans who suspected that the main purpose behind it was to provide a concubine for the head of the household" (Roy Stokes, personal communication 1983). Allowing the category "other men" to include Europeans, I suggest that several additional factors influenced African men's attitudes toward women's work in white homes. Their reluctance to send wives, sisters, and daughters into white households may reflect their unwillingness to expose women to a demeaning work relationship in which very low wages were paid. The matter of wages was never addressed in the debate. The few African women who did participate in a short-lived African charwoman scheme in the copperbelt town of Ndola in 1954 preferred to change from an hourly to a full-time work basis. Their preference implies that part-time household work hardly was worthwhile economically.

But perhaps most important, paid household work-conflicted with the demands placed on African women's own domestic labor as broadly defined in cultural terms among the region's different ethnic groups. Those demands did not yet differ much by class, as reflected for example in the reactions of these African men, members of the up-and-coming elite, who in 1952 took part in a radio debate on women servants. They objected to the idea of African women going into household work because they had enough to attend to in their own homes.[10] When colonial authorities constantly complained that African women in towns were idle and lazy, they failed to recognize the time-consuming nature of food processing and preparation and the constant demands that children and their care placed on women's attention and time. The demands of child care were particularly incompatible with paid household work for most African women began bearing children early and continued to have children at two- to three-year intervals throughout their childbearing years. Although authorities mentioned the need for daycare crêches, it was never attended to.

The single most disturbing fact of the debate was that African women never were called on to express their own viewpoint. They were assumed, without questions being raised, to wish to do household work. That assumption is faulty for it fails to consider that African women might have placed a higher priority on their own household affairs and on activities they might pursue within the new urban socioeconomic environment in which they lived. From the perspective of African women in the towns in the early 1950s, the division of labor which had existed in rural societies had been racially transformed. In the towns, African women and men were grappling with how to arrange their urban households, relations among themselves, between themselves and dependents, as well as to others in towns, including whites. Women's choice not to do wage labor as household workers represents their attempt to resist any further loss of the limited independence they were establishing for themselves within their everyday management of urban household and money-earning activities. No one wanted to labor in an occupation where so much of one's time was controlled by another person. Although census recording methods are unreliable and likely to underestimate the size of the household work sector, the recorded gender gap remained conspicuous. The proportion of men to women workers grew between 1951 and the high point of the African womanpower campaign in 1954 from 30,000:250 to 30,000:850. When the campaign lost its momentum in 1957, the number of African men household workers had grown to 33,000 and that of women had fallen to 800 (Northern Rhodesia 1951–57).

The dismal failure of the effort to recruit African women into household work was not due, as claimed, to lack of suitable housing for women workers, their lack of education, or their men's opposition. Although these factors influenced the outcome, they masked the more sensitive issue of sexuality. White women preferred not to have African women in their homes, and authorities continued to view urban African women chiefly in terms of their sexual functions. Beyond African men's sexual needs for women, authorities drew no conclusions about contending claims on women's labor from within their own households. And African women themselves were not keen on taking paid household work. When the labor shortages were replaced by unemployment by the mid-1950s and the towns' labor pools were full of able-bodied men, African women were no longer called on for household employment.

Postcolonial Continuities and Changes in Household Work

The gender gap in postcolonial household work in Zambia remains large. In this respect there is persistence, for at the last tabulation of household work with a breakdown by gender in Zambia in 1968, 36,491 men were employed as compared to 1,758 women (Government of the Republic of Zambia 1968). According to my own estimate, more than 100,000 persons worked as paid household workers in Zambia in the mid-1980s of whom between one-fourth and one-fifth were women.[11]

The persistence of this pattern is deceptive. It hides changes which when taken together amount to a transformation of this occupation in postcolonial Zambia. The economy has changed, what appears as conventional social practices in this field of employment are assuming different meanings, and quaint sexual images have become accentuated.

Today in Zambia race no longer structures the world of work although access to opportunity continues to be differentially available. When overall employment in the paid labor force decreased in the wake of the mid-1970s economic slow-down, the decline did not affect all sectors and regions in the same fashion, neither did it have the same effects on distinct age groups nor on the two sexes. The urbanization rate accelerated. As in the past, household work remains the chief avenue through which rural migrants and persons with little education and few saleable skills seek to enter the wage labor force. The demand for servants has continued, due largely to the entry of more Zambians into the middle and upper ranks of public and para-statal sectors. Some still find employment in non-African households which, as a proportion of the total population, have declined considerably. Adult men and women and young school dropouts of both sexes today glut the household work market in their search to make a living. The conditions under which they work have worsened, and the gap between their wages and those of other segments of the wage-labor force has widened. Last, but not least, the terms on which women enter the occupation differ significantly from men's, in ways that contribute to the construction of a reshaped gender role within an existing field of employment.

The old colonial standards of proper and gracious living and the legal mechanisms that propped them up have crumbled in independent Zambia. Staffs have been reduced. Household heads who belong to the upper ministerial or managerial ranks often get their household workers' wages paid as part of the employment contract, and may employ three workers: a cook, an indoor servant, and a gardener. These are mainly men, as are the household workers, typically employed in the much larger number of middle-income households who form the majority of today's employer population. These households employ a general servant, who works inside the house *and* on the grounds. The hierarchical specialization and differentiation of tasks between several men has largely disappeared and the contemporary household worker's job has become degraded.

This degradation is not due to improvements in household technology. Most work is manual and done without the aid of labor-saving devices. If employers own such devices, for example washing machines and vacuum cleaners, not to mention kitchen gadgets, they often do not allow their employees to use them. Household workers continue to be considered simpleminded and clumsy and employers fear they may break the gadgets. Some employers do not use their household devices, assuming, with good reason, that spare parts will be unavailable in case of breakdown. The general servant thus is a manual worker who cleans the house with broom and rags, and polishes by hand; does the laundry and hangs it out to dry; irons every item of clothing to prevent putsi flies from surviving;[12] sets the table; washes dishes; sometimes prepares vegetables for cooking; and works in the garden, using a *panga* to cut the lawn and a hoe to turn the soil in the vegetable yard. The general servant often cooks in Zambian households, which, means making tea and preparing maize porridge and a side dish of stewed vegetables, meat, or fish. In return he receives a substandard wage that rarely covers his own household's subsistence costs.

The opportunity for long-time employment with the same employer, which some men enjoyed during the colonial period, is largely gone. The occupation today is characterized by much turnover among both workers and employers. Household workers shop for better employers and higher wages, and employers rarely remain long in one place. Zambian employers are often transferred from one town to another. Most of today's expatriate employers are employed on short-term contracts, and few of them make Zambia their permanent home.

General servants who move between households acquire few special skills, and what they might have learned in one job easily becomes irrelevant in the next. This applies especially to cooking. With the decrease in the number of white households, previously skilled cooks have had to enter the general servant market to take positions in which their skills become redundant. The cooking routine in most Zambian households is less complicated, and in many expatriate households wives today prefer to do their own cooking. This is partly a cost-saving measure as prices on food items have skyrocketed. It is also influenced by periodic shortages of the very basics needed for cooking. The tiny proportion of the expatriate population with access to commissaries and diplomatic stores form the exception to this. They still wine and dine in style, and among them the shrinking supply of well-trained cooks is in high demand.

This general degradation of household work is one of the chief changes in the occupation in postcolonial Zambia. Today's workers are rarely uniformed and they may wear shoes while on the job. The employment relationship and household management practices no longer revolve around the need to uphold racial distinctions, yet remain couched in a master-servant discourse. While they grumble about their substandard wages, workers' chief complaint is the treatment they receive. Regardless of race, most employers continue to deal with their men household workers as a piece of inventory to be ordered around and considered available at their personal whims. The social practices that guide postcolonial household management remain hierarchical in most Zambian and non-Zambian households, although the terms that are used to rationalize these practices have been somewhat reshaped. Workers themselves say their job is like slave-work, for household work never stops. Employers consider their employees simpleminded, lazy, untrustworthy, and complain that they must constantly remind them of duties they have charged them with numerous times before. It remains bad manners for household workers to involve themselves in conversation unless prompted, and if they do, they are considered rude.

Households are no longer as much on public display as during the colonial period. Frequent incidents of burglaries and armed robberies make householders wary of displaying their furnishings and valuables. More areas of homes are locked up and workers are let in only at preset times for cleaning purposes. They still make beds and wash underwear in most expatriate households, whereas bedrooms in most Zambian households, for reasons attributed to "custom," are defined as off-limit for men household workers, and women and teenage daughters wash and iron their own underwear. In Zambian households where some employers are addressed by honorific terms of seniority or by classificatory kinship terms for father and mother, complications often arise when the employee speaks the same local language as his employers. Perhaps this is the reason why many Zambian employers prefer to hire men from different ethnic groups than their own. Workers' statements that they are not treated like human beings in Zambian households highlight lack of consideration for their personal circumstances. It points out that the claim on kinship which the use of kin-like terms implies has no meaning. The employment relationship does not promote reciprocal loyalty, and household workers remain units of labor. As in the colonial past, the relationship between employee and employer remains hierarchical. Unlike the past, it is no longer legitimated in the language of race; subordination is accounted for in class-like terms of inferiority and is said to result from different life-chances, and lack of education and opportunity.

Most of today's male household workers would do other work if they had a choice. The chief attraction of the job is the living quarters that often still comes with it, for urban low-income housing is in short supply in Zambia. Given the depressed economic situation in the country in general, men such as these have few viable alternatives. Their lack of saleable skills and of opportunity to accumulate start-up capital for an informal sector enterprise of their own or to finance a move to a village to begin small-scale farming, cattle-holding, or fishing make household work a way of life for many. Because of their low wages, they become dependent on intermittent handouts of food and of money from their employers to tide over their own households from one month to the next. For this reason many men consent to the hierarchical labor process in household work, although they may voice complaints to an outsider. While deference remains the face of the postcolonial worker/employer relationship, its substance is lack of alternative.

Women's Entry into Household Work after Independence

African urban women to whom the call for household work was directed in the postwar years are likely to have shared the view of the occupation held by the women I interviewed in 1983-84 and in 1985: a woman with small children just does not leave her own household to attend to someone else's. And if she does, it is as a last resort, for who wants to be ordered around by another woman all the time on a slave wage? Men, when all else has failed, and because in Zambia they are normatively defined as heads of households, continue to enter household work because the economy has offered them few other wage labor opportunities.

Women are not replacing men in household work; they are supplementary actors in an already existing, although transformed, field of employment. In the main, women work as nannies who relieve other women of child care responsibilities. The increase in the number of women in paid household work after independence must be viewed against the background of several factors. The first factor concerns the Zambianization of the employer class. In contrast to the colonial period when few white wives worked for wages away from home, middle- and upper-income Zambian households often comprise two wage earners. Zambians in general have more children than had colonial white householders. The latter helped solve their child care problems during the daytime by relegating infants at a tender age to crèches, and for child care at home they more frequently employed "nanny boys" than African women. Their Zambian sisters today are unable to follow this strategy. The creation of crèches and nursery schools has been out of step with the population increase and, where available, too expensive for the majority of Zambians with large families. They find it cheaper to employ nannies.

A second factor contributing to the growing number of women in household work is change among the expatriate population. Some British and white South Africans have remained in the country after independence, but the majority of today's expatriates come from western and eastern Europe, North America, Australia, New Zealand, and southwest and southeast Asia. Among them, far fewer than the employers of the past have lived in racially structured colonial settings. Comparatively few today have ever employed paid household workers. They rarely accept the received wisdom passed down by the previous colonial generation about the problems involved in employing African women. Surprised by seeing so many male household workers, they wonder about the lack of availability of African women, whom several on arrival have no qualms about wanting to employ. Expatriates who accept contracts in Zambia rarely are young householders at the beginning stage of their families' development cycle. Their teenage children often attend boarding schools in their home countries and their needs for household help thus differ from that of most Zambians. Those who do have small children sometimes employ nannies, and some let women household workers do general work inside the house, occasionally including cooking. Women workers rarely excel in this field, however, and most employers will readily tell you that Zambian women "cannot cook." If they do employ nannies, they have turnover problems due to the same factors as those of Zambian women householders. In the past as at present, Asian householders hardly ever employ African women.[13]

Circumstances that characterize the livelihood of low-income Zambian women comprise the third factor that influences their entry into household work. Women do not turn to such work out of choice but as a last resort, particularly in situations of family crisis, and because they have few alternative wage labor options. My earlier work in urban Zambia has shown that many women over the course of their adult lives intermittently launch small-scale trades from their homes, in streets, or at markets (Hansen 1980a, 1980b, 1984). No matter how small in scale their enterprises are, they need start-up capital for this purpose. The lack of it prompts some to seek work in homes, particularly women newly arrived from the countryside, or women who have no other adult household support. Few will wish to follow a lifetime career as household workers. The hours are long, remuneration poor, and the work conflicts with the demands of married life as culturally defined in most ethnic groups in Zambia. Although these demands limit women's interaction in ways that differ by class, rural versus urban residence, and by age, most women are fairly autonomous in the management of their own domestic work. In paid household work they lose autonomy. They have their own household duties to attend to, once the day's paid work has finished. Unlike those married men household workers who carry out economic activity "on the side" as tailors or tinsmiths and who have wives to do their own household's work, women household workers have little time to spare for income-supplementing activity.

The women who do household work fall into two broad categories. First are young school dropouts from rural areas who have recently come to town, sometimes leaving a child behind with relatives. They work in very low paid jobs, primarily as nannies in Zambian households and often live-in there. Second are middle-aged, close to or beyond the end of their child-bearing years, long-term urban residents, often single heads of households because of divorce or death of a spouse. They work as better paid, indoor household workers, especially in expatriate households, and live-out with children and dependents supported by their work.

Men's and women's household work thus differs in many respects. Women's activities focus on child care and tasks associated with it; their jobs have the highest turnover rates; and they earn, with a few exceptions, the lowest wages. Their wages are generally lower than men's since they are assumed by employers to "last" for a shorter time, due to their personal problems in separating from or finding husbands, and to have higher absentee rates caused by their own child care problems. Fewer women than men household workers, proportionately, live in. Women's employers frequently do not pay the statutory housing allowance due to low-income workers on the assumption that women are wives or dependent members of households and therefore have shelter elsewhere.

Low-income women's desire to secure their own and their dependents' livelihood by support from a spouse or consort clashes with middle- to upper-income Zambian women's needs for child care. The woman who takes a job as nanny seeks to quit as soon as she has some economic support in her own household. In the view of Zambian women householders, the "woman problem" in household work is due to the easy virtue of their female employees who are always on the lookout for a man either to marry, or to "keep them nicely." Being kept nicely in Zambia means receiving shelter, food, and occasional clothing.

The "nanny problems" of Zambian women who work away from home begin at the birth of their first child. At this point in their family development cycle they typically secure a distant female relative from the countryside, often a teenage girl who has dropped out of school, or whose parents are unable to pay for her education. She is fed and clothed and shares sleeping space with other members of the household, and is at their beck and call. She rarely stays from the birth of one baby to the next, or at most from two to three years. Problems of discipline arise, for the young girls dislike being ordered around and want to do things their own way. They want freedom to explore the city as well. If they last for three years, they are soon returned by their urban relations or fetched by their parents, the rationale being not to "detain" them for too long in the household since this may reduce their marriage chances. The longer they stay in town, the more likely they are to become "spoiled," that is, made pregnant, which reduces the size of the bridewealth their fathers or guardians may claim. Because of distant kinship, Zambian women can neither command the complete obedience nor control the full labor of these young relatives of whom they may have several come and go during their early years of childbearing.

After their trials with young relatives, they next turn to paid women employees, and their problems with nannies grow rather than lessen. Many prefer country women new to town, whom they assume to be less venturesome in seeking male partners. They deliberately do not keep them too long, for with length of stay develops familiarity and a fear of likely intimate encounters with the male household head. These problems last for as long as they have children of preschool age and they typically "go through" more nannies than they care to remember.

Once their last-born child has entered school, or the older children are considered to be responsible enough to watch over their younger siblings, Zambian women employ only men household workers. They recount their experience of employing female workers in a troubled voice: insolent and cheeky, women employees only do the work they feel like doing; in addition they steal; they go through your panties and toiletries. But worst of all, before you know it they move into the bedroom and take over the house. Part of the collective consciousness of Zambian women who employ their fellow countrywomen are stories of women household workers who usurp the place of the wife. Such stories are frequently featured in popular newspaper columns and women's magazines. The sexuality issue thus continues to shape the gender role attributed to women household workers in contemporary Zambia, although those who frame it have changed in terms of race.

But for women whom circumstances leave no other option than household work, this shift is largely irrelevant. Their gender role continues to be construed in sexual terms. As discussed above, this has consequences for their wages and housing, as well as their treatment as employee. The ideology which is buried in stories about the easy virtue of female household workers becomes socially relevant whenever a Zambian woman employs a fellow country woman. In the Zambian view, such women workers ought to be wives, kept nicely by their husbands; if they are not, obviously they have failed in some respect and must be seeking a new partner. This, and their problems with their own children, accounts for their unreliability. Spoken of in invidious terms, evaluated poorly, and paid miserably, such work does not in the Zambian view properly constitute women's work, for it is not considered "natural" for a woman with small children to leave her own household to attend to someone else's.

Conclusion

Household work is not everywhere considered women's work. Although such tasks as cooking, cleaning, and child care are practiced in all societies, they are not allocated to males and females in the same way across space and time. The contents and meaning of such work may differ between societies, as may the social and cultural context in which they are performed. In colonial Northern Rhodesia, the dominating whites construed household work so that it became associated with men, and not with women. For African men, paid work in homes was just a job, an attempt to make a living. Because of the lack of employment alternatives it continues to be so, and men still remain part of the household inventory among the employer population in postcolonial Zambia. Having African women on the household staff was too close for comfort for white colonial women as it is today for many Zambian women who do employ women household workers. Neither they nor the women they hire seek out each other's company by choice, but only as a last resort: the employer in her need for child care, and the worker in her need for an income. When they do have choices, they organize their individual household activities such that their mutual work arrangements do not throw them together: the employer engages a male employee, and the woman worker becomes the mistress of her own household. Like a previous generation of white colonial women, today women employers find men more tractable and easier to control in the day-to-day management of households. Indeed, in the discourse of both generations of women householders, men appear "naturally" to be more suited for household work.

The processes described in this paper have concerned the social and cultural construction of gender roles against the background of demographic, economic, and political changes in Zambia. My analysis adds a different twist to the prevailing trend in recent studies to feminize the study of household work. I invite other researchers to tease out the complex interweaving of biological and social forces in the gender allocation of household work elsewhere. In the Zambian case, the "naturalness" with which men are held to be suited for the occupation reverses conventional biological arguments about the close link between females and household work. The "oversexed" role attributed to women workers by colonial and postcolonial female employers makes biological sex a political means to lessen the prospects for compromising sexual involvements. At a time when more women than ever before are entering household employment, this strategic "sexualization" of their work is adding another dimension to the already existing gender division of labor in this occupation, and may feed into gender construction more broadly. The processes I have delineated do not comprise a gender transition but rather a recomposition by gender in which men remain the chief players in household work, and more and more women work as nannies, a socially constructed gender role that exaggerates their easy virtue.

The subordination which both men and women household workers experience in Zambia has less to do with patriarchy than it has with class. It is kept alive and grows because of global economic forces which continue to keep developing countries dependent. This, coupled with local stratification dynamics, helps extend internal inequalities in many ways. Today more Zambians than ever before have no other way of making a living than by laboring in homes for better placed fellow citizens, and class, not race, distinguishes household worker from employer.

Notes

Acknowledgments. The fieldwork portion of this research under United States National Science Foundation grant no. BNS-8303507 was carried out during 1983–84 and the summer of 1985. In Zambia I was a research affiliate of the Institute for African Studies at the University of Zambia in Lusaka. Archival research was conducted in England in 1982 under a grant-in-aid of research from the Graduate School at the University of Minnesota, and in 1983, 1984, and 1985 under the NSF grant and a Faculty Research Grant from Northwestern University. I interviewed retired colonial officials and previous residents in Northern Rhodesia in England during the summer of 1986 under a Faculty Research Grant from Northwestern University. This paper offers an expanded version of a presentation, delivered at the annual meeting of the American Anthropological Association, December 1985, in Washington, DC, which has appeared in print (Hansen 1986a).

1. Some of the monographs on household work published prior to this recent wave of studies are referred to in the main body of the paper. A fair number of journal articles and book chapters exist on this topic as well.

2. In her cross-cultural background discussion of household work, Rollins notes the presence of men servants in India (citing a 1951 study) and South Africa (1985:42–48) and refers to the "feminization" of the occupation in South Africa. Similarly, Glenn notes the employment of Chinese and Japanese men on the West Coasts of California and Washington state before the turn of the last century (1986:105–109). In neither work, however, are questions about the social practices that influence these employment traditions taken up as issues for investigation; they are explained by reference to demographic and economic forces.

3. During 1983–84, I carried out two large surveys on household worker management and employment practices in Lusaka. The first was a ten percent sample survey in high-income areas, residentially mixed in terms of national, racial, and ethnic composition. Here the chief household worker and his or her employer were interviewed separately in 167 households. Twenty household workers employed by residents were also interviewed in apartment complexes which government and private industry let to middle-level employees. The second survey was a ten percent household sample in two low-income African residential areas where a total of 270 householders were interviewed about their own experience with household work, as employees or employers, or both, and as "keepers" of children of relatives for purposes of household work.

4. Emily Bradley, the author of a 1939 book on household management, was the wife of a long-term colonial official in Northern Rhodesia. Her second book, *Dearest Priscilla: Letters to the Wife of a Colonial Civil Servant* (1950), takes the form of letters to a fictitious young woman friend going to join her husband in some African colony. It offers a lively description of the do's and don'ts of a young wife in a racially structured colonial setting and of the swirl of the social life in which she was to participate.

5. *Kitchen Kaffir*, also known as *Chilapalapa* or *Fanagolo*, is a hybrid language, consisting of Zulu, English, and Afrikaans terms.

6. In contrast to India, where colonial wives considered it a must to learn one of the local languages (Allen 1985:90), comparatively few white women in Northern Rhodesia bothered with language studies. Their husbands were often transferred across different language areas within the country, and wives may not have considered the learning of a local language worth their trouble.

7. This demarcation of public and domestic spheres in gender terms has been viewed as too simplistic. For a discussion of the relativity of space and its social and ideological partitioning, see Ardener (1981).

8. *Incorporated wives*, the term used by the editors of a recent collection of articles on women whose ascribed social character is a function of their husbands' occupation and culture (Callan and Ardener 1984), had a role beyond wifehood. Their unpaid work revolved around day-to-day reproduction of labor, and social reproduction of a racially divided and class structured colonial society.

9. My discussion of this debate summarizes information contained in several files deposited in the National Archives of Zambia, contemporary newspaper accounts, and magazine articles. The chief documents consulted are listed under the National Archives of Zambia entry among the references at the end of this paper.

10. Their discussion was reported and commented on in the January 1952 issue of a magazine for the African radio audience, called *The African Listener.*

11. Household workers or servants have not been enumerated as a separate category of the labor force by the Central Statistical Office (CSO) in Zambia since 1968, after which date no comprehensive numerical data on shifts in their employment patterns compared to other occupational specializations has been released. Quite recently the CSO publication, *Monthly Digest of Statistics,* has begun to list servants in a separate table, using figures provided by the Zambia National Provident Fund (ZNPF). These figures encompass only registered servants, who numbered 45,760 in June 1983 (Government of the Republic of Zambia 1984). In my 1983–84 survey, about one-third of the household workers interviewed were registered with the ZNPF. The ZNPF figures thus severely underreport the magnitude of total employment in homes which I estimate to be at least three times the size of the ZNPF figures, that is, about 100,000. Even this number excludes young relatives who do household work without pay.

12. Putsi flies are insects that lay their eggs in wet clothing. Their larvae may infest the human body, causing boil-like blisters. To prevent this, all items of clothing, sheets, towels, etc., are usually ironed.

13. The chief study of Asians within this region of Africa offers the following explanation: "males must be hired as African nursemaids are virtually impossible to obtain, and the few who are available are expensive by local standards" (Dotson and Dotson 1968:278). Extremely few of the Asians interviewed in 1983–84 had ever employed African women as household workers. They typically argued that men are able to carry out more, and heavier, tasks in and around the house, that Zambian women do not want to work, and that they make excuses because of their own problems with husbands and children.

References Cited

Allen, Charles, ed.
    1985[1976]   Plain Tales From the Raj: Images of British India in the Twentieth Century. London: Futura.
Ardener, Shirley, ed.
    1981   Women and Space: Ground Rules and Social Maps. New York: St. Martin's Press.
Becker, Jerome
    1887   La Vie en Afrique ou Trois Ans dans l'Afrique Centrale. 2 vols. Paris: J. Lebèque et Compagnie.
Bigland, Eileen
    1939   The Lake of the Royal Crocodiles. Norwich: Hodder and Stoughton.

Bradley, Emily
1939 A Household Book for Africa. London: Oxford University Press.
1950 Dearest Priscilla: Letters to the Wife of a Colonial Civil Servant. London: Max Parrish.

Bunster, Ximena, and Elsa M. Chaney
1985 Sellers and Servants: Working Women in Lima, Peru. New York: Praeger.

Callan, Hillary, and Shirley Ardener, eds.
1984 The Incorporated Wife. London: Croom Helm.

Chauncey, George, Jr.
1981 The Locus of Reproduction: Women's Labour in the Zambian Copperbelt, 1927–1953. Journal of Southern African Studies 7:135–164.

Clarke, Duncan G.
1974 Domestic Workers in Rhodesia: The Economics of Masters and Servants. Gwelo: Mambo Press.

Cock, Jacklyn
1980 Maids and Madams: A Study in the Politics of Exploitation. Johannesburg: Ravan Press.

Dotson, Floyd, and Lillian O. Dotson
1968 The Indian Minority of Zambia, Rhodesia and Malawi. New Haven: Yale University Press.

Dudden, Faye E.
1983 Serving Women: Household Service in Nineteenth Century America. Middletown, CT: Wesleyan University Press.

Fairchilds, Cissie
1984 Domestic Enemies: Servants and Their Masters in Old Regime France. Baltimore: Johns Hopkins University Press.

Gaitskell, Deborah, Judy Kimble, Moira Maconachie, and Elaine Unterhalter
1984 Race, Class and Gender: Domestic Workers in South Africa. Review of African Political Economy 27/28:86–108.

Galton, Francis
1893[1854] The Art of Travel; or, Shifts and Contrivances Available in Wild Countries. London: John Murray.

Glazer, Nona
1980 Everyone Needs Three Hands: Doing Unpaid and Paid Work. *In* Women and Household Labor. Sarah F. Berk, ed. Pp. 249–273. Beverly Hills: Sage.

Glenn, Evelyn Nakano
1986 Issei, Nisei, War Bride: Three Generations of Japanese American Women in Domestic Service. Philadelphia: Temple University Press.

Government of the Republic of Zambia
1968 Annual Report of the Labour Department. Lusaka: Government Printer.
1984 Monthly Digest of Statistics XX, supplement.

Grossman, Allyson Sherman
1980 Women in Domestic Work: Yesterday and Today. Monthly Labor Review 103:17–21.

Hansen, Karen Tranberg
1980a When Sex Becomes a Critical Variable: Married Women and Extra-Domestic Work in Lusaka, Zambia. African Social Research 30:831–850.

1980b   The Urban Informal Sector as a Development Issue: Poor Women
and Work in Lusaka, Zambia. Urban Anthropology 9:199–225.
1984   Negotiating Sex and Gender in Urban Zambia. Journal of Southern
African Studies 10:119–138.
1986a   Household Work as a Man's Job: Sex and Gender in Domestic Service in Zambia. Anthropology Today 2(3):18–23.
1986b   Domestic Service in Zambia. Journal of Southern African Studies
13:57–81.
Hecht, Jean H.
1980[1956]   The Domestic Servant Class in Eighteenth Century England.
London: Routledge and Kegan Paul.
Heissler, Helmuth
1974   Urbanisation and the Government of Migration: The Inter-Relation
of Urban and Rural Life in Zambia. New York: St. Martin's Press.
Maza, Sarah
1983   The Uses of Loyalty: Domestic Service in Eighteenth Century France.
Princeton: Princeton University Press.
McBride, Theresa
1976   The Domestic Revolution: The Modernisation of Household Service
in England and France 1820–1920. London: Croom Helm.
National Archives of Zambia
1943–57   NR 3/143 md/14. Labour Department. Native Labour Conditions.
Woman Power.
1949–51   SEC 5/331 Native Labour. General Policy.
Northern Rhodesia
1948   Report on the Education of Women and Girls in Northern Rhodesia.
Lusaka: Government Printer.
1949   Annual Report of the Labour Department. Lusaka: Government
Printer.
1950   Northern Rhodesia Handbook. Lusaka: Government Printer.
1951–57   Annual Reports of the Labour Department.
Ortner, Sherry, and Harriet Whitehead
1981   Introduction: Accounting for Sexual Meanings. In Sexual Meanings:
The Cultural Construction of Gender and Sexuality. S. Ortner and H.
Whitehead, eds. Pp. 1–27. Cambridge: Cambridge University Press.
Palmer, Phyllis
1984   Housework and Domestic Labor: Racial and Technological Change.
In My Troubles are Going to Have Trouble with Me. Karen B. Sacks and
Dorothy Remy, eds. Pp. 80–91. New Brunswick, NJ: Rutgers University
Press.
Rollins, Judith
1985   Between Women: Domestics and Their Employers. Philadelphia:
Temple University Press.
Rosaldo, Michelle Z.
1974   Woman, Culture, and Society: A Theoretical Overview. In Woman,
Culture, and Society. Michelle Z. Rosaldo and Louise Lamphere, eds. Pp.
17–42. Stanford: Stanford University Press.
Rotberg, Robert I.
1965   Christian Missionaries and the Creation of Northern Rhodesia 1880–
1924. Princeton: Princeton University Press.

Simpson, Donald
  1975   Dark Companions: The African Contribution to the European Exploration of East Africa. London: Paul Elek.
Sacks, Karen B.
  1982   Sisters and Wives: The Past and Future of Sexual Equality. Urbana: University of Illinois Press.
Sutherland, Daniel E.
  1981   Americans and Their Servants: Domestic Service in the United States From 1800 to 1920. Baton Rouge: Louisiana State University Press.
van Onselen, Charles
  1982   The Witches of Suburbia: Domestic Service on the Witwatersrand, 1890–1914. *In* Studies in the Social and Economic History of the Witwatersrand 1886–1914. Vol. 2: New Nineveh, ed. Pp. 1–73. London: Longman.
Weinrich, A. H. K.
  1976   African Domestic Servants in Fort Victoria: Their Employers. *In* Mucheke: Race, Status and Politics in a Rhodesian Community. Pp. 215–229. New York: Holmes and Meier.
  1976b African Domestic Servants in Fort Victoria: The Servants Themselves. *In* Race, Status and Politics in a Rhodesian Community. Pp. 230–243. New York: Holmes and Meier.

8

Female Household Workers in Industrializing Malaysia

M. Jocelyn Armstrong
University of Illinois

This paper examines some implications of the contemporary industrialization process for the experience of female household workers in urban Malaysia. In the West, work in homes was among the occupations that declined numerically with growth in industrialization (Collver and Langlois 1962). Malaysia is in an early, transitional stage of industrialization during which the occupation continues to be a significant source of employment for women. It is also subject to considerable modernizing in form, content, and other features (compare Chaplin 1978; Coser 1973; Katzman 1978).

Here I will look in particular at the implications of industrialization for: (1) the general conditions of household work; (2) the actual tasks involved; (3) the advantages and disadvantages associated with being a household worker; and (4) the future of the occupation as industrialization continues. Some comparisons will be made of the experiences and views of Malay, Chinese, and Indian household workers—women of Malaysia's three main ethnic groups—and between the Malaysian and other Southeast Asian situations.

Since World War II and especially since independence in 1957, Malaysia has undergone relatively rapid modernization and economic growth, to the point of becoming, after Singapore, the most developed nation in Southeast Asia. Industrialization has played a major role in development plans during this period, and due to incentives given multinational industries to establish factories in Malaysia, expanded markedly during the 1970s. Despite the relatively rapid and high level of development, the direct employment of women has been slow, beginning later and remaining less than that of men (Manderson 1979; Wong 1979). For the first two decades of planned development, women's first role was seen as supportive. Most women in the workforce continued in the traditional female occupational categories—agricultural work in rural areas, service occupations in urban centers.

By the 1970s, the expansion of female education during the 1960s had led more women into white-collar careers in both public and private sectors, and the multinational direction of industrial development had incorporated large numbers of young women as "factory girls" working in light industry. Most development policies incorporate a measure of privilege for the indigenous Malay population. By the end of the 1970s, ethnic comparisons of women in the urban labor force, for example, showed similar overall rates of participation (Jones 1984) but noticeably higher proportions of Malay women in professional and technical occupations, and more Malay than Chinese or Indian women working in industry (Khoo and Pirie 1984). However, one-fourth of all women—Malay, Chinese, and Indian—in the urban workforce remained in service occupations, with 60 percent of them employed as household workers.[1]

This paper draws on a study of the lives of female workers in homes completed in 1980 in the city of Kuala Lumpur. Kuala Lumpur is Malaysia's capital city, its largest city by far and also the leading location of industrial development. The study focused on 30 women (10 Chinese, 10 Malay, and 10 Indian) and combined participant observation with in-depth interviewing, informal one-to-one conversations, and additional small group discussions. Some of the participants I had met before during previous periods of research in Malaysia, at their former workplaces or in nonwork situations. I also informally interviewed the members of families for whom the women worked and of other families employing other household workers. During 1980 and earlier, for a total of three years, I was the employer of a household worker myself.

The women ranged in age from 20 to 55 years, but most of them (60 percent) were in their late twenties or their thirties. In terms of marital status, 16 of the women were married at the time of the study or had been married previously, and 14 had never married. Only four had been born in Kuala Lumpur, but half had lived there for 10 or more years, and half of these for 20 or more years. Only five were new arrivals, having been in the city for less than five years. There was a considerable range of experience in terms of number of years in household work. One young Indian woman was completing her first year of work while the oldest participant in the study had worked in homes for more than 40 years. Approximately one-third of the women had been in the occupation for less than 10 years; one-third for between 10 and 20 years; and one-third for 20 years or more. The women's work

experience was thus distributed across the time span of Malaysia's period of industrialization.

The General Conditions of Household Work

One key "modernizing" effect in the process of industrialization
is change in the relationship between employer and employee. In
household work, this involves a shift from a traditional status, a
pseudo-kin relationship, to the contractual one that obtains in most
modern (postindustrial) occupational arrangements (Aubert 1970;
Chaplin 1978; Coser 1973). A contractual pattern, being less exploitative, is seen as an improvement in conditions from the viewpoint of
the employee.

There are two dimensions of industrial development in Malaysia
that have helped modify the employment patterns of household workers. The rapid expansion of multinational light industries in and
around urban areas such as Kuala Lumpur had opened up tens of
thousands of new jobs by the end of the 1970s, most of them for
women. Historically, as the availability of factory work has increased,
women workers have found it an attractive alternative. Accordingly,
the supply of female household workers has been reduced and those
remaining in the occupation have used the new seller's market to up-
grade their conditions of work through more contractual arrangements (Coser 1973; Katzman 1978). In the developing nations of
Southeast Asia today, industry's demand has been for the low-cost,
high-quality labor of young women. In Malaysia, to meet the government's employment quota for the Malay ethnic group, this has meant
primarily Malay young women. While some urban women have been
drawn into employment or from other employment, for the most part
the demand for "factory girls" has been met by the migration of
women from rural areas. To women seeking work, the advantages of
factory work over household work are, at best, unclear. It is well documented that the conditions of work in the multinational factories are
no less exploitative (Ariffin 1984; Grossman 1979; Lim 1978). The pay
is poor; the tasks are monotonous; some work is physically impairing
(notably of vision); overtime is compulsory; and there is no job security. It is low status work, and women must contend with public opinion of "factory girls" as, individually, social misfits and, collectively,
a social problem.

Among the 30 Kuala Lumpur household workers I interviewed, 8
had previously worked in factories but had found the work "too difficult," or "too strenuous," or had discovered that it brought "little

pay but many expenses." A young Indian woman had considered working in a factory, but an elder brother had advised her that she would be "safer and happier in a house." A Malay woman aged 35 felt that factory work was for young girls, that she herself was "too old to work in a factory." Kuala Lumpur household workers were, however, well aware of the increasing availability of factory work, and of the greater personal freedom and more modern lifestyle that it offered.

To the would-be employers of workers in homes, the rapid expansion of factory jobs presented a real threat. One of them expressed a widely held opinion when she said: "The young girls of today are not interested in domestic service. They prefer to work in factories because they have more freedom, and a chance to meet boys and to go out more." All in all, the availability of factory work has had sufficient impact on both employee and employer to prompt change in some of the conditions of work. It is generally the case now that wages, hours, and holidays can be negotiated and, given a lasting relationship, that there will be annual increments.

Another dimension of industrial development in Malaysia that has implications for the conditions of household work is a continuing foreign, especially "European," presence. Since independence in 1957, development policies have favored the Malaysianization of industry's personnel, but the involvement of foreigners has by no means ended. In Kuala Lumpur, British, American, and other "expats" have continued to form a sizeable community of "Europeans." Others remain in commerce, education, and diplomacy. Like their counterparts of the colonial period, they represent a significant source of employment for household workers. Unlike their colonial predecessors, however, the expats of today are not usually practiced as employers, and most of them have more egalitarian attitudes than prevailed among the Europeans of colonial times, or still prevail in Malaysian society today. As one of today's expat employers has written, she and her kind enjoy the benefits of household workers (more leisure time and less strain, for example), but most have a problem in "how to handle them," how to establish the mistress/servant relationship "that the locals take for granted" (Craig 1979).

Malaysian urban household workers often prefer European families as employers. Their range of demands may be less predictable or familiar, but they are considered usually to agree to shorter hours, more time off, and more flexible working arrangements. In the experience of one Malay woman worker in Kuala Lumpur, expatriates made the better employers because "they follow the rules; Malaysians do not." Several Chinese household workers expressed strong disinclination to work for members of their own ethnic group because they were "too strict" and demanded "round-the-clock service." The future of a resident foreign presence in Southeast Asian cities is uncertain, but it has already been an influence for change in the established working conditions of household workers beyond Malaysia, in the more developed and industrialized, but also formerly colonial, cities of Singapore (Lebra 1980) and Hong Kong (Salaff 1981; Sankar 1978).

Kuala Lumpur's household workers give expression to their own perception of changing employer/employee relations in the English-language names they use for their occupation. Rather than "servant" or the Cantonese loan-word *"amah"* which, following British colonial usage, is today widely applied to female household workers of all ethnicities in Malaysia, the Kuala Lumpur women I studied preferred "houseworker" or "housekeeper," or a description of themselves as "working for a family."

Their recruitment to household work shows elements of choice—as in the preferences for work in homes over a factory job reported earlier, and the experiences of two Chinese women who had first worked as salesclerks but moved to household work because it offered better pay and more job security. Women of all three ethnicities said they had chosen their occupation because they liked performing its tasks. There were also instances of "involuntary" recruitment, however, insofar as women felt they were not qualified for any other type of work, or had accepted household work as their destiny. As one Chinese woman who had followed both parents and two elder sisters into the occupation explained, it was "the family work." Of the 30 women, eight had had a parent in household work, and 17 had a sister working in homes at the time of the study.

Kuala Lumpur's "modern" household employees work for wages. The wages are low, but during the 1970s they had doubled and, in 1980, were usually higher than the wages earned by "factory girls." Without exception the workers in my study also received some traditional-style payment in kind. The provision of room and board was commonplace. In addition, 20 women had had medical or dental services provided by their employer. Several reported the provision of transport, for example, being driven to a movie theater or to the home of a relative in their employer's car on their day off. Clothes were a fairly common gift. In the case of expatriate employers, when the time came to return home, it was not uncommon for their employee to inherit a sizeable amount of household equipment and furnishings. Some of the women workers had been able to arrange for members of their family to share their living quarters. The expatriate employer of one of the younger Indian household workers supplied her with "everything for daily living," and the Malay employers of a younger Malay woman provided "everything I need, even the toothpaste."

Whereas under traditional employment patterns "servants" made long-term and even lifetime commitments to a particular "master," a high turnover rate is characteristic of the contemporary situation as employees seek to better their working conditions (Katzman 1978). Today's female household workers in the Philippines clearly appear to be following this pattern (Brandewie 1973; Palabrica-Costello 1984). Among the Malaysian women I studied, a history of multiple jobs was typical. Only 5 of the 30 had held only one household work position, but the length of service ranged widely, from 1 to 22 years. For the 25 women who had held multiple jobs, 20 had stayed in one of those jobs for only a year or less, but terms of up to 12 years were also represented, and terms of 5 years or more were common. When the woman herself chose to leave a job, it was sometimes for personal, family reasons, and sometimes because she had been working for a long time and wanted a break. For 12 of the women, in at least one instance of job termination dissatisfaction with employers who practiced what was felt to be over-supervision, or who made excessive demands, was paramount. Also as often, however, the changes from one job to another had been occasioned by Malaysian employers moving away from Kuala Lumpur, or expatriate employers returning to their home country.

Most Malaysian household workers are still live-in employees, a situation that can easily perpetuate the more traditional conditions of work (Aubert 1970; Coser 1973). Employee and employer are more likely to relate to one another as pseudo-kin; the employee's privacy and freedom are inevitably curtailed; and the understandings about working hours and days off are likely to be less clearly defined, and more commonly violated. Twenty of the women in my Kuala Lumpur study had known only live-in positions, seven more had taken a combination of live-in and live-out jobs. Only three (all working mothers with young children) had confined themselves to live-out jobs. The conveniences and securities of living in made it the more attractive arrangement to most of the women. Not only were housing expenses taken care of (sometimes for members of the worker's family as well as herself), but the accommodation was usually comfortable, and often located in the city's "nicer" and safer suburbs. Single women without family or relatives to live with in Kuala Lumpur did not consider living out an option: living in met the still-strong expectation that Malaysian females live "at home" until they marry. Most of the women saw living out and having to travel to and from work each day as inconvenient, and some considered it "unsafe." A Malay woman in her 40s who had done household work for 22 years explained that she was "used to living in now and wouldn't want to try any other way." I found the preference for live-in work to be still strong for women in all three ethnic groups.

In the typical employer's view, Kuala Lumpur's household worker has initiated her own "modernization" (compare Chaplin 1978). This view is of an informed and self-confident young woman who cleverly manipulates the fact that she is a scarce commodity to achieve increasingly modern employment arrangements. At the time of my study, "the domestic help problem" was receiving frequent attention in the news media. Newspaper articles highlighted the short supply and high turnover issues with headlines like "Help, the maid is walking out on us again!" The typical modern-day household worker was presented as one who named her price, expected to work unsupervised, and knew how to make an employer feel guilty for "exploiting" her.

A magazine feature claiming to take "a lighthearted look at a vanishing breed" invited Malaysia's mistresses to sort their present servants into one of several types. These types, based on perceived common shortcomings, included the truant (who always took more than the agreed-on time off), the shrinker (who skipped the housework to spend most of her time on the phone), and the gossip monger (for whom the word discreet did not exist). In neighboring Singapore, even older household workers had, in the eyes of their employers, become "tough nuts" who had reneged on the tradition of loyal and faithful service and would move on as soon as a better job presented itself (Lebra 1980). A Kuala Lumpur newspaper columnist commenting on the local situation described groups of employers preparing lists of "musts" and "must nots" so that a would-be employer could be "ready with the right answers when a prospective servant came to interview her for suitability as an employer" (Sri Delima 1978:88). The list of "musts" emphasized the modern household worker's high expectations regarding wages, hours, and holidays; the list of "must nots" emphasized complaints about a worker's performance and restraints on her independence.

From the employees' side, work can be said to be more contractually patterned but to still contain a good many features of the older preindustrial pattern. Some, such as living-in and being paid partly in kind, are features that the present population of employees seems to prefer. But, such inclinations aside, more contractualization is unlikely since all employer/household worker "contracts" remain at the level of private, informal agreements. Malaysia is typical of developing countries in having no legislation that requires the employers of household workers to employ them on a contracted basis. In the absence of a written contract, the only rights workers in homes are afforded under the law are payment of wages and due notice of termination (Rafiah Salim 1984). Recently passed rest day, holiday, and maternity leave laws which improved the conditions of hotel and restaurant workers do not extend to household workers. The law specifically excludes such employees from two major government benefits available to other workers—an employees' provident fund (established in 1951) and the social security scheme (begun in 1969). Malaysia is also typical (cf. Chaplin 1978; Palabrica-Costello 1984) in having no household worker union through which pressure for more contractual arrangements might be applied. Given the government's extensive restrictions on unionization, and its rigid control of unions generally, worker organization as a way to better working conditions seems remote.

The Tasks of Household Work

Household workers produce goods and services for the household that employs them. With contemporary industrialization, their duties can be expected to narrow to the personal and family needs that are most resistant to mechanization or, outside the home, to commercialization (Chaplin 1978). In Malaysia, the commercialization of child care has begun, but remains limited. The facilities are few in number, they are expensive, and parents are not accustomed to them. In addition to household machines, some modern commercialization of housecleaning has occurred in Kuala Lumpur in the appearance of cleaning agencies, and there are caterers offering home meal delivery. But to rely on such outside services is beyond the means of many of the urban middle class; the more relaxed lifestyle offered by live-in household employees remains the general preference.

The prevailing position on child-care services was reflected by a young Malaysian Indian employer when she observed that: "Today, most employers are looking for someone to look after the children. We have machines to do the other things—cooking, cleaning, washing—so it is the ability to look after children that is our first requirement." A wealthy Chinese businessman whose children were grown commented on the substituting of "servants" by machines: "But someone has to be there to push the buttons. The wife will have to stay home to push the buttons!"

His comment was only half in jest for he raises two important obstacles to change in domestic life in urban Malaysia. More and more middle- and upper-class Malaysian men accept the idea of a working wife, but they do not expect to share the routine household chores. Surveys have shown that among the husbands of working women who do help, Malay men do the most, Chinese men do the least, and Indian men fall in the middle (Noor Laily Abu Bakar and Raj Hashim 1984). Men of all ethnicities are united in the view that the household remains the woman's domain (Strange 1981). Most of the working wives, on the other hand, entered the workforce and built careers with employment of a household worker as a given. Life without it would not only be less convenient; it is hard to imagine.[2]

In the course of industrial development elsewhere, the private home is one of the last places to change materially (Katzman 1978). The presence of a household worker delays the change further since it removes much of the pressure or interest to adopt household machinery and packaged services. The worker is thus likely to continue doing traditional preindustrial tasks, and in much the same way.

The developing nations of today, of course, can borrow home machinery from already industrialized societies. In urban Malaysia during the 1970s and 1980s, however, there has been only a limited shift to machines, most often a refrigerator, rice cooker, washing machine, and vacuum cleaner, usually in that order. Some of Kuala Lumpur's employers indicated that their employees demanded the machines as labor savers, and some felt that they had been persuaded to acquire the new equipment by a household worker whose first concern was that "her" household should be as well equipped and "modern" as others in the neighborhood.

From the viewpoint of the workers, however, there had not been much mechanization of their work. Those who could look back over five or ten years of household employment were in general agreement that wages had increased and that some improvements had been made in hours and time off. There was no consensus about the introduction of labor-saving devices. In the experience of most women, expatriates were more likely to have appliances, but "only" the Americans had washing machines and vacuum cleaners. Malaysian homes generally had less in the way of modern equipment; the Chinese homes in particular had "no" labor-saving equipment. There were also household workers of each ethnicity, and various ages, who expressed conservatism about the modern machines that were available to them. A younger Malay woman, not new to household work but with only three years of employment in the modern urban setting of Kuala Lumpur, felt uncomfortable using an automatic washer for laundry. A Chinese woman in her thirties acknowledged the washer as a labor saver but remained to be convinced of its superiority over her traditional overnight-soak-and-scrub technique. An experienced Indian household worker in her forties who had held 13 different jobs in the households of both expatriates and Malaysians was pleased to recount that there had been no machines in any of them.

A manual of information and advice prepared to help Americans establish themselves in Kuala Lumpur in the 1960s and early 1970s listed and described the duties of seven different types of "servants" that could be employed (American Association of Malaysia 1972). These were named in Malaysian English as cook, general *amah*, baby *amah*, wash *amah*, gardener, driver, and houseboy. The list is almost identical with one of the servants employed in the homes of Europeans in Malaysia 50 years earlier (Butcher 1979). With industrialization, however, as the female labor market has diversified and the supply of household workers has decreased, there has been a reduction in the number of workers per household (Chaplin 1978). In Malaysia today, only some upper-class Malaysian families retain staffs of workers, and among European families, only those do who have the resources and a perceived need, for example some who do extensive entertaining. By far the most common situation is employment of one "general" household worker. Of the 30 women in my Kuala Lumpur study, 18 had been employed only as general workers and the remainder had all held general jobs as well as specialized ones.

As described by the women themselves, the duties of a present-day general household worker always include cooking, cleaning, and laundry, nearly always child care, and often marketing. Other tasks which had been required or expected in some jobs included sewing, gardening, carwashing, backyard chicken-raising, and cat, dog, bird, or other pet care. A general household worker could be called on to do "whatever needs doing" but the "outside jobs" (gardening, carwashing) were excluded by some, and counted as extras by others. Since most urban employers are absent during the day, the employee is also expected to receive service people, accept deliveries, take phone messages, relay instructions to a part-time gardener, and so on. During an employer's extended absences, the household worker is likely to be left with general responsibility for the house. Half of the women in my study had been taken along on one of their employer's trips, including trips abroad. In most cases, the trips were seen as "work," or a "working holiday," because it was expected that the woman would take care of the children, or provide her employer with companionship and personal services.

Job descriptions as offered by employers are much less complete. Cooking is almost always specified. Most Europeans find cooking for themselves with the unfamiliar supplies and outdated equipment difficult or undesirable. Malaysian employers feel that the "fussy" and "tedious" methods of Asian cooking *"require* servants." Beyond cooking, employer job descriptions may specify, for example, "light housework" or "day-time babysitting only," but the performance of other tasks in addition to cooking is just as likely to be taken for granted.

By 1980, the household worker's traditional responsibility for household marketing was in the balance. One-third of my Kuala Lumpur employee group still considered it one of their tasks, but employers were increasingly inclined not to "allow" the employee to do the marketing. The reasons usually offered were that the worker spent too much money, that she was not a good judge of quality, or, especially when new, that she did not know the household's likes and dislikes well enough. But it was also becoming more socially acceptable for members of the urban middle and upper classes to do their own marketing. With more wives working, it was often convenient for them to shop at one of the better, central markets rather than make do with the limited neighborhood one. And the multiplication of Western-style supermarkets in the city was adding a new and attractive dimension to marketing that employers wanted to explore. For the most part, however, Kuala Lumpur employers still seem to assume, as household workers do, that their employee will do "whatever needs doing."

The Rewards of Household Work

Under the traditional, preindustrial pattern of employment, Asian household workers gave service in return for the safety and stability of a pseudo-family situation. As a "family member," the worker received little or no cash payment but instead was paid in kind with room and board, accorded some family-style respect and consideration, and cared for in old age. Today this pattern is the exception. The typical modern household worker has a career of multiple jobs and works for wages. But beyond wages, what are the rewards and satisfactions of household work today? Everywhere, in the developed and developing worlds alike, it is one of the poorest paid occupations, near the bottom of occupational hierarchies. Viewed in local context and from the inside, however, such disabilities can appear less severe.

According to the Kuala Lumpur women workers I studied, some of the traditional rewards remain important. First, the home-like environment of household work, and the security and safety it provided, was valued by women of all three ethnic groups. Protection from the perceived risks of big-city living was stressed by recent rural migrants and somewhat more so by Malay women who, as a group, are the most recent to experience urban living. The women were aware that they enjoyed better living conditions than other Malaysians at their socioeconomic level. In some cases, respite from the crowded or otherwise unattractive home environment of their own family was appreciated. An Indian woman in her twenties expressed a general sentiment in her appreciation of "the restful atmosphere of the homes and neighborhoods" her work placed her in.

Benefits also were seen to derive from a personalized relationship with one's employer, as when an employer is "kind" or "good" and takes an interest in the worker's well-being, and sometimes in the well-being of members of her family too. Enjoyment of close relations with an employer's children was another common experience. This set of advantages was most obviously associated with live-in employment but not exclusively so. Day household workers in stable work situations could draw such satisfactions too.

Another source of rewards was the independent nature of household work. The Chinese women were especially vocal about the satisfactions of being one's own boss, and being able to plan one's own day, but Malay and Indian women joined them in valuing the responsibilities that working alone granted. As Katzman suggests (1978), when industrialization creates alternative occupations for women, the household worker may be disadvantaged in control over her personal life, but relatively advantaged in the measure of control she has over her task performance. She is generally left to her own initiative and judgment in cooking, cleaning, and laundry, and often in infant and child care too. In urban Malaysia today, household work compares favorably with the occupations of salesgirl and "factory girl" in these terms. With urban employers away at their own jobs all day, the measure of control increases; with employer mobility, it can extend to longer periods of full responsibility for the house.

Another kind of independence that several participants in my study recognized was separation, if not freedom from female subordination within their own families. Malaysian women of all three ethnic groups, Malay, Chinese, and Indian, are subject to male authority and can expect a close monitoring of their behavior by fathers and elder brothers and, with marriage, by husbands. My study participants communicated a continuing respect for male authority but they were not unaware of, nor unwilling to talk about the restrictions and inequalities it implied, and the "traditional" stamp it gave their lives in the modern urban setting of Kuala Lumpur.

The variety of duties built into household work was another recurring satisfaction. Sometimes a comparison with the monotony and tedium of assembly line work in the multinational factories was made, but in most cases the women claimed to enjoy doing the various tasks of housekeeping. They were interested in doing them efficiently and well, and in taking the opportunities their work provided to develop their homemaking skills. The variety of people and lifestyles to which their work exposed them was also generally enjoyed. Some of this kind of reward came from simply being resident in Kuala Lumpur, always Malaysia's most cosmopolitan city and, in 1980, its undisputed pacesetter for change. Household workers employed by persons of another ethnicity were usually expanding their horizons since interethnic mixing in Malaysia has long been limited and remains so for most people. The employees of expatriate households participated in even more different ways of living. A frequently mentioned specific reward was the chance most European homes offered to become a better speaker or reader of English. Beyond being a useful qualification for future jobs, competence in English is one of the badges of being a "modern" urban Malaysian.

These kinds of rewards have been noted historically in the United States (Katzman 1978) and, in Asia today, in the Philippines (Brandewie 1973) and Hong Kong (Salaff 1981). Access to such rewards is increased for those household workers who have relatively more job mobility, whose working conditions offer relatively greater freedom of movement, and who have the most time and money and inclination for independent outings and entertainment outside the home. In Kuala Lumpur, Chinese women workers were somewhat more adventurous in this respect.

The social isolation of household work was not a commonly felt disability. Time off was always adequate for regular contact with family or friends. Daily work routines allowed sufficient exchange between the household workers of a neighborhood for feelings of solidarity to develop. In addition, the Kuala Lumpur employees took precautions against isolation. Nearness to other women workers who were friends, or friends of friends, was a common factor in job selection. So, too, was accessibility to public transport. While, as already mentioned, the Chinese household workers generally had more fully developed social lives, most of the women were in the habit of evening or weekend outings with friends or relatives to a restaurant, movie, or shopping mall. Even the disadvantage of being in a low status occupation was somewhat tempered because the main alternative occupation, factory work, was of even lower status. The "factory girls" were seen as relatively unprotected from the evils of big-city living, ascribed low reputations, and viewed collectively as one of Kuala Lumpur's leading social problems (cf. Ariffin 1984; Daud 1985).

As may be characteristic in the transitional phase of industrialization, the wages of Malaysia's urban household workers in 1980 were still better than those of women in the alternative newer occupations of factory and sales work. With payments in kind (room and board and so on), all the Kuala Lumpur women household workers I knew were able to save money. They were also able to maintain adequate, up-to-date wardrobes, to own a television set or cassette player, invest in jewelry, enjoy gambling, or maintain their own separate housing, and still meet major expenses such as dental work, eyeglasses, or unexpected travel.

All of the women planned to continue working, about half of them for "as long as I can." Two-thirds, including more or less equal numbers of Malays, Chinese, and Indians, expected to remain in household work. Only one, a 20-year-old Malay woman with a high school education, was intent on finding a "better" job. The other women were either not sure about their work future or had not given the matter serious thought. The prevailing expectation of continuing to do household work could be partly explained by the facts that alternatives remained limited, that few of the women were, or felt they were, qualified for other work, and that some of the women considered themselves too old to change occupations. But the perceived advantages and satisfactions of household work in urban Malaysia today were also at issue.

The Future of Household Work

What can be said about the future of household work in urban Malaysia as industrialization increases and the female labor force continues to diversify? In the past, in the Western experience, and in parts of the developing world, private household work has become "a declining type of employment" as the level of industrialization has increased (Collver and Langlois 1962; Jones 1984). As is characteristic of declining occupations, it has been marked by "casualization" (Chaplin 1978), becoming predominantly a part-time, short-term, secondary, or moonlighting occupation. And in a parallel, recurrent trend, household work has become increasingly an occupation of ethnic minorities or recent international immigrants.

In the opinions of most Kuala Lumpur household workers in 1980, the demand for the occupation would continue not only into the near future (five to ten years), but also through their own lifetimes and into their daughters' and nieces' working lifetimes, if not indefinitely, or "always." These opinions may read as mere wishful thinking, but the women's comments in support of them were considered and sound. Most of the women had experienced multiple employer requests for their services, or had been in a position of being able to choose among several openings when looking for a new job. They felt confident that the demand for household workers remained healthy, that there were still "plenty of jobs."

Some of the women could see their work as supporting development and modernization. They referred in particular to the expanding opportunities in higher education for women and the consequent entry of more and more women into white-collar occupations and the professions. As working wives and mothers these women would "need" household workers. Some of the older women in the Kuala Lumpur study sensed less willingness to do household work among today's young women, and some hoped that their daughters and nieces would move into other, "better" jobs. Given the reduction in competition, the older women nevertheless could look with confidence to the continuation of employment in homes for themselves. The Malaysianization of industry and commerce was noted as perhaps reducing the European community as a source of employment, but it was not perceived as an immediate or major threat to the need for household workers.[3]

No ethnic group was more optimistic or pessimistic than the others about the future of household work in urban Malaysia. It was common knowledge that in Kuala Lumpur Chinese women commanded the highest wages, partly because of the reputation of their ethnic group as "hardworking." But not all employers could or wanted to afford a Chinese household worker in 1980 and, for Malaysian employers, religious and other ethnically specific restrictions in diet and other behaviors put limits on the cross-ethnic recruitment of employees. There were as many openings for Malay and Indian household workers as for Chinese. Outside competition from immigrant women was not of any consequence. A limited amount of recruitment of young women from Sabah and Sarawak in East Malaysia and from neighboring Indonesia occurred, but Malaysia's strict immigration laws prevented any significant importation of household workers. The pattern of a substantial displacement of local workers by employer imports (Filipinas in Hong Kong, and Sri Lankan women in Singapore, for example) seemed unlikely to be paralleled in Malaysia.

As indicated earlier, most of the employer population wanted to retain household workers. As they saw it, the competition for employees in Kuala Lumpur in 1980 was serious, meaning that there was at least a shortage of what employers considered "good" workers at the price they wanted to pay. Some casualization was envisaged, mainly a move away from live-in servants to employment on a day basis only. Some casualization was in place, as in live-out and part-time general household workers who served single households, and in specialized workers (mainly washerwomen) who served several employers.

A few well-off Malaysians may be learning to live without household help. I knew two mature professional couples, both spouses still working and with no children living at home, who used commercial laundry services, ate out at restaurants, and employed caterers for their entertaining. A small number of younger middle-class women had found less costly methods. One of them presented her "formula" as: "Buy a washing machine, rely on gadgets, eat simple meals, organize your life." Overall, however, there was more talk than action about managing without household workers. Beyond convenience, or real or imagined need, the status dimension of having a "servant" is still significant, and seems likely to persist. To return to a view from the employee side, from an Indian household worker in her middle twenties: "For as long as girls want to do housework, people will want them to."

Malaysia is still in the early phases of planned industrialization. Development plans for the 1990s involve the introduction of heavy industries. Further distinctively Malaysian consequences for the occupation of household work can be expected. A follow-up study of household workers in Kuala Lumpur in the year 2000 would be worthwhile.

Notes

Acknowledgments. The research for this paper was completed with support from the U.S. National Science Foundation (Grant No. NSF-SOC 79-10521). I am grateful to all Malaysians who participated, and owe special thanks to Narindar David for competent and interested interviewing assistance.

1. Other women workers categorized as "service workers" are waitresses, hairdressers, policewomen, and women in the armed forces (Khoo and Pirie 1984).

2. Strange (1981:186) reports on a meeting of university women during the 1970s at which each participant was asked to fill out a questionnaire about her educational/occupational background. One question provided a checklist for each woman to show who had been most-to-least important in helping her achieve her goals—husband, parents, friends, colleagues, other. A professor looking at the list said, "My *amah* was by far the most important!" The women around her laughed but agreed.

3. By 1985, the Malaysianization of industry and commerce had in fact slowed. Economic growth had fallen short of targets and the government had relaxed its restrictions on foreign investment and foreign-owned companies as part of recovery efforts.

References Cited

American Association of Malaysia.
   1972   Selamat Datang. Kuala Lumpur.
Ariffin, Jamilah
   1984   Migration of Women Workers in Peninsular Malaysia: Impact and Implications. *In* Women in the Cities of Asia: Migration and Urban Adaptation. J. T. Fawcett, Siew-Ean Khoo, P. C. Smith, eds. Pp. 213–226. Boulder, CO: Westview Press.
Aubert, Vilhelm
   1970   The Housemaid—An Occupational Role in Crisis. *In* Society and the Legal Order. R. D. Schwartz and J. H. Skolnick, eds. Pp. 149–158. New York: Basic Books.
Brandewie, Ernest
   1973   Maids in Cebuano Society. Philippine Quarterly of Culture and Society 1:209–219.
Butcher, John G.
   1979   The British in Malaya 1880–1941: The Social History of a European Community in Colonial South-east Asia. Kuala Lumpur: Oxford University Press.
Chaplin, David
   1978   Domestic Service and Industrialization. Comparative Studies in Sociology 1:97–127.
Collver, Andrew and Eleanor Langlois
   1962   The Female Labor Force in Metropolitan Areas: An International Comparison. Economic Development and Cultural Change 10:367–385.
Coser, Lewis
   1973   Domestic Servants: The Obsolescence of an Occupational Role. Social Forces 52:31–40.
Craig, Jo Ann
   1979   Culture Shock! What Not to Do in Malaysia and Singapore, How and Why Not to Do It. Singapore: Times Books International.
Daud, Fatimah
   1985   "Minah Karan": The Truth about Malaysian Factory Girls. Kuala Lumpur: Berita Publishing.
Grossman, Rachael
   1979   Women's Place in the Integrated Circuit. Southeast Asia Chronicle 66:2–17.
Jones, Gavin W.
   1984   Economic Growth and Changing Female Employment Structure in the Cities of Southeast and East Asia. *In* Women in the Urban and Industrial Workforce: Southeast and East Asia. G. W. Jones, ed. Pp. 17–59. Canberra: Australian National University.

Katzman, David M.
    1978   Seven Days a Week. Women and Domestic Service in Industrializing
    America. New York: Oxford University Press.
Khoo, Siew-Ean and Peter Pirie
    1984   Female Rural-to-Urban Migration in Peninsular Malaysia. *In* Women
    in the Cities of Asia: Migration and Urban Adaptation. J. T. Fawcett, Siew-
    Ean Khoo, P. C. Smith, eds. Pp. 124–142. Boulder, CO: Westview Press.
Lebra, Joyce
    1980   Bazaar and Service Occupations. *In* Chinese Women in Southeast
    Asia, by J. Lebra and J. Paulson eds. Pp. 66–96. Singapore: Times Inter-
    national Books.
Lim, Linda Y. C.
    1978   Women Workers in Multinational Corporations: The Case of the
    Electronics Industry in Malaysia and Singapore. Michigan Occasional Pa-
    pers in Women's Studies, No. IX. Ann Arbor: Women's Studies Program,
    University of Michigan.
Manderson, Lenore
    1979   A Woman's Place: Malay Women and Development in Peninsular
    Malaysia. *In* Issues in Malaysian Development. J. C. Jackson and M. Rud-
    ner, eds. Pp. 223–271. Kuala Lumpur: Heinemann Education Books
    (Asia).
Noor Laily Abu Bakar and Rita Raj Hashim
    1984   Child Care for Working Women. *In* Women in Malaysia. Hing Ai
    Yun, Nik Safiah Karim, Rokiah Talib, eds. Pp. 78–93. Kuala Lumpur: Pe-
    landuk Publications.
Palabrica-Costello, Marilou
    1984   Female Domestic Servants in Cagayan de Oro, Philippines: Social
    and Economic Implications of Employment in a "Premodern" Occupa-
    tional Role. *In* Women in the Urban and Industrial Workforce: Southeast
    and East Asia. G. W. Jones, ed. Pp. 235–250. Canberra: Australian Na-
    tional University.
Rafiah Salim
    1984   The Legal Status of Women in a Multi-racial Malaysian Society. *In*
    Women in Malaysia. Hing Ai Yun, Nik Safiah Karim, Rokiah Talib, eds.
    Pp. 187–201. Kuala Lumpur: Pelanduk Publications.
Salaff, Janet W.
    1981   Working Daughters of Hong Kong: Filial Piety or Power in the Fam-
    ily? Cambridge: Cambridge University Press.
Sankar, Andrea
    1978   Female Domestic Service in Hong Kong. *In* Female Servants and Eco-
    nomic Development. Michigan Occasional Papers in Women's Studies,
    No. I. Pp. 51–62. Ann Arbor: Women's Studies Program, University of
    Michigan.
Sri Delima
    1978   Help, the House-Help's Gone. *In* As I Was Passing, Vol. 2. Sri De-
    lima, ed. Pp. 82–85. Kuala Lumpur: Berita Publishing.
Strange, Heather
    1981   Rural Malay Women in Tradition and Transition. New York: Praeger.
Wong, Aldine K.
    1979   The Changing Roles and Status of Women in ASEAN. Contemporary
    Southeast Asia 1:179–193.

9

Household Workers in Urban Martinique

Michel S. Laguerre
University of California, Berkeley

The presence of female household workers in middle- and upper-class homes is a familiar part of urban life in the Caribbean. In urban Martinique, two historical factors have shaped contemporary household work: the colonial past, and the transformation of the island into a Department of France in 1946.[1] The colonial period accounts for the cultural mold in which employers and workers created the symbolic and behavioral content of their asymmetric relationships. With departmentalization, social security laws defined a new social context, and new modes of interaction.[2]

Departmentalization has transformed Martinique from a plantation economy to one heavily subsidized by Paris.[3] Since 1946, the civil rights of Martinique's household workers have been officially recognized by the state. Household workers are protected by the law against such abuses as firing without notice or sexual harassment. Legislation also provides these workers with economic protection should they lose their jobs or become disabled, and calls for employers to pay social security benefits on their behalf.

Yet in urban Martinican society, paternalistic relations toward household workers continue to be common. While the laws limit the possibilities for exploitation in terms of working hours and workplace conditions, and introduce paid fringe benefits, such laws do not change employers' attitudes and patterns of behavior. The macrosystem of capitalist exploitation finds its micro-expression in the domestic unit.[4]

In the employer's household, the household worker is both an insider and an outsider. She is an outsider in that she is not a blood relative; she was not born into the family, and has been incorporated as a teenager or adult. But she is also an insider, especially in upper-class families, in that she plays a key role in nurturing and feeding the family. Over time, the household worker may become closer to the employer's family, and increase the emotional content, both positive and negative, in her relationships with each of her employing household's members. However, in many contemporary households, the relations between the worker and the employing husband and wife remain paternalistic in form. The worker is often reminded subtly that she is a lower-class member of the household.

As a partial insider in her employing household, and a full-time insider in her own, the household worker is a link between the two homes. Her employment experience has an impact on her own family. In cases where the worker lives in, the connection between the two families is complex. For example, if the worker has dependents, and is the only paid worker in her own family, any financial difficulty encountered by her employer will have immediate consequences on her own family. Any interpersonal problems the worker may have with her employers can also have ramifications for her relationships with her own family. In cases where the employee works days and returns home at evening, or works for multiple employers, the relationship between the two households may be more distanced.

Typology of Household Workers

Our focus here is on female household workers in private homes. The Martinique census of 1982 reports a total of 4,934 household workers living and working in the metropolitan area of Fort-de-France. Some 878 were male, and 4,056 female. The census also shows that in the city 11 percent of all working women were household workers, and that 60 percent of the female population was not employed (*Institut National de la Statistique* 1983:104).[5] To understand the work roles these women may play, we begin with a typology of household workers.

First there are young women placed voluntarily or involuntarily in urban homes to cook, clean, and babysit, and who are provided in turn with shelter, room, and board. For the most part, they tend to be orphans or young persons whose parents are too poor to care for them. Interviews with several informants indicate that this pattern is declining. Foster children from lower-class families who are placed in middle- and upper-class homes—unless they are related consanguineally to the household residents—end up doing household work, similar to those young women recruited expressly for this purpose.

Second are the full-time adult household workers, women who are paid for their services. They are told before being hired the tasks and working hours that compromise their jobs. They have freedom to organize their time after work, and may refuse to do additional jobs beyond those specified at the time they are hired. They receive a monthly salary, and the employer pays social security on their behalf.

Third are part-time paid workers, individuals who are hired, for example, for half-days. They do not eat lunch at their employer's house, and the same individual may be engaged by more than one household, and have social security paid by each, or by only one, of their employers. Some of these part-time workers are specialists rather than general household workers.[6] Those who babysit or iron clothes are members of this category. In one case, a woman spent three hours in three different homes during a work day. In other cases, women combined part-time work in private homes with work in private enterprises or the public sector.

In all three categories of household work, the quality of worker-employer relations is affected by length of employment. Usually a household worker who has been working for a family for several years develops close ties to them. She has invested time, and made some commitment to the life of the family. In such cases, when problems arise, both employer and worker build on intentions to work out differences and satisfy each other's expectations. This is the ideal commitment of the colonial period *gouvernante* or *da* household worker toward her *patron*. Such relationships are declining in frequency, however, in contemporary Martinique.

Today relationships are more short-term, often because either worker or employer is not forthcoming about the length of their commitment to the relationship. I found cases, for example, where a household worker takes a job on a temporary basis without informing her employer of her intention. Her level of job commitment is very low, knowing that she is not going to stay for long. There was also a case of a family who hired a household worker for a few weeks, misleadingly stating that they intended this to be a permanent position.

Recruitment Patterns

In bringing together household worker and employer, Martinicans used five methods of recruitment. I discuss each in some detail.

Informal contacts. Some workers are found through a third party, a friend, or an acquaintance. A prospective employer may ask a friend for help, informing him or her that the employer is looking for a household worker. Sometimes the employer may be told of the availability of a worker, or the household worker may be referred to the employer.

It is common that an employer family will help an employee no longer needed to find a new place of work. And if a household worker decides to leave her job, she may introduce a relative to the employer to replace her.

Door-to-door canvassing. Some household workers offer their services door-to-door. This is done frequently in Didier, a neighborhood that still has several *Béké* families, the descendants of French colonists. Getting hired in this way is a matter of presenting oneself at the proper time, when a family is looking for a household worker.

Newspapers. Household workers and employers increasingly use the columns of the newspapers *France-Antilles* and *Von Von* to meet their requirements. Usually those who seek employment in this manner tend to be well-educated, and could easily work in another sector of the economy if jobs were available. During the month of July 1985, there were several young women who looked for a household worker position by placing advertisements in these newspapers. From their descriptions of their qualifications, several were trained as secretaries.

Employment agencies. *Métro* families, migrants from metropolitan France, including civil servants and army personnel, frequently use the Agence Nationale Pour L'Emploi (ANPE) to find household workers. Often these employers are newly arrived, and do not have a network of informal contacts to turn to. Some women who have no direct contact with this section of the employer market find jobs directly through ANPE. This is usually a last resort for the experienced household worker; there are more risks involved as *Métro* employers do not always know the conventions of Martinican society or its employer-household worker codes of relationship.

Countryside visiting. The fifth mode of recruiting a household worker has a long tradition in Martinique. Some employers visit the countryside in search of a household worker. These employers believe that young women from the urban area are more difficult to deal with. Such employers prefer to hire a rural woman because they believe that she is likely to be more modest, less demanding, and more respectful. Even if untrained, she is viewed as being malleable.

Changes in Employer-Household Worker Patterns

Household work has recently gained a new popular image as a legimate endeavor. This evolution of the household worker's status in Martinique can be related to a series of factors, including the restructuring of the economy, protective laws, technological changes, and the attitudes of both employers and household workers toward the job. This evolution is also registered in the common terms by which the worker is referred to. In the predepartment era, Martinicans referred to them as *da* (domestic servant), *bonne* (domestic), or *gouvernante* (live-in maid). Now Martinicans use *femme de ménage, gens de maison,* or *femme de maison* (all translatable as housekeeper). This is understood to be a paid job, based on an informal contract sanctioned by the law.

There has also been an evolution in the employer's needs, and in the kind of work requested from the household worker. This is partly related to technological change. For example, the household worker is no longer requested to wash clothes by hand since the washing machine will do the same amount of work in a shorter period of time. Gas or electric stoves are less demanding than coal or wood-burning stoves. In the past, employees used to work for patrons who lived in their own private home, with large families. Now the employing family tends to be small, and many of them live in apartments.

In historical terms, departmentalization caused an occupational shift in the household worker-employing *Béké* segment of Martinican society. Prior to 1946, these local whites were mostly plantation owners, and each *Béké* family had two or more household employees. With departmentalization, many have shifted to industries and to the import/export sector of the economy. In the process of that change many have sold their large homes in Didier. According to the 1982 census, those still living in Didier now employ no more than one household worker, and occasionally a gardener.

As the number of household workers in *Béké* families has become smaller over the last three decades, new employers have also emerged. Many are members of the new Martinican middle class, individuals who have benefited from the expansion of the Martinican economy, or who lived abroad for a period of time. Many of these families, especially those with young children and a working wife, have hired household workers. These families tend to have a tight budget and they pay their workers less, even if they show more understanding or sensitivity to the worker's plight, than do the rich bourgeois families.[7]

According to my interviews, the employers with whom workers feel most comfortable are the *Métro* families who, given their education and European upbringing, hold liberal and democratic ideas and are less prejudiced toward their employees.[8] For example, the household worker is invited to eat with them, and the female employer may ask the household worker to call her by her first name, thus reducing the distance between them.

There is thus a diversity of employers (local whites, metropolitan whites, and Martinicans) which in part reflects class differences between middle- and upper-class employing families. Diversity is also seen among the household workers. One finds both rural and urban lower class Martinicans, and also foreign immigrants such as St. Lucians, Dominicans, and Haitians.

While the old type of household workers tended to be individuals with little formal education who could not compete well in the labor market for other jobs, the new type is educated. She may have worked in another type of job (secretary, salesclerk); may specialize in one form of household work (babysitting, cooking); and may take the job on a temporary basis.[9] These are individuals who, under other circumstances, would not do such work, and who consider the job a temporary position. These young women dress in such a way so as to convey to the employer that this is a job they accept by necessity, not by choice. They are victims of cyclical constrictions of the labor market.

All employers, old and new, hold a common perception of the evolution of the household worker. For them, before departmentalization the worker was a faithful servant; now she does it primarily for the money, and demands more benefits, such as better living quarters. Employer-worker conflict is no longer a private matter resolved by the employer, but may now involve the courts. As an informant from Didier said, if you fire a household worker without advance notice, "the entire administration would rise against you."

Ecological and Social Stratification

A family home is usually zoned ecologically in terms of the use of each room and its social functions for family members. Where there are live-in workers, the house is further divided into family rooms and the household worker's room. While the family rooms are centrally located in the house and better furnished, the worker's room may be marginal to the rest of the house, near the back door, or in a separate unit in the yard. The space occupied by the household worker has a symbolic value different from that of the rest of the house.

There are many reasons why the household worker occupies a space marginal to the house. First this allows the employers more privacy in movement and in interacting with visitors. It also allows the household worker to have a separate space of her own. One worker said that she was very grateful to her employer for such privacy because she was able to receive her friends and parents and invite her boyfriend for the night. After work, she can leave and return without disturbing the peace of the rest of the house. Another informant was told: "If you want to sleep out, do as you please provided that you do come back by the morning to prepare breakfast for the children." The household worker's room within the house is foreign territory for the rest of the family. It is a space that the members of the family are not expected to use routinely as they do other rooms.

The structure of apartment life, however, does not always allow such spatial separation between workers and employers. When the employing family lives in an apartment, the worker may even use the same bathroom facilities as the rest of the family.

Whether in a house or an apartment, the position of the household worker is also situated in time. She wakes before the other members of the family to prepare breakfast for them. Her entire day is constructed around other people's needs. Her own volition is subordinated so that she can be useful, someone always·ready to receive orders.

The separation of the employing family and the worker is operational in still other ways. The household worker does not eat at the same time and in the same room as the employers. She eats either before or after the rest of the family has completed its meal. Sometimes the worker serves the food and later eats the leftovers. The worker may not get anything if the family likes the meal. An informant recalled, "Once I served or placed everything on the dining table, and they ate it all. I was obliged to go to the shop to get something for myself. I ended up eating two eggs and some bread, because I was too tired to cook for myself."

The inequality of status is also maintained in address. The worker refers to the employers as Mr. X and Mrs. X, while the employer calls the household worker by her first name. Even when a kinship term is used, it reflects condescension and paternalism. It is a way of easing the tension that can develop between the employer and the worker. It may be seen as a mask for exploitation.

Work Tasks and Salary

The work schedule of the household worker can be a point of contention and conflict in the household.[10] Sometimes the work is not precisely defined and the employee is expected to do whatever comes up. In the more traditional form of household work, the worker is called on to do everything. Thus she cooks meals, washes and irons clothes, and takes care of children. Nowadays the work is more often defined in terms of times and content. The worker may be told she is expected to work from 8:00 a.m. to 7:00 p.m., or if it is a part-time job, the precise hours. When the work is so defined, additional tasks are paid for. The worker may do whatever she wants with her time after she has completed the household work.

It is mostly in upper-class families that one finds full-time general household workers. In middle-class homes, specialists tend to work on a part-time basis. Some are hired as cooks, and others as gardeners. Still others are hired to iron clothes once a week, or to babysit a number of hours per day, or a couple of days per week. In any case, paid household workers are hired to work only from Monday through Friday or Saturday noon, following the work schedule of the public and private sectors. Even live-in workers are given free time and are no longer expected to work all day and night as in the colonial period.

The average salary of a household worker is between 1000 and 1500 francs (US$117.65–176.48) per month. In addition, their social security benefits are paid by the employers, and they are entitled to five weeks of vacation per year. If they work full-time, they may also sleep and eat in their workplace. Household workers who do not have a large number of dependents sometimes are able to save money and achieve upward mobility.

Sometimes there are informal monetary arrangements made between employers and employees. There are cases where the employer, instead of paying social security for the worker, pays her in cash half the amount required for social security. Both parties feel they win something in this case—the employer pays less, and the employee gets more cash. The woman who enters such an agreement may already have been covered by her husband's social security. In any case, the state is the loser, and the employer is the winner since she pays less.

Conclusion

To the degree that the household worker participates in her own exploitation by accepting to work in an inferior position in someone else's household, her decision is conditioned by her inability to find a job in another sector of the economy. Few household workers choose this occupation when other work is available. There are forms of labor that place people in a position of inferiority and also make them aware of their status, and household work is one such form of labor.

Household work reduces the official rate of urban unemployment and the pressure on the state to provide jobs to its people. Smith (1973:192) found that, "domestic service operates as an effective mechanism by which the national capital of Lima is able to accommodate at least a part of the flood of migrants to the city from the provincial regions of the country." Household work takes an entire segment of the population out of competition for jobs in the public sector and places them as workers in private homes.

Hiring household workers allows the employing wife to move into the nondomestic work arena. Indirectly, it liberates her from housework duties. At the same time, she may continue to look down on housework and household workers.

While the legislation around such matters as social security, firing without advance notice, and sexual harassment has no doubt provided some protection to household workers and improved their status, both paternalism and exploitation continue in a variety of forms. The socially inferior position of the household worker in the employer's household is spatially, linguistically, and psychologically reinforced.

Household work is a form of socially tolerated exploitation. For the majority of workers, especially those with dependents, household work allows them to remain at a basic subsistence level. Few save any money. Their monthly salary is used to take care of food and shelter. They do not learn skills that could make them competitive in the open job market. As the years go by, they have few alternatives other than to work in more than one home. Whichever way one looks at their situation, household workers are placed in a job structure that reproduces poverty. However, many household workers are determined that through their sacrifices, this poverty will not continue into the next generation, and that their children will not have to experience similar hardships. Some succeed, but others do not.

Notes

This research was carried out from June 25 to August 10, 1985, in three neighborhoods of Fort-de-France, namely Didier, Sainte Thèrése and Volga Plage. I conducted most of the interviews with both the employers and the household workers. A few interviews were also conducted by 11 University of California Research Expeditions Program volunteers who accompanied me in the field. I later rechecked these interviews for accuracy. I am indebted to Roger Sanjek and Shellee Colen for insightful comments and editorial assistance and to Louis Suivant, director of the urban planning agency in Fort-de-France, for logistic support. The research was sponsored by the University Research Expeditions Program and the Committee on Research of the University of California at Berkeley. This essay is an abbreviated version of a chapter from my book, *Urban Poverty in the Caribbean* (1990).

1. Martinique became a Department of France on March 19, 1946. For a historical sketch of the history of Martinique from 1635 to 1946, see Achéen 1983:1815–1835.

2. On the departmentalization question, see the very useful book by Sable 1955.

3. One essay, by Benoist (1968) and another by Petitjean-Roget (1983:1852–1871) place in its ecological context the evolution of the economy of Martinique.

4. The literature on kinship and family organization in the English-speaking islands is reviewed by Smith (1963), and in Haiti by Laguerre (1978). On the lower-class families in Martinique, see Dubreuil (1965), Horowitz (1967) and Slater (1977). On family organization among the *Béké* segment of Martinican society, see Kovats-Beaudoux (1969).

5. The situation here is not too different from that of household workers in the Dominican Republic. Duarte (1976:86) has found that in 1970 there were 31,115 female household workers in Santo Domingo, comprising 12 percent of the population of women in the labor force.

6. For example, while the general household worker is called on to do everything, the specialist is asked either to cook, babysit, iron, clean the house, or take care of the garden. Individual household workers may be hired for each one of these tasks. See also Duarte (1976:92).

7. Similarly, Duarte (1976:95) has found that in Santo Domingo middle-class families are more flexible in regard to their household workers, and sometimes even provide them the opportunity to learn a trade or to attend school.

8. In Malaysia household workers show a similar preference for European employers, and for similar reasons; see Armstrong, this volume.

9. The status of household workers in secondary cities of the Caribbean has evolved more slowly than in the capitals. For example, a study of household workers in Santiago de los Caballeros, Dominican Republic, found that the majority lived in, and made in 1968 an average of 15 pesos per month (Lanz 1969:197–207).

10. For comparative materials on household workers in Haiti, France, Ecuador, and the United States, see Katzman (1978); Martin-Fugier (1979); Nett (1966); Rollins (1985); Salmon (1897); Scott (1939); Taylor (1976); and Vernet (1935).

References Cited

Achéen, René
    1983   Pour une Grammaire de L'Histoire Antillaise: 1635–1946. Les Temps Modernes 39 (441–442) Avril-Mai: 1815–1835.
Benoist, Jean
    1968   Types de Plantations et Groups Sociaux à la Martinique. Montréal: Centre de Recherches Caraibes, Université de Montréal.

Dubreuil, Guy
    1965   La Famille Martiniquaise: Analyse et Dynamique. Anthropologica
    7:103–129.
Duarte, Isis
    1976   Condiciones Sociales del Servicio Domestico en la Republica Dom-
    inicana. Realidad Contemporanea I (3–4) Diciembre: 79–104.
Horowitz, Michael M.
    1967   Morne-Paysan: Peasant Village in Martinique. New York: Holt, Rine-
    hart and Winston.
Katzman, David M.
    1978   Seven Days a Week: Women and Domestic Service in Industrializing
    America. New York: Oxford University Press.
Kovats-Beaudoux, Edith
    1969   Une Minorité Dominante: Les Blancs Créoles de la Martinique. Ph.D.
    dissertation, University of Paris.
Institut National de la Statistique et des Etudes Economiques
    1983   Martinique: Résultat du Recensement de la Population dans les Dé-
    partements D'Outre-Mer, 9 Mars 1982. Aix-en-Provence: Centre National
    Informatique.
Laguerre, Michel S.
    1978   Ticouloute and His Kinsfolk: The Study of a Haitian Extended Fam-
    ily. *In* The Extended Family in Black Societies. Demitri B. Shimkin, Edith
    M. Shimkin, and Dennis A. Frate, eds. Pp. 407–445. The Hague: Mouton.
    1990   Urban Poverty in the Caribbean. New York: St. Martin's Press.
Lanz, Gregorio
    1969   Servicio Domestico: Una Esclavitud? Estudios Sociales II (4) Di-
    ciembre: 197–207.
Martin-Fugier, Anne
    1979   La Place des Bonnes. Paris: Bernard Grasset.
Nett, Emily M.
    1966   The Servant Class in a Developing Country: Ecuador. Journal of In-
    ter-American Studies 8:437–452.
Petitjean-Roget, Bernard
    1983   Pour Comprendre la situation Economique des Antilles. Les Temps
    Modernes 39 (441–442):1852–1871.
Rollins, Judith
    1985   Between Women: Domestics and Their Employers. Philadelphia:
    Temple University Press.
Sable, Victor
    1955   La Transformation des Isles d'Amérique en Départements Français.
    Paris: Editions Larose.
Salmon, Lucy Maynard
    1897   Domestic Service. London: MacMillan Co.
Scott, George T.
    1939   Symposium on Household Employment. New York: Federal Council
    of Churches.
Slater, Mariam K.
    1977   The Caribbean Family: Legitimacy in Martinique. New York: St. Mar-
    tin's.
Smith, Margo L.
    1973   Domestic Service as a Channel of Upward Mobility for the Lower-
    Class Woman: The Lima Case. *In* Female and Male in Latin America. Ann
    Pescatello, ed. Pp. 191–207. Pittsburgh: University of Pittsburgh Press.

Smith, Raymond T.
  1963 Culture and Social Structure in the Caribbean: Some Recent Work on Family and Kinship Studies. Comparative Studies in Society and History 6:24–45.
Taylor, Pam
  1976 Women Domestic Servants 1919–1939. Birmingham: Centre For Contemporary Cultural Studies, University of Birmingham.
Vernet, Elie Louis
  1935 La Domesticité Chez Nous: Question Sociale Haitienne. Port-au-Prince: Imprimerie du Collège Vertières.

Conclusion

10
At Work in Homes II: Directions

Shellee Colen
Roger Sanjek

This volume has focused on household workers, their work, and their relations with employers in a variety of settings. Linked to flows of capital and labor in a global economy, household work reflects and intensifies dominant lines of social differentiation and power in the local societies in which it exists. Several axes of inequality—class, race, ethnicity, age, gender, and migration status—structure recruitment and workplace relations. Hiring a worker to perform household reproductive tasks serves to maintain or advance the class position and lifestyle of employers, but such work also constrains the choices household workers can make about their own household and family relationships. The essays, drawing on several unfamiliar or little-studied cases of household work, expand the terrain for analysis and generalization about the global phenomenon of household work. In this conclusion, we wish to identify several directions for continuing work—theoretical approaches, the household as workplace, household worker careers, and contemporary trends of change.

Three Theoretical Approaches to Household Work

We find household workers around the globe, in the past and present. In calling for more ethnographic and historical study, we see a need to transcend gap-filling, to move beyond discovering patterns of household work in countries and regions as yet ethnographically invisible. Each new study should also be a venture in theory-building and conceptualization. With the harvest of household work studies during the 1980s (see final chapter), the time is ripe for consolidation, comparison, and posing questions for exploration in field and archive. Bringing together the studies in this volume has raised more questions for us than we can answer. It has also reminded us that some approaches are more productive than others.

The first theoretical approach, which we do not favor, is the "modernization" framework that proposes uniform, country-by-country stages of development and change in household work (Boserup 1970; Chaplin 1978; Coser 1973).[1] This scenario usually begins with male household workers, replaced in turn by females as factories and alternative employment appear, and replaced in the end by household workers from "outside," and usually "of color." While this sequence may have occurred historically in parts of Europe and North America, we question its inevitability or naturalness, either there or in other times and places. The historical evidence from Zambia and Ghana in this volume, or from South Africa (Cock 1980), Jamaica (Higman 1983), and Hong Kong (Watson in press) does not fit the modernization scenario. We question the ahistorical notion of comparing local sequences of household work in order to factor out a universal pattern. There is no universal pattern.

The second theoretical approach, which we favor, obviates the first. Here, household work is viewed historically, locally, and contextually within a capitalist world system. Our cases, from Africa, Asia, the Caribbean, and the United States, occur in particular places and moments within this larger picture.[2] As capital grows and recomposes, booms and busts, develops and underdevelops, spurs emigration and immigration, builds cities and depopulates villages, it shapes local demands for labor. These labor demands include not only waged labor in the formal sector, to which much "labor history" is confined, but also waged and unwaged labor in the informal sector. New households form; old households are transformed as external labor allocation calls forth reorganization, and may impose new internal demands for household workers. Wealth in the booming, upswinging centers creates new varieties of household work. Labor in underdeveloped, stalled peripheries holds on to what it can, sometimes including household work in old or novel forms.

"Household work" is not a unitary phenomenon. It is part of many local demands and supplies of labor, here and there, overlapping with yet others. As each local labor market changes, men and women, adults and children, natives and foreigners, and first-class or second-class citizens may each take up household work, or leave it. When local economic conditions are waxing in particular sectors, and demand for certain kinds of waged labor is high (as in Nyishang, Kuala Lumpur, New York City), working conditions improve, or new sources of household workers are tapped, locally or from outside (Cooke; Armstrong; Colen, this volume). When local economic conditions are waning, and demand for waged labor is low (as in Zambia or Martinique), household workers come to potential employers, looking for work (Hansen; Laguerre, this volume).

At the same time, local economic conditions elsewhere may decline or improve, creating new pools of potential household workers ready to migrate, or rendering "traditional" sources of household labor dry. Changes in household composition, gender relations, and the balance between leavers and stayers may follow; elaboration or impoverishment of community social forms may result. The sources of such ups and downs, and the changes in who fills the household worker role, lie not in a "modernization" script, repeated country by country. They lie, rather, in the growth, the uneven development, and the movement of capital on a worldwide scale.

This second approach is most evident in the essays of Sanjek and Colen, our own contributions to the volume.[3] We believe this approach also helps explain the particularities of the growth of household work elsewhere—in Zambia and Nyishang for example, where the standard modernization scenario clearly does not apply. The world economic system approach, we believe, would also illuminate the trajectories of household work in Malaysia and Martinique; Armstrong, indeed, presents striking evidence of the role of international capital and labor flows in shaping household work in Kuala Lumpur. This second approach might again be helpful in understanding the intensification of demand for female household workers in 19th-century Kano, and subsequent decline, although that is not the objective of Mack's paper in this volume.

A third approach, which we also favor, takes the participant's point of view, and examines the conditions of work and recruitment, the costs and benefits of becoming or remaining a household worker, the constraints on leaving the role, and the extra-work social arenas of the workers themselves. This actor-centered approach complements the second. It is most clearly represented in Rollins's paper, but also figures into each of the other essays, notably those of Mack and Colen. In the considerations of "Household as Workplace" and "Household Worker Careers" that follow, we offer points that may further analysis using this third approach.

Household as Workplace

The dichotomy of domestic and public domains elaborated by Rosaldo (1974)—reproductive and productive, female and male, household and workplace—has by now undergone much rethinking and recasting, by Rosaldo herself (1980), as well as many others. All to the good. Yet the significance of household work and workers for these theoretical considerations has not received the attention it deserves (Hansen, this volume). Employer-worker relations are part and parcel of the organization of many households on every continent. They figure into the decision-making, and financial bases, of still other households from which household workers originate, or in which they reside or visit.

What the essays in this collection, and the recent household worker literature, force us to acknowledge is that, worldwide, millions of homes are workplaces, and millions of workplaces are homes.[4] All this interweaves persisting statuses, kinship, and verbal agreement, with social security and immigration legislation, and pervasive capitalist commoditization. Our considerations in this section derive from the question: what are these workplaces like *as workplaces*, rather than as homes.

First, as many point out, they are workplaces marked by isolation from other workers.[5] Few household workers in the cases considered here work in the large servant staffs of Europe past (Coser 1973; Hecht 1956; Luton 1977), or early colonial Zambia (Hansen, this volume). This creates difficulties for organizing household workers as workers.[6] It also gives the worker-employer relationship a personalistic quality that is absent when workers confront bosses as work gangs, unions, or classes.[7]

The physical presence and attitude of the employer is thus central to the calculus of "good" or "bad" working conditions. The relative satisfaction Malaysian household workers enjoy is due in part to the autonomy they experience in running the household—their workplace—while their working-woman employer is out of the house (Armstrong, this volume). Evaluations of the employer are crucial in staying or leaving where household workers can entertain this option.[8] Where they cannot, a demanding, insensitive employer grates on and frustrates the household worker.[9]

Household workers must operate within a different social geography of the home from those who live, not work, there. As several studies show, household workers are restricted in where they may eat, sleep, rest, and use toilet facilities; they may work in some places within the home, but not sit down or even speak there (Hansen; Laguerre; and Rollins, this volume).[10] This geography is also time-linked: there are times when household workers may be in certain spaces within the home, or may eat with household members; and there are other times when they may not.

Demeaning traditional names for the role are resisted nowadays. Latin American household workers prefer *empleada* to *criada, servienta,* or *muchacha* (Bunster and Chaney 1985; Nett 1966; Rubbo and Taussig 1977; Smith 1978). In Martinique, they prefer *femme de maison* to *da* or *gouvernante* (Laguerre, this volume). Malaysian household workers prefer "housekeeper" to *amah* or "servant" (Armstrong, this volume).[11] In contrast, however, in Kano it is "royal slaves" (though no longer slaves in Lovejoy's sense), not masters, who insist on this term and its entitlement to household work; a less "traditional" status would place them outside the palace and its privileges (Mack, this volume).

No matter how old the household worker may be, first names and familiar forms are widely employed to address them (Nett 1966; Rollins 1985)—and made-up first names in South Africa and colonial Zambia at that (Cock 1980; Hansen 1989; van Onselen 1982). "Girl" and "boy" may be terms of reference and address (Cock 1980; Rollins 1985). Distancing terms of address, however—"madam," "Mrs. X," or their equivalents—must be used for the employer.

A household worker, especially one who lives in, is part of the employing household in her or his role as worker. But in spite of any rhetoric of kinship, or terms of address and reference that may mystify the worker-employer relationship, household workers are never really "one of the family" (Childress 1956; Colen 1989). Only rarely are the actual kinship terms used for consanguineal household members employed; few Ghanaian girls, for example, only those who join their mistresses between ages 2 and 8, are referred to and treated as "daughters." An ironic reversal of this occurs in some white families employing African-American and Caribbean women household workers: here the employer's children refer to the worker as "mother," a usage consonant with the role performances involved (Colen 1989; Dill 1980; see also Ruiz 1987). In South Africa and the United States when a household worker is said by the employer to be "one of the family," the manipulative aspect of the statement is not lost upon the employee.[12]

Greater degrees of terminological incorporation, and family-like ideology, appear to be attached to live-in than to live-out work. The Ghanaian and Hong Kong (Watson in press) girls who work in homes throughout their childhoods, and the Kano household workers there for their lifetimes, are most firmly household members. For those women who do household work for limited periods in their late teens and early adulthood, employment is ordinarily live-in, and extra-workplace social life correspondingly restricted.[13]

For other adult women who take on household work as a career, or for an indefinite period, live-in work is resisted and disliked, and only put up with when it is the best alternative available. These women prefer to live in their own homes in which they may nurture their own families.[14] Only in Kuala Lumpur, where household workers have more of a sellers' market for their labor, and working (and living) conditions are better than most other cases, do long-term household workers prefer live-in employment. Both our examples of male household workers also involve live-in arrangements (Cooke and Hansen, this volume).[15]

Whether live-in, or live-out, household work polarizes households in each society where it is found. Some supply household workers, and others employ them (Rubbo and Taussig 1977). For live-in, older women household workers, their job totally restructures their own reproductive activities with respect to their children, husband, and kin. Visits may be short, and ill-timed; physical and psychic energy may be spent on the employer's household, and the child-care responsibilities located there (Preston-Whyte 1978). Reproductive work at home also may be a live-out worker's full responsibility, and several studies deal with this domestic side of the household worker's life.[16] For undocumented West Indian women in New York and Canada, newly arrived and separated from their families, the hope of reconstituting their households motivates them to do household work for others (Colen, this volume; Silvera 1983).

Unlike concubines (Mack, this volume; Watson in press), female household workers do not provide sexual services as part of their role. Yet, in most if not all places studied, sexual advances from males, harassment, and rape, occur in some household workplaces, and this threat or danger is widely appreciated by women household workers.[17] Male household workers in turn-of-the-century South Africa also faced advances from women employers, or accusations of making advances toward them (van Onselen 1982).

A second aspect of sexuality linked to asymmetrical power relations is the limits employers attempt to place on the sexual and intimate relations household workers choose for themselves (Brandewie 1973; Bunster and Chaney 1985). Sanjek (this volume) raises this issue for Ghanaian teenage household workers. For adult women in live-in employment, both the day off and control of one's live-in room are points of contention with employers (Laguerre, this volume).[18]

Payment for household work, beyond room and board, may go to the parents of girl workers (Sanjek, this volume; Watson in press), or to the worker herself or himself. Wages usually are very low compared to other available work; Malaysia is again the exception (Armstrong, this volume). Employers often justify low wages by their culturally ingrained views of both the occupation and the social backgrounds of household workers, and by their self-serving character assessments of individual employees. Further, they place value on the "gifts" they bestow—typically cast-off clothing or unwanted household goods, often equally unwanted by the recipients.[19] Finally, theft by household workers is often suspected. Silverware, penny jars, and liquor bottle levels are watched assiduously; accusations, like those of witchcraft, are made when a deeper social crisis in the employer-employee relationship is ready to burst.[20] Some household workers, no doubt, do steal, with a sense of Robin Hood justice observers might judge understandable (Cooke, this volume).

Most worker-employer relations in the formal sector are today penetrated by state regulation; indeed, that is what makes such work "formal." Household work, in most settings, remains informal, with terms and conditions negotiated by each worker and employer, orally more often than on paper, with little legal force attached to such contracts. Household workers, United States government statistics show, collectively work below the minimum wage (Rollins, this volume), a situation of socially dispersed employer lawlessness. In the United States, Martinique, and Peru, social security benefits are attached to household employment, but depend upon employer contributions that often go unpaid, frequently with the consent of the worker.[21] Ominously, Colen (1986, this volume) shows that immigration legislation, in the context of the present United States demand for household workers, operates to ensure a buyers' market (compare Silvera 1983 for Canada). These aspects of state legal structures, like pass laws in South Africa (Cock 1980, 1981; Preston-Whyte 1978), affect the conditions, supply, and individual experience of household workers in the modern world.

Household Worker Careers

As we have seen, some enter household work during their childhoods, others for a short stint in early adulthood, others for varying periods as adults, and still others as long-term occupation. While workers hold task and working condition preferences, there is no career mobility ladder in household work, no expectable promotion to higher positions. Despite recommendations (Spofford 1977[1881]) and attempts (Palmer 1984) to professionalize household work in the United States, or elsewhere, little headway has been made. There remain many questions about household work as career that we hope others will address in historical and ethnographic research.

We know little in a systematic sense about recruitment to household work. The kinship ties between household workers used to locate and fill job openings among African-American women in Washington, DC (Clark-Lewis 1985, 1987), are no doubt typical of many other settings. Katzman (1978) provides information on agencies and advertising in the 19th-century United States, and Laguerre (this volume) in contemporary Martinique; Okediji (1981) on recruiting and training networks in Nigeria; and Tellis-Nayak (1983) on the role in India of Roman Catholic nuns in directing young female household workers to middle-class homes. More case-based portrayals are needed for comparison of how children, women, and men seek and find household work, or how employers seek and find household workers.[22]

Similarly, broader quantitative assessments of the ages at which household workers enter and leave live-in, live-out, or day work employment would be useful. There are problems, however, in using census occupational categories, and problems of undercounting. Yet research in this area is needed for wider comparisons of the place household workers occupy in labor markets, and in the life career pathways of the social groups from which they are recruited.

While we believe that household work is, in essence, a dead-end job, there is evidence in the literature that for those who take it on as a long-term occupation, there is some inward, if not upward, mobility. We refer to the shifting of jobs that such workers may use to improve their working conditions and pay.[23] Workers search for employers who provide the combination of pay, respect, autonomy, work pacing, tasks, sick days, and leave for family concerns that make one workplace better than others. Some of this involves a subtle training of the employer by the worker, a testing and response that may result in heightened workplace commitment. "People managing" is an underappreciated aspect of household work in most settings.

Household work is not monolithic—scrubbing floors or ironing are different from child care. There are hierarchies of tasks, variable culturally and from person to person, involved in assessing household work by workers. Child care rates above house cleaning for West Indian women in New York City (Colen 1986, this volume); and live-out laundering above live-in maid-of-all-work employment for Peruvian women in Lima, or African-American women in the early 20th-century United States (Bunster and Chaney 1985; Katzman 1978). What a household worker will and will not do; what tasks are added on after employment begins; what standards of acceptable work are imposed or changed by each employer—all are present in the logics of workplace evaluation used by household workers.[24]

"Casualization," the processes of dividing household work into separate jobs by the employer, and of multiple day or half-day employment for the worker, is changing household work careers in the

United States, Latin America, Martinique, and Hong Kong.[25] How does this process translate into control of the labor process by the worker, and by the employer? How is this in turn affected by the local demand and supply of household labor? What does casualization imply for commercialization through subcontracting agencies, and for employer-worker relations? What will be the longer term implications of casualization for attempts to organize household workers, and to bargain for better working conditions with state regulators and legislators?

Finally, there are questions about the relationship of household work employment and careers to the workers' broader social goals. We agree that the achievement of social mobility through household work,[26] and the desire for it engendered by work in homes,[27] have both been exaggerated. This latter aspect of household work may be most important for the teenage and young adult women for whom household work, urban migration, and widened worlds are intertwined. Yet similar desires mark young urban arrivals who work in factories, workshops, and market commerce.

Long-term household workers may have more mundane goals: survival where the job market and their educational backgrounds offer few alternatives; and upward mobility for their children, whose education depends upon their parent's labor.[28] This is probably especially so for women of color in the United States, where opportunities to move from household work into better paid, higher status occupations have been minimal until recently.[29]

Trends in Household Work

What are the global trends in household work? Are numbers of household workers increasing? How are the tasks and conditions of work in homes changing?

Several scholars assert that numbers of household workers are increasing in many countries.[30] Sanjek's figures for Ghana between 1960 and 1970 (this volume), and Robertson's (1984:79) for Accra in the 1970s, lend support to this argument for one African nation, but also demonstrate the difficult nature of assessing the evidence. In the Third World the numbers of household workers may be rising while the very conditions of work deteriorate, as in Zambia. Research, as we have noted, is needed at all levels on the social scale where household workers are employed, at the top (Armstrong, this volume) as well as the middle and bottom (Sanjek, this volume).

Commoditization of reproductive labor, including care of children and the frail elderly, is today occurring in a context of changing labor force composition, and changing household and family experiences. Sassen-Koob (1981, 1984), using a variety of data, argues that the gentrification of New York City in the 1980s produces its own increasing demand for household workers and other low-waged service labor. Colen shows what this means in practice (1986, 1989, this volume).

The forms of household work are changing, and several forms may coexist. An upper middle-class New York City household in 1990, for example, may employ a child care worker from 8 a.m. to 7 p.m., five days a week; this worker may also do grocery shopping and local errands. Another household worker will be hired one day a week to do housecleaning and laundry. The household also will pay a commercial cleaning service to wash windows and polish floors monthly.

With growing numbers of elderly persons receiving varieties of home care, the expansion of in-home services to families in distress, and the dehospitalization of patients under current U.S. cost-containing health-care regulations, more and more women (and mainly women) find themselves at work in homes (Colen, this volume; Dinkins 1988). They provide personal care—bathing, feeding, body work, companionship—as well as shopping, cooking, and "light housekeeping" (Rollins 1985; Silvera 1983). There is today in the United States a continuum that includes child-care workers, house cleaners, home health-care workers, and other household workers.

This volume has presented studies of household workers around the globe. It reminds us that certain elements of household labor are salient despite differences of culture, geography, and ongoing transformations. Household work always occurs within a global political economy that structures many of its features. Differences of class, race, ethnicity, gender, age, and migration status are translated into hierarchical relations within this context, and they are reinforced by the social relations of household work. States may act to ensure supplies of workers, and protect some while disadvantaging others. Household work provides choices to employers, who maintain position and lifestyle with the paid labor of household workers, but its cost is often the restriction of life choices to those who do this work. We hope this volume will be read by scholars, household worker organizers, employers and workers themselves, and their family members and friends. Activism, worker organizing, new social policy, education, consciousness-raising, and improved pay and working conditions are all required to promote social justice for those at work in homes.

Coda

A particularly poignant recent press account brings together the connections between household work, international inequalities, migration, class, and wartime displacement in the contemporary world.

Americans Find the Good Life in Guatemala

ANTIGUA, Guatemala—The attractions are obvious in this picturesque colonial town. Spanish-style mansions, with two acres of gardens and pools, can go for the equivalent of $20,000. Live-in servants are paid about $40 a month. And two-bedroom garden apartments rent for $33 a week.

The lure of life is so strong, that many Americans have foregone suburbia, big-city living or retirement in California and Florida to settle in what has become one of Latin America's strongest American communities. . . .

"One of the benefits you can't deny is the servant help. What we pay in a month here you would pay in one day or a week in the States." . . .

Antigua in the early 1980s had only a handful of Americans. . . . Violence under military rule was on the rise, Guatemalans were disappearing, and business was drying up.

Such violence left as many as 100,000 people killed, and more than 440 villages destroyed. . . .

The contrast between the lives of the Americans and the Guatemalans is striking.

Many Guatemalans live in wooden huts in the mountains without running water or enough food. Many Americans live in mansions that used to house five or six Guatemalan families. . . .

Many Guatemalans say that while they appreciate the jobs Americans provide, they resent their control of local industries and their comfortable style of life that is beyond what Guatemalans can afford. . . .

"Most Americans live here because they want slaves," said one foreigner who has lived in Antigua for several years. "You thought slavery ended? It hasn't." . . .

At the same time, another American . . . said, "I've had rich Guatemalans tell us that our living quarters were too good for the servants and that we were ruining them." [Nix 1987]

Notes

1. References to all works cited in this conclusion are found following the final essay, "Household Workers in World Perspective."

2. We have come across no studies of household workers in the socialist societies of the Soviet Union, Eastern Europe, the Peoples Republic of China, or Cuba.

3. See also Cock (1980, 1981), Gaitskell et al. (1984), Jelin (1977), Luton (1977), and Rubbo and Taussig (1977).

4. We note also the resurgence of home-as-workplace in the return of light industrial homework, and in computer-based homework, in both of which women predominate, and in home-managed businesses of many sorts.

5. See Bunster and Chaney (1985), Mohammed (1983), Rollins (1985), and van Onselen (1982).

6. Chaney and Garcia Castro (1989), Cock (1980), Gaitskell et al. (1984), Hansen (1986b), Palmer (1984, 1987).

7. Cock (1980), Rollins (1985, this volume), Romero (1987, 1988), Silvera (1983), Smith (1978).

8. Colen (1986, 1989), Glenn (1986), Rollins (1985), Romero (1987, 1988).

9. Cock (1980), Colen (1986, 1989, this volume), Silvera (1983).

10. See also, Graham (1988), Hansen (1989), Tellis-Nayak (1983).

11. By the 1880s, "servant" had acquired a derogatory connotation in the United States (Spofford 1977 [1881]).

12. See Childress (1956), Cock (1980, 1981), Colen (1986, 1989), Glenn (1986).

13. Brandewie (1973), Bunster and Chaney (1985), Glenn (1986), Katzman (1978), Luton (1977), Palabrica-Costello (1984), Riegelhaupt (1967), Rubbo and Taussig (1977), Smith (1973, 1978), Tellis-Nayak (1983).

14. See Bunster and Chaney (1985), Clark-Lewis (1985, 1987), Cock (1980), Colen (1986, 1989, this volume), Glenn (1986), Marshall (1959), Preston-Whyte (1978), Rollins (1985), Romero (1987, 1988), Silvera (1983).

15. Bits and pieces are found in the literature about male household workers in Italy, colonial Hong Kong, Lagos, Lima, and for Chinese and Japanese men, the United States (Bunster and Chaney 1985; Glenn 1986; Luton 1977; Okediji 1978; Sankar 1977; Spofford 1977 [1881]). A sustained comparative discussion, taking into account the work of Bujra, Hansen, and van Onselen will not be attempted here.

16. See Bunster and Chaney (1985), Cock (1980), Dill (1980), Glenn (1986), Graham (1988).

17. See Brandewie (1973), Bunster and Chaney (1985), Clark-Lewis (1985), Cock (1980), Hansen (1989), Rollins (1985), Rubbo and Taussig (1977), Ruiz (1987), Silvera (1983), Smith (1973), Watson (in press).

18. See also Colen (1986), Katzman (1978), Palmer (1987), Silvera (1983).

19. Brandewie (1973), Cock (1980), Cooke (this volume), Coser (1973), Rollins (1985), Romero (1987), Silvera (1983), Tellis-Nayak (1983), van Onselen (1982).

20. Brandewie (1973), Cock (1980, 1981), Colen (1986), Graham (1988), Hansen (this volume), Mohammed (1983), Spofford (1977 [1881]).

21. See Bunster and Chaney (1985), Laguerre (this volume), Rollins (1985, this volume), Ruiz (1987).

22. See also Brandewie (1973), Bunster and Chaney (1985), Glenn (1986), Ruiz (1987).

23. Armstrong (this volume), Clark-Lewis (1987), Cock (1980), Colen (1986, this volume), Glenn (1986), Rollins (1985), Romero (1987, 1988), Silvera (1983), Smith (1973).

24. Cock (1980), Colen (1986, this volume), Glenn (1986), Rollins (1985), Silvera (1983).

25. For examples, see Chaney and Castro (1989), Glenn (1986), Laguerre (this volume), Rollins (1985), Romero (1987, 1988), Salaff (1981), Sankar (1977). Casualization of the live-out, multiple employer variety seems to mark laundering in many places (Atkins 1986; Brandewie 1973; Katzman 1978; van Onselen 1982), with commercial laundries later competing with and displacing individual launderers in South Africa and the United States.

26. Bunster and Chaney (1985), Jelin (1977), Smith (1973, 1978).

27. Brandewie (1973), Nett (1966), Rubbo and Taussig (1977), Tellis-Nayak (1983).

28. Cock (1980), Colen (1986, this volume), Dill (1979), Glenn (1986), Hansen (1986b, 1989), Laguerre (this volume), Marshall (1959), Rollins (1985), Preston-Whyte (1978), Silvera (1983), van Onselen (1982).

29. Dill (1980), Glenn (1986), Romero (1987, 1988).

30. Bunster and Chaney (1985), Hansen (1989), Rollins (this volume); but see Cock (1981) on declining numbers in South Africa.

11

Household Workers in World Perspective

Roger Sanjek
Shellee Colen

In this final essay, we provide a brief review of the literature on household workers since the late 1960s. This body of work, including more than a dozen books published during the 1980s,[1] arose from both scholarly and political commitments. It emerged, as did much critical reassessment of race, class, and gender, from the practice and theory of the social movements of the 1950s, 1960s, and 1970s. Three tributaries were of particular importance in feeding the stream of household worker studies in the past two decades.

Racial and Ethnic Studies. Race and ethnicity are primary factors determining recruitment to household work in the United States, and social movements concerned with these dimensions of inequality have stimulated several investigations of work in homes. Prompted by the Civil Rights movement, one current of scholarship on household work has addressed persisting racial inequality, and reclaimed episodes of African-American and other ethnic histories (Clark-Lewis 1985, 1987; Dill 1979, 1980, 1988; Glenn 1986; Hamburger 1977, 1978; Harris 1982; Katzman 1978; Palmer 1984; Rollins 1985; Romero 1987, 1988). Similar conditions in South Africa underpin the study of household workers there (Atkins 1986; Cook 1980, 1981; Gaitskell et al. 1984; van Onselen 1982).

Feminism. In the early 1970s, political and scholarly feminist attention focused on household reproductive labor in general, but rarely addressed *paid* reproductive labor by nonhousehold members (e.g., Benston 1971; Dalla Costa and James 1972; Gardiner 1975; Oakley 1974a, 1974b; Prescod-Roberts and Steele 1980). As the scope of attention to household labor widened, feminists came to see that household work has been a major form of women's paid employment in the West for two centuries, and remains so in many areas around the world. By the 1980s, a global feminist perspective had inspired many studies of

paid household work in Africa, Asia, Latin America, and the Caribbean (Bunster and Chaney 1985; Chaney and Garcia Castro 1989; Cock
1980, 1981; Colen 1986, 1989; Gaitskill et al. 1984; Goldsmith n.d.; Mohammed 1983; Sankar 1977; Silvera 1983).

Social History. The "bottom up" social history of Hobsbawm,
Thompson, and Gutman emerging in the 1960s also stimulated research on household workers. Local history, and studies of laboring
classes and communities, provide the matrix in which the lives of
household workers are studied by Graham (1988), Hansen (1989), and
van Onselen (1982), who well represent this tradition.

Just as people of color, women, and working classes are no longer
"hidden from history," workers in homes are no longer "part of the
household inventory." The essays in this collection are part of a recent
efflorescence of studies of household workers by anthropologists, historians, and sociologists. While some recent work draws upon the historical and worldwide scope of this literature (e.g., Rollins 1985; Hansen 1986a, 1989), most scholarship has developed within national and
regional research agendas. The United States, Europe, and Latin
America are better represented in this work than are Africa and Asia,
but research is growing in all world areas.

In the United States household work and its discontents stimulated a vast popular and applied research literature in the 19th- and
20th-century United States (and a new popular literature, from the employer's perspective, in the 1980s; see Hansen 1989). On the popular
side, Spofford (1977[1881]), written from the female employer's point
of view, reveals much of the organization and labor relations of household work at a time when Irish women had replaced northern European Protestant immigrants, and reform and new sources of workers
(Chinese male household workers in California, for example) were
topics in the air. Salmon (1972[1897]) is a landmark in the applied, re-
formist tradition; data from surveys of 1000 Vassar alumnae employers
and from more than 700 household workers was accompanied by historical and economic background material in order to stimulate discussion and eventual reform.

A variety of studies have probed the history and transformations
of household work in the United States. Dudden (1983) focuses on the
19th-century shift in household work from the native-born rural
"help" or "hired girl" to the immigrant woman "domestic servant."
As this transition occurred, at varied tempos in different cities, household work became more "demanding and demeaning" (Dudden
1983:7), and less preferable than the alternative work opportunities
outside homes provided by an evolving industrial capitalism. Sutherland (1981) analyzes 19th-century household work as well. Katzman

(1978) traces the 19th-century development of live-in household work, linked to an expanding urban middle class, through its 20th-century succession into live-out household work for a single employer, and then day work for multiple employers. He focuses not only on the changing nature and social relations of household work, but also on the movements in and out of the occupation of white native-born women; Irish, German, Scandinavian, and other immigrant women; Chinese men; and African-American women. Palmer (1987) surveys attempts at organizing and writing worker-employee contracts for household work during the 1930s.

Katzman pays close attention to the involvement of African-American women in household work from slavery through emancipation in the South, and their movement into work in middle Atlantic and northeastern homes as they migrated north, from Reconstruction through the Great Migration of the 1910s and 1920s. Clark-Lewis (1985, 1987) portrays the experience of two dozen African-American women who made this south-north migration for household work in Washington, DC. She highlights their strong preference for live-out work, the norm by the 1920s; tellingly, live-in employment was referred to as "working out" in the African-American community. Opportunities for employment other than household work were severely limited for African-American women, as they were for those immigrant West Indian women who first arrived in significant numbers of U.S. cities after World War I (Reid 1939). In the 1930s, both groups of Black women found themselves seeking day work in the Depression-era "slave markets" of Brooklyn and the Bronx (Connolly 1977:116–117; Lerner 1972:229–231; Marshall 1983:4).

Palmer (1984) traces organizational and technical aspects of the changing condition of African-American women household workers. Dill (1979, 1980, 1988) has studied the household work experience of African-American women in two northern cities, revealing the texture of their relations with adults and children in both their own and their workplace homes. Rollins (1985, this volume) focuses on the complex relationships of African-American household workers and their white employers in the Boston area. Coley's dissertation (1981) presents additional data on African-American household workers.

In recent decades, the numbers of African-American women in household work have dropped nationwide as other jobs became available. For example, in Brooklyn "[i]n 1940 nearly two-thirds of employed black women worked as domestics. . . . one-third in 1950 . . . one-fifth in 1960 . . . less than one in ten by 1970" (Connolly 1977:186–187). Yet, in 1970, African-American women still accounted for half of all private household workers, while constituting only 11 percent of the female paid labor force (Almquist 1979:53).

Some white American women continue to fill the other half of household worker ranks, but several studies point to the crucial role race and migration play in the recruitment of household workers in the United States. Glenn (1986) covers the 20th-century history and circumstances of Japanese immigrant and Japanese-American women household workers in the San Francisco Bay area. Romero (1987, 1988) has studied Chicana day household workers in Denver, covering both their work and home lives. Ruiz (1987) sketches the situation of El Paso Mexican and Mexican-American household workers, and the role of immigration policy in this subminimum wage border city.

In the past two decades, increasing numbers of Caribbean immigrant women have come to North America and found employment as household and child care workers. Colen (1986, 1989, this volume), documents West Indian women's confrontation with legal immigration procedure, and their experiences at work and with their own and their employers' families. Clarke's novel, *The Meeting Point* (1967), the first of a trilogy, focuses on the life of a Barbadian live-in household worker in Toronto. Silvera (1983) presents oral histories of West Indian household workers in Canada, while Henry (1968) discusses the Canadian "domestic scheme" that brought them there.

Silvera's book is complemented by several insiders' accounts of household work in the United States. A short story by Yezierska (1979) gives us a turn-of-the-century view of household work for an Eastern European Jewish immigrant woman. The household work experience of African-American women is represented in many novels, stories, and memoirs. Childress's *Like One of the Family* (1956) presents a biting vision of household work from a worker's perspective. Morrison, in several novels, especially *The Bluest Eye* (1970), offers searing images of work in homes. Marshall (1959, 1983) gives us glimpses of West Indian household workers in New York from the 1930s to the 1950s. Harris in *From Mammies to Militants* (1982) provides a comprehensive montage of images of household workers in novels by African Americans.

The history of household work in England and France, from the 18th century on, has been well studied in recent decades. Maza (1983) outlines the changing relations between household workers and their employers in 18th-century France as the bourgeoisie replaced the aristocracy as the primary employing class, household work became feminized, households became more spatially segregated, and ideologies of family privacy developed. Fairchilds (1984) complements Maza, discussing forms of household work—including the taking on of "poor relations"—and the movement from patriarchal, paternalistic relations to waged household work by the end of the century. Hecht (1956), Horn (1975), and McBride (1976) cover similar terrain for England, together tracing the movement from large staffs of servants in the 18th century, to employment in Victorian middle-class households. Several historians have studied ideologies of gender and household work in Victorian England (Davidoff 1974, 1979; Gillis 1979).

For anthropologists and sociologists, the perspective of Scott and Tilly (1975) on 19th-century European household economies and opportunities for daughters' employment as household workers or factory workers has been influential (e.g., Lamphere 1987; Salaff 1981). In northern Europe the likelihood of household work during the early phases of a woman's life cycle has declined drastically over the last 150 years. "[I]n 1851, 905,000 women in Britain were employed as domestic servants, plus 128,000 servant girls on farms; by the 1961 Census, there were no more than 103,000" (Goody 1982:163). In southern Europe, a period of household work remained the norm among poor rural families until more recently (Luton 1977; Riegelhaupt 1967), but by the 1970s, Luton could report that Calabrian "[u]pper middle class women continually complain about their inability to find decent domestic help 'these days' " (1977:80).

Beginning with Nett's (1966) paper on Ecuador, the literature on household workers in Latin America has focused on the institution as an instrument of national and interclass integration, as well as on other issues (Goldsmith n.d.; Jelin 1977; Rubbo and Taussig 1977; Smith 1973, 1978). Bunster and Chaney (1985), documenting household work in Lima, Peru, offer the fullest study of household workers in Latin America. The introduction and papers in Chaney and Garcia Castro's collection (1989) provide coverage of household work for contemporary Latin America and the Caribbean unparalleled by the literature for any other continent. An historical study of the household work labor force in Rio de Janeiro, Brazil, from 1860 to 1910, depicts indoor and outdoor work assignments, and the increasing prevalence of live-out employment as free women replaced enslaved women in the occupation (Graham 1988).

Higman (1983) has traced household work in Jamaica from 1750, finding that models of household work in England and North America do not fit this Caribbean case. Mohammed (1983) summarizes current conditions of household workers in the Caribbean with a focus on legislative developments, and a concern for improved work conditions. Members of Sistren, a Jamaican women's theater collective, have written (in Patois) and performed the play, *Domesticks*, and published essays and articles on Jamaican household workers (Sistren and Ford-

Smith 1987; Sistren 1988). Laguerre's paper (this volume) on Martinique, adds to the picture in the Caribbean.

For Africa, much research remains to be done. Young female
household workers are ubiquitous in west African cities, and Okediji's
misleadingly titled paper (1978) is a fascinating study of the recruitment and training networks that bring these household workers to urban employment in Lagos, Nigeria. Sanjek (this volume) discusses
fostered child household workers in a Ghanaian urban neighborhood,
and appraises the relevant literature for that country. The allocation of
household work in relation to varieties of female servitude and freedom for the traditional northern Nigerian elite is analyzed by Mack
(this volume).

The household work picture for southern Africa is much clearer.
Hansen, in a series of publications (1986a, 1986b, 1989, this volume),
details the past and present of household work in Zambia, where
adult men are the typical role incumbents. Bujra (n.d.) provides com-
plementary coverage for neighboring Tanzania. For South Africa, regional differences, historical trajectories, gender and race shifts, and
current tragedies are all given due in the rich literature now available
(Atkins 1986; Cock 1980, 1981; Gaitskell et al. 1984; Preston-Whyte
1978; van Onselen 1982). Cock's major book (1980), combining thorough ethnography, a full history of household work in the Eastern
Cape, and analysis of exploitation under apartheid, is especially noteworthy, as are van Onselen's historical studies (1982) of turn-of-the-
century male household workers and washermen in Johannesburg.

The literature for Asia is most meager of all, though we suspect
that a thorough combing and commissioning, as Chaney and Garcia
Castro have done for Latin America and the Caribbean, could produce
handsome results. Three studies cover urban and rural Hong Kong
(Salaff 1981; Sankar 1977; Watson in press), together providing a view
from the mid-1800s through the contemporary period. Brandewie
(1973) for the Philippines, and Tellis-Nayak (1983) for India, hint at
regional variations beyond the Bisayan and Kerala Christian specific-
ities they depict (see also Ramu's comment in Tellis-Nayak 1983;
Mehta 1960, cited in Rollins 1985; Palabrica-Costello 1984). Finally,
Armstrong (this volume) provides a detailed account of household
work in Kuala Lumpur, Malaysia; and Cooke (this volume) charts the
emergence of new patterns of male household work, where one might
least expect to find it, in rural Nepal.

Notes

1. Three additional books that came to our attention after completing this
essay are Palmer (1989), Tucker (1989), and Van Raaphorst (1988).

References Cited

Almquist, Elizabeth McTaggart
  1979 Minorities, Gender, and Work. Lexington, MA: Lexington Books.
Atkins, Keletso
  1986 Origins of the AmaWasha: the Zulu Washerman's Guild in Natal, 1850–1910. Journal of African History 27:41–57.
Banton, Michael
  1983 Racial and Ethnic Competition. Cambridge: Cambridge University Press.
Benston, Margaret
  1971 The Political Economy of Women's Liberation. *In* Roles Women Play: Readings Toward Women's Liberation. Michele Hoffnung Garskof, ed. Pp. 194–205. Belmont, CA: Brooks/Cole Publishing Company.
Berk, Sarah Fenstermaker, ed.
  1980 Women and Household Labor. Beverly Hills: Sage.
Boserup, Ester
  1970 Woman's Role in Economic Development. New York: St. Martin's Press.
Brandewie, Ernest
  1973 Maids in Cebuano Society. Philippine Quarterly of Culture and Society 1:209–219.
Bujra, Janet
  n.d. Men at Work in the Tanzanian Home: How Did They Ever Learn? (Manuscript, files of the author.)
Bunster, Ximena, and Elsa M. Chaney
  1985 Sellers and Servants: Working Women in Lima, Peru. New York: Praeger.
Chaney, Elsa M., and Maria Garcia Castro, eds.
  1989 Muchachas No More: Household Workers in Latin America and the Caribbean. Philadelphia: Temple University Press.
Chaplin, David
  1978 Domestic Service and Industrialization. Comparative Studies in Sociology 1:97–127.
Childress, Alice
  1956 Like One of the Family. Brooklyn: Independence Publishers.
Clarke, Austin C.
  1967 The Meeting Point. Toronto: Macmillan of Canada.
Clark-Lewis, Elizabeth
  1985 "This Work Had a' End": The Transition from Live-In to Day Work. Working Paper 2. Memphis: Center for Research on Women, Memphis State University.
  1987 "This Work Had a' End": African-American Domestic Workers in Washington, D.C., 1910–1940. *In* "To Toil the Livelong Day": America's Women at Work, 1780–1980. Carol Groneman and Mary Beth Norton, eds. Pp. 196–212. Ithaca: Cornell University Press.
Cock, Jacklyn
  1980 Maids and Madams: A Study in the Politics of Exploitation. Johannesburg: Ravan Press.
  1981 Disposable Nannies: Domestic Servants in the Political Economy of South Africa. Review of African Political Economy 21:63–83.

Colen, Shellee
    1986   "With Respect and Feelings": Voices of West Indian Child Care and
           Domestic Workers in New York City. *In* All American Women: Lines That
           Divide, Ties That Bind. Johnetta Cole, ed. Pp. 46–70. New York: Free
           Press.
    1989   "Just a Little Respect": West Indian Domestic Workers in New York
           City. *In* Muchachas No More: Household Workers in Latin America and
           the Caribbean, Elsa M. Chaney and Maria Garcia Castro, eds. Pp. 171–
           194. Philadelphia: Temple University Press.
Coley, Soroya Moore
    1981   And Still I Rise: An Exploratory Study of Contemporary Private Black
           Household Workers. Ph.D. dissertation. Bryn Mawr College.
Connolly, Harold X.
    1977   A Ghetto Grows in Brooklyn. New York: New York University Press.
Coser, Lewis
    1973   Servants: The Obsolescence of an Occupational Role. Social Forces
           52:31–40.
Dalla Costa, Mariarosa, and Selma James
    1972   The Power of Women and the Subversion of the Community. Bristol,
           England: Falling Wall Press.
Davidoff, Lenore
    1974   Mastered for Life: Servant and Wife in Victorian England. Journal of
           Social History 7:406–429.
    1979   Class and Gender in Victorian England: The Diaries of Arthur J.
           Munby and Hannah Cullwick. Feminist Studies 1:87–141.
Davis, Angela
    1971   Women, Race, and Class. New York: Vintage.
Dill, Bonnie Thornton
    1979   Across the Boundaries of Race and Class: An Exploration of the Re-
           lationship between Work and Family among Black Female Domestic Ser-
           vants. Ph.D. dissertation. New York University.
    1980   The Means to Put My Children through: Child-rearing Goals and
           Strategies among Black Female Domestic Servants. *In* The Black Woman.
           LaFrances Rodgers-Rose, ed. Pp. 107–123. Beverly Hills: Sage.
    1988   "Making Your Job Good Yourself": Domestic Service and the Con-
           struction of Personal Dignity. *In* Women and the Politics of Empower-
           ment. Ann Bookman and Sandra Morgen, eds. Pp. 33–52. Philadelphia:
           Temple University Press.
Dinkins, David
    1988   Plight of the Home Care Worker: Report of the Manhattan Borough
           President's Hearing on April 29, 1987. New York: Manhattan Borough
           President's Office.
Dudden, Faye
    1983   Serving Women: Household Service in Nineteenth Century America.
           Middleton, CT: Wesleyan University Press.
Edholm, Felicity, Olivia Harris, and Kate Young
    1977   Conceptualising Women. Critique of Anthropology 9–10:101–130.
Fairchilds, Cissie
    1984   Domestic Enemies: Servants and Their Masters in Old Regime
           France. Baltimore: Johns Hopkins University Press.

Gaitskell, Deborah, Judy Kimble, Moira Maconachie, and Elaine Unterhalter
1984   Class, Race and Gender: Domestic Workers in South Africa. Review of African Political Economy 27/28:86–108.

Gardiner, Jean
1975   Women's Domestic Labor. New Left Review 89:47–71.

Gillis, John
1979   Servants, Sexual Relations, and the Risks of Illegitimacy in London, 1801–1900. Feminist Studies 5:142–173.

Glenn, Evelyn Nakano
1986   Issei, Nisei, War Bride: Three Generations of Japanese American Women in Domestic Service. Philadelphia: Temple University Press.

Goffman, Erving
1963   Stigma: Notes on the Management of Spoiled Identity. Engelwood Cliffs, NJ: Prentice-Hall.

Goldsmith, Mary
n.d.   Paid Domestic Labor in Mexico. New York: Women's International Resource Exchange.

Goody, Jack
1982   Cooking, Cuisine and Class: A Study in Comparative Sociology. Cambridge: Cambridge University Press.

Graham, Susan Lauderdale
1988   House and Street: The Domestic World of Servants and Masters in Nineteenth-Century Rio de Janeiro. Cambridge: Cambridge University Press.

Hamburger, Robert
1977   A Stranger in the House. Southern Exposure 5(1):22–31.
1978   A Stranger in the House. New York: Macmillan.

Hansen, Karen Tranberg
1986a   Household Work as a Man's Job: Sex and Gender in Domestic Service in Zambia. Anthropology Today 2(3):18–23.
1986b   Domestic Service in Zambia. Journal of Southern African Studies 13:57–81.
1989   Distant Companions: Servants and Employers in Zambia, 1900–1985. Ithaca: Cornell University Press.

Harris, Trudier
1982   From Mammies to Militants. Philadelphia: Temple University Press.

Hecht, Jean
1956   The Domestic Servant Class in Eighteenth Century England. London: Routledge and Kegan Paul.

Henry, Frances
1968   The West Indian Domestic Scheme in Canada. Social and Economic Studies 17:83–91.

Higman, B. W.
1983   Domestic Service in Jamaica since 1750. *In* Trade, Government, and Society in Caribbean History 1700–1920: Essays Presented to Douglas Hall. B. W. Higman, ed. Pp. 117–138. Kingston, Jamaica: Heinemann Educational Books.

Hochschild, Arlie Russell
1983   The Managed Heart: The Commercialization of Human Feeling. Berkeley: University of California Press.

Horn, Pamela
  1975   The Rise and Fall of the Victorian Servant. New York: St. Martin's
         Press.
Horowitz, Michael
  1974   Barbers and Bearers: Ecology and Ethnicity in an Islamic Society. Af-
         rica 44:371–382.
Jelin, Elizabeth
  1977   Migration and Labor Force Participation of Latin American Women:
         The Domestic Servants in the Cities. Signs 3:129–141.
Joshel, Sandra R.
  1986   Nurturing the Master's Child: Slavery and the Roman Child-Nurse.
         Signs 12:3–22.
Katzman, David
  1978   Seven Days a Week: Women and Domestic Service in Industrializing
         America. New York: Oxford University Press.
Kelly, Joan
  1979   The Doubled Vision of Feminist Theory: A Postscript to the Women
         and Power Conference. Feminist Studies 5:216–227.
Lamphere, Louise
  1987   From Working Daughters to Working Mothers: Immigrant Women
         in a New England Industrial Community. Ithaca: Cornell University
         Press.
Lerner, Gerda
  1972   Black Women in White America. New York: Vintage.
Lovejoy, Paul
  1983   Transformations in Slavery: A History of Slavery in Africa. Cam-
         bridge: Cambridge University Press.
Luton, Susan Berkowitz
  1977   Female Servants in Southern Italy: The Changing Configurations of
         Honor and Power. Michigan Discussions in Anthropology 3:66–86.
Marshall, Paule
  1959   Brown Girl, Brownstones. Old Westbury, NY: Feminist Press.
  1983   From the Poets in the Kitchen. *In* Reena and Other Stories. Pp. 3–12.
         Old Westbury, NY: Feminist Press.
Maza, Sarah
  1983   The Uses of Loyalty: Domestic Service in Eighteenth Century France.
         Princeton: Princeton University Press.
McBride, Theresa
  1976   The Domestic Revolution: The Modernization of Household Service
         in England and France, 1820–1920. New York: Holmes and Meier.
Mehta, Aban
  1960   The Domestic Servant Class. Bombay: Popular Books Depot.
Mohammed, Patricia
  1983   Domestic Workers in the Caribbean. Concerning Women and Devel-
         opment. Women and Development Unit, Extra-Mural Department, Uni-
         versity of the West Indies, Barbados.
Morrison, Toni
  1970   The Bluest Eye. New York: Washington Square Press.
Nett, Emily
  1966   The Servant Class in a Developing Country: Ecuador. The Journal of
         Inter-American Studies 8:437–452.

Nix, Crystal
　1987　Americans Find the Good Life in Guatemala. New York Times. 10
　September.
Oakley, Ann
　1974a　The Sociology of Housework. New York: Pantheon.
　1974b　Housewife. London: Penguin.
Okediji, Oladejo O.
　1978　On Voluntary Associations as an Adaptive Mechanism in West Af-
　rican Urbanization: Another Perspective. *In* The Processes of Urbaniza-
　tion: A Multidisciplinary View. Joyce Aschenbrenner and Lloyd Collins,
　eds. Pp. 195–221. The Hague: Mouton.
Origo, Iris
　1955　The Domestic Enemy: The Eastern Slaves in Tuscany in the Four-
　teenth and Fifteenth Centuries. Speculum 30:321–366.
Palabrica-Costello, Marilou
　1984　Female Domestic Servants in Cagayan de Oro, Philippines: Social
　and Economic Implications of Employment in a "Premodern" Occupa-
　tional Role. *In* Women in the Urban and Industrial Workforce: Southeast
　and East Asia. G. W. Jones, ed. Pp. 235–250. Canberra: Australian Na-
　tional University Press.
Palmer, Phyllis
　1984　Housework and Domestic Labor: Racial and Technological Change.
　In My Troubles are Going to Have Trouble with Me: Everyday Trials and
　Triumphs of Women Workers. Karen Brodkin Sacks and Dorothy Remy,
　eds. Pp. 80–91. New Brunswick: Rutgers University Press.
　1987　Housewife and Household Worker: Employer-Employee Relation-
　ships in the Home, 1928–1940. *In* "To Toil the Livelong Day": American
　Women at Work, 1780–1980. Carol Groneman and Mary Beth Norton,
　eds. Pp. 179–195. Ithaca: Cornell University Press.
　1989　Domesticity and Dirt: Housewives and Domestic Servants in the
　United States, 1920–1945. Philadelphia: Temple University Press.
Prescod-Roberts, Margaret, and Norma Steele
　1980　Black Women: Bringing It All Back Home. Bristol: Falling Wall Press.
Preston-Whyte, Eleanor
　1978　Families without Marriage: A Zulu Case Study. *In* Social System and
　Tradition in Southern Africa: Essays in Honor of Eileen Krige. John Ar-
　gyle and Eleanor Preston-Whyte, eds. Pp. 55–85. Cape Town: Oxford
　University Press.
Rapp, Rayna
　1978　Family and Class in Contemporary America: Notes toward an Un-
　derstanding of Ideology. Science and Society 42:278–300.
Reid, Ira DeA.
　1939　The Negro Immigrant: His Background, Characteristics, and Social
　Adjustment, 1899–1937. New York: Columbia University Press.
Riegelhaupt, Joyce
　1967　Saloio Women: An Analysis of Informal and Formal Political and Eco-
　nomic Roles of Portuguese Peasant Women. Anthropological Quarterly
　40:109–126.
Ringer, Benjamin
　1983　"We The People" and Others: Duality and America's Treatment of its
　Racial Minorities. New York: Tavistock.

Robertson, Claire
    1984   Sharing the Same Bowl: A Socioeconomic History of Women and
        Class in Accra, Ghana. Bloomington: University of Indiana Press.
Rollins, Judith
    1985   Between Women: Domestics and Their Employers. Philadelphia:
        Temple University Press.
Romero, Mary
    1987   Domestic Service in the Transition from Rural to Urban Life: The Case
        of La Chicana. Women's Studies 13:199–222.
    1988   Day Work in the Suburbs: The Work Experience of Chicana Private
        Housekeepers. *In* The Worth of Women's Work: A Qualitative Synthesis.
        Anne Statham, Eleanor M. Miller, and Hans O. Mauksch, eds. Pp. 77–91.
        Albany: State University of New York Press.
Rosaldo, Michelle
    1974   Woman, Culture and Society: A Theoretical Overview. *In* Woman,
        Culture and Society. Michelle Rosaldo and Louise Lamphere, eds. Pp. 17–
        42. Stanford: Stanford University Press.
    1980   The Use and Abuse of Anthropology: Reflections on Feminism and
        Cross-cultural Understanding. Signs 5:389–417.
Rubbo, Anna, and Michael Taussig
    1977   Up Off Their Knees: Servanthood in Southwest Colombia. Michigan
        Discussions in Anthropology 3:41–65.
Ruiz, Vicki
    1987   By the Day or Week: Mexicana Domestic Workers in El Paso. *In* "To
        Toil the Livelong Day": American Women at Work, 1780–1980, Carol
        Groneman and Mary Beth Norton, eds. Pp. 269–283. Ithaca: Cornell Uni-
        versity Press.
Salaff, Janet
    1981   Working Daughters of Hong Kong: Filial Piety or Power in the Fam-
        ily? New York: Cambridge University Press.
Salmon, Lucy Maynard
    1972[1897]   Domestic Service. New York: Arno.
Sanjek, Roger
    1984   Review of Michael Banton, Racial and Ethnic Competition. American
        Ethnologist 11:629–631.
Sankar, Andrea
    1977   Female Domestic Service in Hong Kong. Michigan Discussions in
        Anthropology 3:87–98.
Sassen-Koob, Saskia
    1981   Exporting Capital and Importing Labor: The Role of Caribbean Mi-
        gration to New York City. Occasional Paper No. 28. New York: Center for
        Latin American and Caribbean Studies, New York University.
    1984   The New Labor Demand in Global Cities. *In* Cities in Transformation.
        Michael P. Smith, ed. Pp. 139–171. Beverly Hills: Sage Publications.
Scott, Joan, and Louise Tilly
    1975   Women's Work and the Family in Nineteenth Century Europe. Com-
        parative Studies in Society and History 17:36–64.
Secombe, Wally
    1974   The Housewife and Her Labour under Capitalism. New Left Review
        83:3–24.

Silvera, Makeda
 1983   Silenced. Toronto: Williams-Wallace.
Sistren
 1988   Sistren 10(2/3).
Sistren, with Honor Ford-Smith
 1987   Lionheart Gal: Life Stories of Jamaican Women. Toronto: Sistren Vision Black Women and Women of Colour Press.
Smith, Margo Lane
 1973   Domestic Service as a Channel of Upward Mobility for the Lower-Class Woman: The Lima Case. *In* Female and Male in Latin America: Essays. Ann Pescatello, ed. Pp. 191–207. Pittsburgh: University of Pittsburgh Press.
 1978   The Female Domestic Servant and Social Change: Lima, Peru. *In* Urbanization in the Americas from the Beginnings to the Present. Richard Schaedel, ed. Pp. 569–585. The Hague: Mouton.
Spofford, Harriet Prescott
 1977[1881]   The Servant Girl Question. New York: Arno.
Sutherland, David
 1981   Americans and Their Servants from 1820 to 1920. Baton Rouge: Louisiana State University Press.
Tellis-Nayak, V.
 1983   Power and Solidarity: Clientage in Domestic Service. Current Anthropology 24:67–79.
Tucker, Susan
 1989   Telling Memories among Southern Women: Domestic Workers and Their Employers in the Segregated South. Baton Rouge: Louisiana State University Press.
van Onselen, Charles
 1982   Studies in the Social and Economic History of the Witwatersrand, 1886–1914. Vol. 2: New Ninevah. London: Longman.
Van Raaphorst, Donna L.
 1988   Union Maids Not Wanted: Organizing Domestic Workers 1870–1940. Westport, CT: Greenwood Press.
Watson, Rubie S.
 in press   Wives, Concubines, and Maidservants: Kinship and Servitude in the Hong Kong Region, 1900–1940. *In* Marriage and Inequality in Chinese Society. Rubie S. Watson and Patricia B. Ebrey, eds. Berkeley: University of California Press.
Yezierska, Anzia
 1979[1923]   America and I. *In* The Open Cage: An Anzia Yezierska Collection. Alice Kessler-Harris, ed. Pp. 20–33. New York: Persea Books.

Bitter Money

Cultural Economy and Some African Meanings
of Forbidden Commodities

by Parker Shipton

Bitter Money unites symbolic and economic analysis in exploring beliefs about forbidden exchanges among the Luo of Kenya and other African peoples. Luo classify money as good or evil ("bitter") according to its source. Selling certain commodities, including land, gold, and tobacco, connotes social injustice; and using the money for marriage payments, Luo believe, leads to family tragedy. Possessors of bitter money can be purified by blood sacrifice. Linked purchase and sale prohibitions reveal uncertainties and tensions about individualism and betrayal, involving gender, class, lineage, and religion. A comparative chapter draws parallels and contrasts between East African Christian and West African Muslim variants of "devil's money" beliefs, and between African and South American concepts. Shipton's multiparadigmatic theoretical explanation briefly summarizes a century of anthropological thought about African exchange, while integrating ways of understanding rural African economy, politics, and culture.

American Ethnological Society Monograph Series Number 1.
$7.50 to members, $10.00 to all others.
Please enclose payment in U.S. funds, with all orders.

American Anthropological Association
1703 New Hampshire Avenue, N.W.
Washington, D.C. 20009

Nationalist Ideologies and the Production of National Cultures

Richard G. Fox, Editor

Through case materials from Romania, Israel, India, Guatemala, Tanzania, and Guyana, the essays in this collection investigate and analyze the development of nationalist ideologies and, thence, the production of national culture. Nationalist ideologies, responsive though they may be to material conditions, are nevertheless shown to be contingent and the outcome of processes in history. Each chapter investigates the relationship between nationalist ideology and national culture as contingent in two senses: the outcomes are predetermined neither by a universal form that nationalism must take nor by a compelling cultural tradition.

American Ethnological Society Monograph Series Number 2.
$7.50 to members, $10.00 to all others.
Please enclose payment in U.S. funds, with all orders.

American Anthropological Association
1703 New Hampshire Avenue, N.W.
Washington, D.C. 20009

GENDER

OLOGY

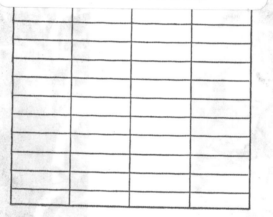

Criti

ching